Y0-BVN-254

THE DE-ESCALATION OF NUCLEAR CRISES

The De-escalation of Nuclear Crises

Edited by

Joseph E. Nation
International Policy Analyst
RAND Corporation

St. Martin's Press New York

Scholarly and Reference Division,
St. Martin's Press, Inc., 175 Fifth Avenue,
New York, N.Y. 10010

First published in the United States of America in 1992

Printed in Great Britain by Billing and Sons Ltd, Worcester

ISBN 0–312–05245–6

Library of Congress Cataloging-in-Publication Data
The De-escalation of nuclear crises / edited by Joseph E. Nation.
p. cm.
Includes index.
ISBN 0–312–05245–6
1. Nuclear crisis control—United States. 2. Nuclear Crisis control—Soviet Union. 3. Nuclear arms control. I. Nation, Joseph E.
JX1974.8.D4 1992
327.1'74—dc20 91–20553
CIP

For Kristen and Alexandra

Contents

Acknowledgments

Editing a volume on nuclear crisis de-escalation has been a tremendous challenge, and I owe a great deal of gratitude to a number of colleagues and friends.

Perhaps most deserving of my thanks was Robert Perry. Bob served as the Executive Director of the California Seminar shortly before his death in 1990, and Bob's encouragement and support were instrumental. Quite simply, without Bob's support, this volume would not have been written.

I owe a special thanks to each of the contributing authors for their diligence and hard work, but Paul K. Davis deserves special thanks for his initial encouragement. In 1986, Paul was an instructor in a RAND Graduate School class for which I originally wrote a very rough paper on the problems of de-escalation. Although the paper had a long way to go, Paul encouraged me to continue work on the subject. Alan J. Vick also encouraged my early work on the subject and provided numerous comments on my earlier efforts. Paul Stockton provided useful comments on my contributions.

The staff of the California Seminar provided valuable assistance in organizing our research conference and with a number of other administrative matters. Special thanks to Margie Milrad, Shirley Gelman, and Kathleen McCallum. I am also grateful for the assistance and advice provided by Simon Winder of St. Martin's and John M. Smith at Macmillan. Finally, thanks to Linda Rudell-Betts for indexing this volume.

Funding for this volume was provided by the United States Institute of Peace and the Rockefeller Foundation. Partial support was also provided by Stanford University's Center for International Security and Arms Control.

Finally, I owe a great deal of thanks to my wife Linda, whose constant support and love mean everything to me.

Santa Monica, CA

List of Abbreviations

ACM	Advanced Cruise Missile
ALCM	Air-launched Cruise Missile
ASW	Anti-Submarine Warfare
C^2	Command and Control
C^3	Command, Control, and Communications
C^3I	Command, Control, Communications, and Intelligence
C^3IW	Command, Control, Communications, Intelligence, and Warning
CBM	Confidence-building Measure
CFE	Conventional Forces in Europe
CINCSAC	Commander in Chief, Strategic Air Command
CSBM	Confidence and Security Building Measure
CSCE	Conference on Security and Cooperation in Europe
DEFCON	Defense Condition
DM	De-escalatory Measure
EAM	Emergency Action Message
EUCOMM	European Command
ExComm	Executive Committee
HML	Hardened Mobile Launchers
HUMINT	Human Intelligence
ICBM	Intercontinental Ballistic Missile
LF	Low Frequency
LOTW	Launch On Tactical Warning
LUA	Launch Under Attack
MBFR	Mutual and Balanced Force Reductions
MIRV	Multiple Independently-targetable Re-entry Vehicles
MOB	Main Operating Base
MX	US 'Peacekeeper' ICBM
NATO	North Atlantic Treaty Organization
NCA	National Command Authority
NEACP	National Emergency Airborne Command Post
NORAD	North American Air Defense Command

NSNC	Non-superpower Nuclear Crisis
NTM	National Technical Means
PAL	Permissive Action Links
ROE	Rules of Engagement
RRC	Risk Reduction Center
SAC	Strategic Air Command
SACEUR	Supreme Allied Commander in Europe
SAG	Surface Action Group
SDI	Strategic Defense Initiative
SICBM	Small Intercontinental Ballistic Missile
SIOP	Single Integrated Operational Plan
SLBM	Sea-Launched Ballistic Missile
SLCM	Sea-Launched Cruise Missile
SNDV	Strategic Nuclear Delivery Vehicle
SSBN	Nuclear-powered Ballistic Missile submarine
SSN	Nuclear-powered attack submarine
START	Strategic Arms Reduction Treaty
VLF	Very Low Frequency
WSAG	Washington Special Action Group
WTO	Warsaw Treaty Organization

Notes on the Contributors

Glenn Buchan is a senior systems analyst at the RAND Corporation, specializing in strategic forces issues. Prior to joining RAND, he worked at the Institute for Defense Analyses and the Central Intelligence Agency.

Richard Darilek is a senior analyst at the US Army's Concepts Analysis Agency. He was previously a program manager at the RAND Corporation.

Paul K. Davis is RAND's Corporation Research Manager for Defense Planning and Analysis. His previous positions include senior analyst and then senior executive in the Department of Defense, senior analyst in the US Arms Control and Disarmament Agency, and senior scientist at the Institute for Defense Analyses. He has published extensively on issues of military strategy and planning, knowledge-based simulation, and models of decision-making.

David Frelinger is a defense analyst at the RAND Corporation, working on strategic nuclear and conventional force employment issues.

William C. Martel is a social scientist at the RAND Corporation. His research interests include foreign policy and national security, and he is involved in studies on nuclear deterrence, arms control and regional issues. Dr Martel has co-authored *Strategic Nuclear War* and *How to Stop a War*, and is currently completing a book on the relationship between force and diplomacy.

Philip J. Romero is Director, Strategic Planning for United Technologies (Carrier Corporation). He has served as an economist and defense analyst at RAND and at Science Applications International Corporation, writing extensively on problems of controlling military forces, on the enforcement of arms control agreements and on land forces doctrine. In 1989–90 he was a Council on Foreign Relations International Affairs Fellow.

Paul N. Stockton is Assistant Professor of National Security Affairs at the Naval Postgraduate School in Monterey, California. He has served as senior legislative assistant for Senator D. P. Moynihan, focusing on military policy, arms control and foreign affairs. Dr Stockton is the author of the Adelphi Paper 'Strategic Stability Between the Superpowers', as well as other publications on arms control and the US policymaking process.

Sergei Y. Tikhonov is a research fellow at the Institute of the USA and Canada, Soviet Academy of Sciences. He has written several articles on the command and control of nuclear forces and accidental war.

Barry Wolf is a student in the RAND Graduate School of Policy Studies. He also has a law degree from Georgetown University Law Center.

Introduction

Joseph E. Nation

We are moving toward a world without wars, a world of equality and freedom. I will take, as a point of departure, the fact that the Cold War is now behind us.

Soviet President Gorbachev,
4 June 1990 at Stanford University

Today, you graduate at an end of an era of conflict ... a cold and abstract war of words and walls. Europe and the world have entered a new era – the Age of Freedom.

US President Bush,
4 May 1990 at Oklahoma State University

In today's era of rapidly improving US–Soviet relations, most laypersons – indeed some defense analysts – undoubtedly view research on how nations might successfully de-escalate a nuclear crisis as an odd and perhaps outdated exercise. Clearly, recent progress in superpower relations makes a US–Soviet nuclear crisis in the next several years seem highly unlikely.

But a less sanguine, and perhaps a more realistic assessment of the potential for nuclear crisis must also be made for the long term. Recent developments could unexpectedly reverse and relations between the superpowers and other nuclear powers could deteriorate. In fact, even if relations improve further, we will continue to be faced with the momentous challenges of avoiding nuclear war involving the superpowers or the emerging nuclear powers, and this challenge will remain one of the most critical facing modern society. Even as relations improve, the nearly 60 000 US and Soviet nuclear warheads and their potential destructive power compel our continued study of nuclear crises. Moreover, the proliferation of nuclear weapons and delivery systems in the rest of the world may result in an increased likelihood of non-superpower nuclear crises, and this requires our continued attention.

MOTIVATION FOR OUR RESEARCH

Over the past 40 years – even though the United States and the Soviet Union have been ideological enemies – the risk of nuclear conflict has been relatively low. A keen recognition of the horrors of nuclear war has certainly played a role in reducing the number of US–Soviet disputes. However, political confrontations, most notably the crisis over the Soviet emplacement of missiles in Cuba in 1962, have from time to time significantly increased the risk of superpower conflict. Shifting political moods, particularly the rise in anti-Soviet attitudes in the United States in the early 1980s, also reportedly convinced many Soviets that the United States was planning a massive 'bolt from the blue' peacetime attack to rid the world of the 'evil' Soviet empire.

As Soviet reforms continue and cooperative military, economic, and political arrangements are established or expanded, the risk of nuclear conflict will probably decrease further and nuclear war – already highly unlikely – may become an even less probable outcome of superpower disputes. The next several years – and perhaps the next several decades – suggest greater superpower cooperation rather than confrontation. And although it now appears unlikely, this could change for the worse. For this and other reasons, continued research on how nuclear crises could begin *and end* is imperative.

Perhaps the first and most important reason for continued research is the recognition that nuclear weapons cannot be disinvented and that they will continue to be used *or threaten to be used* as military instruments. Moreover, the superpowers will almost certainly continue to maintain large nuclear arsenals. Today's US and Soviet arsenals include nearly sixty-odd thousand nuclear warheads, including 27 000 strategic warheads on ICBMs, SLBMs, and strategic bombers.[1] An additional 25 600 tactical nuclear launchers,[2] some capable of delivering more than one warhead, increase the number of warheads in the superpower arsenals to nearly 60 000.

For the first time in our short nuclear history, the number of US and Soviet nuclear weapons will probably decrease in the next several years. But their numbers will decrease only slightly. Although President Reagan and General Secretary Gorbachev agreed at the Reykjavik summit to 50 per cent reductions in strategic nuclear warheads, liberal START counting rules, particularly those affecting strategic bombers, may result in actual reductions of only 10 to 20 per cent. The reductions in the number of tactical nuclear weapons, such as those addressed in the INF Treaty, will similarly result in modest cuts in the total number of superpower warheads. In short, even after US and Soviet negotiators have concluded historic agreements that reduce nuclear arsenals, the total number of warheads will fall only slightly,[3] and the decrease in their potential destructive power will be insignificant.

It is increasingly difficult to imagine a US–Soviet nuclear crisis. Indeed, the risks of crises in the next few years are probably very low. However, just as superpower relations can improve – as evidenced by recent US–Soviet events – they can also deteriorate rapidly. Herein lies a second reason for continuing to research the de-escalation of nuclear crises.

In fact, even if Soviet reforms continue successfully and US–Soviet relations improve further, military power – including the maintenance of formidable conventional and nuclear forces – will remain a key element in the Soviets' superpower status.[4] Military power could become increasingly critical to Soviet superpower status as Moscow struggles with economic restructuring and dramatic internal political changes. This is not intended to suggest a heightened risk of military adventurism by the Soviets. Indeed, the opposite may be more likely, especially in the short term. But Soviet military capabilities will remain very substantial, and in the long term, as Soviet reforms take hold and Soviet leaders are less conciliatory to the West, the risk of conflict could increase.

Internal reforms in the Soviet Union and Eastern Europe and their effects on external relations are a third reason to continue to study nuclear crisis de-escalation. Although it now seems unlikely, these reforms could unexpectedly and paradoxically bring the United States and the Soviet Union close to conflict. In particular, they could lead to greater uncertainty about the rules of superpower behavior, including confusion about spheres of superpower influence, established precedents, and expected behavior. How would the Soviets, for example, react to Hungarian and Rumanian calls for NATO's assistance, including the deployment of a large German contingent, to quash escalating ethnic fighting? And would the Soviets view

NATO's deployment of even a small number of peacekeeping forces a violation of established precedents and a threat to Soviet security?

The point of this and similar scenarios is that now, unlike the last 20 years, the rules of behavior are changing, and these changes could result in greater instability, just as they did in the period following the Second World War. From 1945 until the mid-1960s, military and political crises were almost commonplace. We experienced four serious crises over the status of Berlin, the Cuban Missile Crisis of 1962, and several crises involving the question of Soviet control over Eastern Europe. In the second half of the postwar era, the number of equally dangerous crises, particularly those involving nuclear threats, has been essentially zero.[5] Clearly, the establishment of rules of behavior may not be *the* most critical factor in explaining the sharp fall in the number of superpower crises, but they have certainly played an important *role* in reducing the number of crises. In the next 20 years, predictions about expected Soviet behavior may become more difficult, Soviet commitments to existing spheres of influence may become more tenuous, and currently-established precedents may grow less valid. These factors could increase the risk of unintentional or deliberate conflict involving the Soviet Union, including an increase in risk-taking by traditional Soviet adversaries, and lead to involvement by nuclear powers, including the United States and its allies.

Internal instability in the Soviet Union alone could also increase the risk of superpower conflict in the short term. As opposed to the unlikely, but often-cited scenarios in which anti-western hardliners wrestle power from Gorbachev and his allies, instability could increase greatly if internal controls weakened and the Soviet Union slipped into anarchy or civil war. The control of nuclear weapons in a crumbling Soviet Union that had slipped into civil war would be of particular concern. Nuclear crises between a united or disintegrating Soviet Union and its traditional adversaries appear unlikely. But the threat of nuclear use by a fragmented nation for either domestic or foreign purposes could increase, and the de-escalation of these crises would obviously be of great importance to the United States and other nations.

Although these historic changes may result in some of the increased risks discussed above, they provide even greater *opportunities* for the superpowers to reduce the risk of nuclear conflict. In particular, the Soviet willingness to discuss a wide range of arms control initiatives is a strong reason for continuing to research superpower nuclear crises. Recent Soviet offers to establish cooperative arms control measures, such as intrusive on-site verification regimes, may be very useful in a number of respects, particularly in establishing de-escalatory mechanisms for use in crises. For example, provisions in the INF agreement permit the most intrusive and comprehensive verification regime established, including on-site challenge inspection of most facilities with little notice. Similar provisions involving strategic forces, such as challenge inspections or observations of military operations, and recent Soviet offers to discuss command and control of nuclear weapons provide perhaps a historic opportunity to reduce the risk of war.

Finally, perhaps the greatest argument for continuing research in light of the improvements in US–Soviet relations is the unfortunate fact that, even as the United States and the Soviet Union reduce their nuclear arsenals, membership in the world's nuclear club will undoubtedly increase. These new nuclear powers will develop and maintain far fewer nuclear weapons than the superpowers, but their use of only a small number of weapons will have catastrophic results, and the de-escalation of these crises – even those involving non-superpowers with small nuclear arsenals – will quickly command our attention. One hopes that the concepts that evolve from the research into the de-escalation of superpower crises are equally valid for and applicable to crises involving non-superpowers.

PREVIOUS RESEARCH

The intent of this volume is to break new ground in what is generally a well-researched subject. A number of researchers have written virtually countless volumes and articles about various aspects of the Cuban Missile Crisis,[6] probably the world's closest call with potentially large-scale nuclear conflict. Studies have also been undertaken on lesser-known brushes with nuclear war, such as the 1973 US and Soviet reactions to war in the Middle East. More recently, researchers have focused their efforts on the command and control of nuclear forces and the effects of command and control failures on the probability of war. Others have addressed the origins of crises and conflict, potential consequences of misperceptions, unintended, unauthorized, or accidental conflict, and a host of related issues. Very little research has addressed nuclear crisis de-escalation, particularly the role of military operations in defusing crises and their potential effects on the likelihood of conflict. And to my knowledge, no one has addressed directly or specifically nuclear crisis de-escalation involving developing world nations.

There are several apparent explanations for this limited amount of research. First, some researchers argue that effective crisis management is a virtually impossible task.[7] Soviet researchers have also generally taken up this argument. Others have advanced similar arguments, noting that leaders do not fully appreciate the implications of specific military measures in crises and concluding that attempts to 'fine-tune' military operations to signal intent is perhaps at best futile and at worst potentially dangerous. Skeptics of effective crisis management instead have proposed greater efforts at crisis avoidance and have suggested fundamental changes in international systems and military forces that promote stability. While we recognize the import of avoiding crises and the construction of highly stable environments, it is not satisfying to ignore the possibility of future crises and the potential role of de-escalatory measures. Even with the momentous changes in US–Soviet relations that have occurred in recent years, it is hardly imaginable that serious political disputes – involving the United States, the Soviet Union, or other nuclear powers – and the crises that accompany them, will become remnants of the past.

A second reason for the limited amount of research on nuclear crisis de-escalation and the potentially beneficial role of military operations is an apparent widespread belief that military signaling is less valuable than political bargaining. It is not our intent to dispute the importance of political measures in crisis de-escalation – superpower crises after all originate from political disputes – but de-escalatory measures, including those involving military forces to signal intent, may complement political bargaining effectively and serve as an important management tool. For example, changes in the tempo of nuclear force operations, such as the resumption of strategic bomber training missions, may be useful in signaling resolve or conciliation, especially as a means of illustrating accompanying political intentions. Conversely, the suspension of bomber training could be utilized to signal resolve and a willingness to use force. It is precisely because military operations are complex and not well understood that their potential contribution to de-escalation deserves added research and emphasis.

Finally, the potential usefulness of de-escalatory measures involving nuclear forces is difficult to evaluate since the operational details of nuclear forces are highly classified. As a result, most analyses that address nuclear operations must rely on broad assumptions about how forces would operate in a crisis, and thus only general policy measures can be provided. Even if these highly classified, theoretical operational details were known, they might be at variance with the real world operation of forces. Nevertheless, additional information about the operations of US and Soviet forces has become available in the past several years,[8] and this permits us, at least at a theoretical level, to explore and suggest more specific measures for de-escalation.

The broad objective of this volume is straightforward: to identify and evaluate the potential roles – both positive *and* negative – of de-escalatory measures in past crises and to develop and evaluate their roles in future crises. We pay particular attention to de-escalatory measures involving US and Soviet nuclear forces in *a crisis or a conventional war* and to de-escalatory measures that provide traditional characteristics of confidence-building measures (CBMs) or confidence- and security-building measures (CSBMs). In contrast to structural arms control, CBMs deal more with intent, perceptions, and with the operations of forces than with force structure.

CBMs developed for use in crisis or war have the following broad objectives:

- to signal potential adversaries of their intent to resolve a crisis peacefully
- to reduce the military threat in a crisis, particularly by lowering the probability of a successful surprise attack and by increasing warning time should an attack occur.

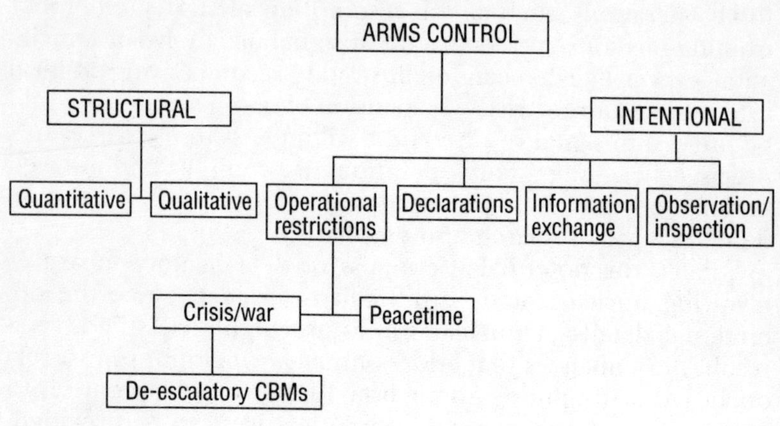

Figure 1 A taxonomy for arms control and CBMs

This volume addresses a range of 'intentional' arms control measures, although much of our emphasis is devoted to operational restrictions on nuclear forces in a crisis or conventional war. Some of the chapters discuss broader CBM concepts, including those that can be applied to the political (e.g. declarations, diplomatic exchanges and meetings) or to the economic arenas (e.g. joint ventures). Figure 1 illustrates a taxonomy of arms control and CBM categories.

RESEARCH GROUND RULES

In this research volume, we examine a range of issues involving de-escalation and confidence building. What roles can or should de-escalatory measures play in nuclear crisis de-escalation? Have these or other measures been useful in the de-escalation of past crises or in the termination of conventional wars? Do Soviet and US views, including those of military leaders, differ about the utility of CBMs? How might behavioral factors influence de-escalation? Are CBMs likely to become more or less useful as force structures are changed? Can we apply the lessons from de-escalating US–Soviet crises to non-superpower crises?

Much of our work focuses on the de-escalation of US–Soviet nuclear crises. These chapters do so under the following assumptions:

- US and Soviet strategic and theater nuclear forces are fully generated.
- The crisis is a serious one – the likelihood of war appears significant and the probability of a diplomatic solution appears low initially. (In short, the crisis is not one of muscle-flexing or posturing.)
- There is an apparent diplomatic breakthrough to the crisis.[9]
- Despite this apparent political resolution, military forces remain on full alert and there are no fundamental changes in operations. Moreover, leaders are not inclined to return their forces to peacetime operations as a hedge against a re-escalation of the crisis.

Under these circumstances, the perceived likelihood of war and the risk of conflict would remain high. Indeed, the proverbial slippery slope that can lead to unintended escalation can also prevent nations from climbing back to a more secure, less threatening situation. Hesitance to order forces back to normal peacetime military operations, especially if they had not received assurances that the other party had done or was planning to do the same, would be commonplace.

Three dangers are immediately apparent. First, the risk of unintended war or unintended crisis re-escalation is significant. In particular, interactions between opposing forces, even if inadvertent, could increase escalatory pressures and lead to conflict. Second, in an extended crisis, the command and control of nuclear weapons may be diffused, increasing the probability of the unauthorized launch of weapons. Finally, in an extended and potentially unresolved crisis, pressure to 'use or lose' military forces (e.g. to use forces at their peak of readiness rather than to risk the loss of capabilities over time because of maintenance problems), regardless of political perceptions, may increase and consequently raise the risk of war.

Other pressures will restrict de-escalatory options and these may also increase the risk of war. Of particular significance, the level of trust between adversaries will be very low and the incentives to de-escalate will be weak. Building trust will be difficult because of the crisis environment. Confidence-building must overcome the suspicion of adversaries who had only recently (at least implicitly) threatened the large use of nuclear weapons. Given this level of mistrust, leaders might fear that an adversary is using the de-escalation process to employ deception, and this could decrease further incentives to de-escalate. Finally, leaders may be overly sensitive to domestic pressures to keep up one's guard, even if an apparent political solution to the crisis had occurred, and this could make de-escalation more difficult.

De-escalatory confidence-building measures may facilitate crisis termination in several respects. Most important, de-escalatory CBMs provide a framework for leaders to make sense of complicated military operations, and they add a semblance of order to the de-escalation process. De-escalatory measures also permit leaders to assess the trade-offs between key factors in the de-escalation process. For example, as nuclear forces are returned to peacetime operations, de-escalatory measures provide a critical management tool to balance the negative effects on one's own forces (increased vulnerability, tightened constraints on their capabilities, etc.) with the positive effects on an adversary's forces (decreases in an adversary's threatening posture, opportunities for further dialogue to de-escalate the crisis, etc.). Balancing these negative and positive effects permits an orderly return of nuclear forces to peacetime operations, permits necessary maintenance, and thus lessens pressures to 'use or lose' weapons. In short, de-escalatory measures provide a mechanism to balance more effectively benefits and risks although, as some of our analysis shows, the introduction of measures in some cases could in fact be risky at best and counterproductive at worst.

Second, some de-escalatory measures can establish operational guidelines for nuclear and conventional forces, including rules of engagement. These guidelines can limit the number of potential interactions between forces and decrease the likelihood that a single, unintended event (e.g. the shooting-down of a reconnaissance aircraft near a naval operations group) will precipitate an escalation of the crisis or result in an accidental war.

Third, de-escalatory CBMs can reduce preemptive pressures. In a heightened crisis, preemption is more likely to occur if an adversary is viewed as preparing for war. Carefully-crafted de-escalatory CBMs can perform a number of functions to decrease these pressures. Their most important contribution is the added insight into an adversary's intentions. De-escalatory CBMs that promote transparency (e.g. increased data exchanges or on-site inspection of facilities, etc.) can provide effective insights into a number of factors that demonstrate an intent to de-escalate.[10] For example, the return of some forces to peace-time training exercises or the return of leaders to normal governmental activities do not offer proof of benign intent, but they certainly offer *evidence* that supports this conclusion and greatly reduce pressures to use nuclear weapons first. If nothing else, de-escalatory measures reduce the pressures for immediate retaliation, such as launch under attack or launch on tactical warning, in response to a suspected attack. In short, de-escalatory CBMs establish firebreaks by removing the incentives to keep forces ready for immediate response, and they provide useful insights into intentions.

RESEARCH OUTLINE

This research volume represents a compilation of individual efforts and chapters, although considerable coordination of these efforts has occurred. Authors have had the opportunity to review all chapters, and as explained in the final chapter, some general themes and conclusions emerge from the contributions.

The volume contains three parts. Part I, 'Perspectives on Crisis De-escalation and Building Confidence', contains four chapters that address broad issues of crisis de-escalation and building confidence. Part II, 'Nuclear Operations and De-escalatory Measures', contains two chapters that describe US and Soviet nuclear operations and outline and assess potential de-escalatory measures. Part III, 'Future Prospects and Conclusions', contains three chapters that assess the future roles of de-escalatory CBMs in superpower and in non-superpower nuclear crises. Part III examines the applicability of de-escalatory CBMs following reductions in strategic nuclear forces, discusses de-escalatory CBMs for non-superpower nuclear crisis de-escalation, and offers general research conclusions.

Parts and chapters

The first Part, 'Perspectives on Crisis De-escalation and Building Confidence', outlines the theoretical underpinnings, strengths, and weaknesses of confidence-building measures, and it addresses broadly Soviet perspectives of crisis management, crisis de-escalation, and means of building confidence. It describes key behavioral factors in crisis de-escalation and also examines de-escalation in past crises and conventional war termination.

Confidence-building measures remain a relatively new concept in arms control and the theoretical underpinnings and history of CBMs are less well-known than those of traditional structural arms control efforts. Chapter 1 examines the gradual evolution of CBM objectives, from the increased transparency of ambiguous military operations to restrictions and bans on specific military operations. It outlines CBM objectives and how these are achieved and it discusses the limitations of CBMs as useful crisis management tools, especially the limitations and inherent dangers of CBMs when they are employed by an adversary bent on aggression. Chapter 1 describes past CBM agreements, including the 1975 Helsinki and 1986 Stockholm Agreements, CBMs in SALT I, II, INF, and other nuclear arms control agreements and discusses strategic nuclear analogues to conventional arms agreements. Chapter 1 also suggests general prospective strategic nuclear de-escalatory CBMs.

Building confidence in crises requires cooperation between potential adversaries and thus Soviet attitudes toward CBMs are an important part of our analysis. Chapter 2 provides an overview of Soviet views on crisis management and building confidence, and it describes Soviet perspectives on CBM benefits and shortcomings, Soviet differences from traditional US views on CBMs, and the evolution of Soviet approaches to CBMs. Chapter 2 emphasizes the continued danger of accidental nuclear conflict between the superpowers, describes potential sources of conflict, and it explains the traditional Soviet emphasis on crisis avoidance rather than crisis management. It describes official and unofficial Soviet views of de-escalatory CBMs, CBM proposals outside the military realm, and it outlines broadly prospective de-escalatory CBMs.

A limited historical database complicates the identification of past de-escalatory measures in nuclear crises; however, an overview of de-escalatory measures in past crises may provide important insight into the future use of de-escalatory CBMs. Chapter 3 provides a historical analysis of de-escalatory measures in nuclear crises, and it also explores de-escalatory measures in conventional war termination as an analogue to nuclear crisis de-escalation. The chapter examines de-escalatory measures in five nuclear crises, some more spectacular than others: Suez/Hungary 1956, Lebanon 1958, Berlin 1961, Cuba 1962, and the Middle East in 1973. It examines decisionmakers' interests and objectives in de-escalation, and the results, and summarizes the risks – apparent and real – and benefits of de-escalatory CBMs.

Nuclear crisis de-escalation is highly dependent on behavioral factors. Anticipating possible behavioral problems and taking measures to avoid or mitigate them may greatly increase the probability of successful de-escalation. For example, what behavioral factors may cause leaders to become skeptical of an adversary's avowed good intentions? How can the negative effects of these factors be mitigated? Chapter 4 describes models of human decisionmaking, their contribution to crisis de-escalation research and perhaps most important, identifies dangerous ideas that can derail the de-escalation process.

Part II contains two chapters that focus on nuclear operations in crises and the assessment of potential de-escalatory CBMs. Chapter 5 identifies potential de-escalatory CBMs from a US military planner's perspective, providing a detailed review of US nuclear operations and outlining and evaluating potential de-escalatory measures. In particular, it describes the objectives of nuclear alerts, such as minimizing force vulnerabilities, increasing warfighting capabilities should deterrence fail, and signaling resolve to opponents. It then examines the effects of specific de-escalatory measures on these objectives and identifies promising de-escalatory CBMs. Chapter 6 parallels Chapter 5, assessing potential de-escalatory CBMs from a Soviet military planner's perspective. Both Chapters 5 and 6 address some of the verification aspects of de-escalatory CBMs.

Part III, 'Future Prospects and Conclusions', contains three chapters that prospectively examine de-escalation and building confidence, first describing how alternative nuclear futures might affect the utility of de-escalatory CBMs. Chapter 7 outlines anticipated reductions in nuclear forces, their effects on crisis stability, and de-escalatory measures involving nuclear forces. It considers reductions under START guidelines and subsequent agreements that reduce sharply superpower nuclear arsenals. In addition to exploring opportunities that force reductions might create for de-escalatory measures, Chapter 7 explores the problems that might result from reductions in nuclear forces.

Although most of our research effort has focused on superpower crises, the concepts we develop may be very useful for non-superpower nuclear crisis de-escalation, and these are explored in Chapter 8. A number of broad issues are addressed. For example, Chapter 8 addresses whether we should be concerned with non-superpower crisis de-escalation, and if so, whether CBMs can play positive roles. Similarly, it asks if the lessons learned from superpower nuclear crises can be applied to non-superpower crises. Chapter 8 discusses the origins of non-superpower crises, probable antagonists, and how doctrine and force structure could influence future non-superpower crises. It addresses how non-superpower crises might be terminated, and outlines the possible role of outside powers in non-superpower crisis de-escalation.

Finally, Chapter 9 ties together general conclusions and offers areas for further investigation.

CONCLUSIONS

Several notable conclusions emerge from this research effort, and they are summarized below:

- CBMs are potentially useful across a broad spectrum, but a strong case can be advanced that political, economic, and cultural CBMs are more important management tools in peacetime than CBMs that involve military forces.
- Nevertheless, CBMs that involve military forces are useful across a wide spectrum – from peace to crisis to war, but their potential contribution may be more significant in avoiding or ending wars than in fostering better relations in peacetime.
- The most important actions in crisis de-escalation may be the

introduction of or the continued adherence to military 'insignificant', or largely symbolic CBMs.

- There is substantial reluctance to consider militarily significant de-escalatory measures, particularly those that increase the vulnerability of forces in a crisis.
- The contribution of CBMs involving military forces to crisis de-escalation is probably marginal since leaders appear to notice only the most serious military developments, but this marginal contribution should be welcomed as a way to reduce the risks of accidental war.
- CBMs are most effective when a comprehensive approach to arms control, including the integration of structural and operational arms control measures is undertaken.
- Large reductions in warhead levels may affect crisis stability and the prospects for crisis de-escalation adversely. START may also pose problems for crisis de-escalation because of its stringent compliance mechanisms.
- CBMs have a number of limitations that sometimes may outweigh their potential benefits. CBMs can send the wrong message, they can be misinterpreted, and their usefulness can vary greatly depending on a number of factors.

NOTES

1. Using SALT counting rules, the US now has 14 500 strategic warheads and the Soviets 12 400. Using the more liberal START counting rules, current warhead levels 'decrease' to 9900 and 11 000, respectively.
2. Consisting of 9900 US and 15 700 Soviet launchers.
3. Follow-on agreements may result in more substantial reductions, but we will without question remain a far cry from a nuclear-free world or a world free from nuclear threats. Even 90 per cent cuts across all weapons categories, for example, leave superpower arsenals of nearly 6000, including about 1000 strategic nuclear warheads.
4. This argument was advanced by Michael Nacht, 'Cold War is Over – Why the Arms Race Is Not', *San Francisco Chronicle,* 25 April 1990, Briefing pp. 1, 5. Soviet military forces will remain the largest in Europe and will probably be second in size only to those of the United States.
5. The 1973 US nuclear alert that occurred in response to the Middle East War was more one of posturing than a real threat to use nuclear weapons.

6. For example, a literature search of Stanford's library system indicates almost 100 books on this subject.
7. The most prominent of these is Lebow. He argues that temporal and other constraints on decisionmaking, organizational complexity, incorrect interpretation of historical events, the irreversibility of some escalatory actions, the inability to control events, and other factors make crisis management very difficult. Lebow argues that effective crisis management requires fundamental changes in force structures, doctrines, and target sets that define strategy. Richard Ned Lebow, *Nuclear Crisis Management: A Dangerous Illusion* (Ithaca: Cornell, 1987), especially pp. 15–28.
8. The most comprehensive sources on nuclear operations are Ashton B. Carter, John D. Steinbruner, Charles A. Zraket (eds), *Managing Nuclear Operations* (Washington, DC: Brookings, 1987); Bruce G. Blair, *Strategic Command and Control: Redefining the Nuclear Threat* (Washington, DC, Brookings: 1985); and Paul Bracken, *The Command and Control of Nuclear Forces* (New Haven: Yale, 1983). The seminal piece on Soviet nuclear operations is Steven M. Meyer, 'Soviet Nuclear Operations', in Carter, et al., pp. 470–534.
9. The difficulty in theory or in practice, of course, is to distinguish between 'apparent' breakthroughs and tactical maneuvers. For the purposes of this research, our general assumption equates apparent political resolutions with events that occurred in the Cuban Missile Crisis. On 24 October, Soviet ships turned back from the US established quarantine line in the first direct confrontation of the crisis. Perhaps even more significant, two days later, Khrushchev wrote to President Kennedy and appeared to give in to US conditions for ending the quarantine.
10. There are also a number of associated dangers that could lead to a re-escalation of the crisis, including insights gained from intrusive on-site inspections. For example, on-site inspections could reveal that preparations for war are continuing, despite other indications of an intent to de-escalate. A number of these dangers are discussed later in this volume.

Part I

Perspectives on Crisis De-escalation and Building Confidence

1 The Theory of Confidence-Building Measures

Richard E. Darilek

1.1 INTRODUCTION

This chapter discusses the theory of Confidence-Building Measures (CBMs) in two ways. First, it employs a top-down, deductively oriented approach to explain CBM theory in terms of the arms control goals and objectives to be achieved, the types of measures to be employed, and the problems or limitations likely to be encountered when applying CBMs to conventional or nuclear forces. The chapter as a whole asks how various types of CBMs might function during a political–military escalation from peacetime to a crisis and beyond (i.e. including conflict), as well as how they might operate in a de-escalatory environment.

In pursuit of these overarching issues, the second section of the chapter raises a fundamental but complicating question: how might the next all-out war actually come about – by unpremeditated escalation resulting from misunderstanding or miscalculation, or by premeditation resulting in a surprise attack? The second section of the chapter addresses this question, explores its various implications for CBMs, and suggests the potential contribution of different types of CBMs toward successful resolution of the issues involved.

A second, more inductively oriented approach to CBM theory follows in the third section of the chapter. This approach attempts to explain the historical development of CBMs – in particular, the creation of various CBM packages or 'regimes' and the theories surrounding them – as they have evolved since the Second World War but, especially, over the past two decades. Most (but by no means all) CBM developments during this period have occurred within the context of conventional military forces and arms control efforts involving those forces in

Europe. The third section of the chapter draws upon that context in its discussion of the history of CBM theory to explain and exemplify the developmental process. At various stages in the discussion, this section of the chapter also extrapolates from conventional to nuclear forces in an attempt to suggest relevant CBM analogues for strategic nuclear forces.

In its fourth and concluding section, the chapter draws upon the discussion of CBM objectives, limitations, and history in the preceding sections to assess, in theoretical terms, the potential role that CBMs might play in nuclear crisis de-escalation and conventional war termination. This section differentiates between an escalation from peace to crisis (and beyond) in which at least some CBMs have remained in force and one in which all existing CBMs have either been ignored or violated. In the first case, the chapter suggests, CBMs can contribute promising mechanisms for successful crisis management on both the upside and the downside of an escalatory ladder.

In the second case, however, where existing CBMs have ceased to function, the chapter contends that subsequent reintroduction of the old CBMs or the invention of new ones on the spur of the moment cannot fully be trusted to play a constructive role in crisis de-escalation. This argues further for maintaining compliance with at least some CBMs throughout an escalatory situation. Nevertheless, the chapter concludes, previously violated or *ad hoc* CBMs may represent the only alternatives available under the circumstances to help support a process of de-escalation. For the most part, such measures might be expected to play this supporting role once de-escalation has been initiated by other means (e.g. a political breakthrough in a crisis, or a ceasefire in a conventional conflict) – not by CBMs themselves.

1.2 A FRAMEWORK FOR THINKING ABOUT CBMs

In a real sense, CBMs relate more to the operations of particular military forces – to how those forces can or should be employed, to what they do or might be capable of doing – than to the military structure of those forces. Such questions as how many forces there are or ought to be, what different types or composition of forces are involved, and how different types might be equipped relate to how a given military force is structured, to what the force 'is', more than to how that force operates, or what it 'does'. When it comes to arms control, therefore, CBMs help define and represent a distinctive category of 'operational' measures. These stand in marked contrast, theoretically, to an equally distinctive set of 'structural' arms control provisions.

Such definitional distinctions extend beyond the realm of theory. As discussed in the next section of this chapter, arms control negotiations themselves have tended to divide along operational and structural lines, even though convincing arguments can, should, and have been made that the proper relationship between operational and structural arms control efforts is a complementary one, that the two approaches are neither antithetical nor sufficient unto themselves, and that arms control agreements should incorporate elements of both to be truly effective.[1] Nevertheless, operational arms control measures like CBMs can achieve many, if not all, of the same goals and objectives that their structural counterparts can and, in theory at least, can do so independently of structural arms control agreements (i.e. those involving force reductions).

CBM objectives

Several broad goals tend to pervade the world of arms control, thereby framing the context within which CBMs attempt to operate and fostering several objectives for them to pursue. Undoubtedly, the first of these goals is to maintain a satisfactory peace. In its purest form – as a concept with its own positive content, not simply as the absence of war – this goal can be expressed in a variety of ancillary ways: to improve political as well as military relationships among states; to limit both the existence and the use of military forces in specified geographic regions; to provide for the settlement of disputes without recourse to force and violence. At a minimum, however, conscientious pursuit of this goal through serious arms control efforts would seem to imply the prevention of political–military crises. Crisis prevention, in other words, is another way of articulating the goal of preserving the peace.

But what if crises do arise, despite concerted efforts to prevent them and maintain peace? A second goal of arms control must surely be to provide tools for the successful management of those crises and, thus, to control or arrest their escalation. An additional aspect of this goal would be to provide mechanisms for safely de-escalating a crisis once its further development has been arrested. A third goal – avoiding war – is suggested by the possibility of crisis management efforts that fail de-escalation: such a failure may not necessarily result in conflict, but instead in further efforts to prevent the outbreak of hostilities. A fourth goal might be provision of war termination measures in the event that none of the other goals can be achieved in a particular case. One way of visualizing these various goals is as a spectrum – running the gamut from peace, to crisis, to war, and beyond – which arms control can conceivably address throughout its entirety.

PEACE			WAR
Preserve peace/ prevent crises	Control escalation/ de-escalation	Avoid war	Facilitate termination

Figure 1.1 Spectrum of arms control goals

In theory, CBMs can promote arms control objectives that improve the prospects of achieving the different goals arrayed along this spectrum. To pursue the goal of preserving peace, for example, CBMs can seek to clarify misunderstandings about the purpose of suspected military activities being conducted by a potential opponent. The hope would be that CBMs could prevent any misunderstandings from arising in the first place. If that objective failed in a particular case, however, the further objective would be to clear up any misunderstanding as quickly as possible through the provision of, or the opportunity to gain access to, additional information about the nature and purpose of questionable military activities.

More complete information on opposing military forces and their activities should work to dispel misunderstandings quickly in a case where no hostile intent exists. But even in cases where hostilities are seriously being contemplated, such information might also help guard against underestimation of a potential attacker's capabilities or intentions. In theory, increasing a potential defender's knowledge of a threatening opponent's military disposition should help that defender respond promptly to the threat. Such action (e.g. mobilization of reserve forces) could increase the chances of war, of course; in practice, however, it could have the opposite effect. Prompt action by the defender could actually deter a potential attacker from initiating conflict against an alert, resolute opponent. CBMs that provide for mutual exchanges of militarily relevant information (e.g. troop strengths, weapons dispositions, exercise plans and activities, doctrinal developments) and that supply ample notification, preferably in advance, of planned military activities – in a word, CBMs that promote military 'transparency' – can conceivably serve the objective of reducing misunderstanding and, thus, the goal of preserving peace and preventing crises.

By providing information, access (e.g. some means of verifying the information), or both on a regular basis, CBMs can serve other arms control objectives as well. A representative listing of such objectives would probably include the following:

- clarify misunderstandings about the nature or purpose of military forces and their activities;
- limit possibilities of using force for political intimidation;
- lessen the dangers of miscalculation of a potential opponent's strengths or intentions in cases where hostilities are being contemplated or at least remain an option;
- reduce chances for offensive military action, especially by surprise;
- create firebreaks to war; in particular, by providing time to negotiate in a rapidly-moving crisis and to react to aggressive or otherwise hostile acts.

The foregoing list does not pretend to be an exhaustive one. Instead it is meant to be representative of the kinds of objectives that might be pursued in a transition from peace to crisis and that can reasonably be derived from the arms control goals discussed above.

In pursuit of these various goals and objectives, various types of CBMs can be variously employed. Transparency measures (e.g. data exchanges, notification of exercises) can provide information that serves the objectives of reducing the chances for misunderstandings and miscalculation. Communication measures (e.g. hotlines) can serve those same objectives, as can observation and inspection measures intended to promote access – i.e. some means of verifying the information communicated. Access measures can also support the objective of lessening possibilities for offensive military action by surprise. Measures intended to enhance stability (e.g. regulations on the call-up of reservists) and constraints on the use of military forces (e.g. restrictions on where troops or weapons can be deployed) would limit specified military activities, ideally in conjunction with arms control agreements that reduce the numbers of forces. Such stabilizing and constraint measures can help control the use of force for political intimidation and provide firebreaks to war, as well as help lower the chances of surprise offensives.

To illustrate these theoretical relationships more clearly, Table 1.1 takes the potential contributions of various types of CBMs to various arms control objectives, as suggested in the preceding paragraph, and depicts them in matrix form.

Just as there are undoubtedly more arms control objectives than those listed here, there are also other types of CBMs that are not represented above. Declaratory measures, for example, such as pledges of no-first-use (of force, of nuclear weapons),

Table 1.1 Illustrative contributions of CBMs to arms control objectives

Types of CBMs	*Clarify misunderstandings*	*Lessen miscalculation*	*Limit intimidation*	*Reduce surprise*	*Establish firebreaks*
Transparency					
Information	X	X			
Notification	X	X			
Communications	X	X			X
Access					
Observation	X	X		X	
Inspection	X	X		X	
Stabilization			X		X
Constraints			X	X	X

are absent from the matrix. Because they are just promises, which are as easy to break as they are to make, and even though they may help promote the goals of arms control (e.g. preserving peace), the likelihood seems low of such measures being able to contribute reliably to the successful management of either an escalatory or a de-escalatory process. Furthermore, the potential contributions indicated by an 'X' in the above matrix represent highly gross judgments; the absence of an 'X' in any cell does not mean that a certain type of measure makes no contribution at all to a particular objective. Rather, the matrix is what it says it is: 'illustrative' or representative. It is not definitive.

The various types of CBMs listed above, moreover, can potentially make their contributions to the various objectives, as indicated, across the entire spectrum of arms control goals presented earlier. For example, CBMs that contain specific stabilizing provisions or constraints can help prevent a crisis from arising in the first place by setting clear limits on what is permissible military activity. CBMs that establish communications facilities (e.g. hotlines) or consultative mechanisms (e.g. predesignated political or military arrangements to get together or, at least, to talk) can also contribute to crisis prevention by helping to clarify the precise nature and avowed intent of each side's moves – in the meantime, serving the secondary objectives of clarifying any misunderstanding and lessening the chances for miscalculation. Furthermore these CBMs, together with the transparency measures noted above, could in theory help both to dampen pressures for escalation of a crisis and to maintain important elements of communication, and even some control, in the event of further escalation or de-escalation.

In the absence of successful crisis management resulting in de-escalation, with an impasse or inflexibility developing on both sides, CBMs can potentially play a role in helping to avoid the outbreak of war. Even if other arms control agreements and other CBM provisions (e.g. notification of exercises) have been violated during a crisis, certain CBMs (e.g. constraints on deployments, reserve call-ups, readiness levels), when combined with trustworthy means to verify that they continue to be observed (e.g. on-site inspections, open-skies overflights), can make it difficult for a potential attacker to contemplate an attack. In particular, such CBMs can lessen the chances of that attack coming as a surprise. They can pose crucial dilemmas for the attacker: violate the measures, do whatever it takes to ready your forces for the attack, provide advance warning to a defender as a result, and forfeit surprise; or maintain surprise, launch the attack with forces that are not well-prepared, and potentially compromise your chances of success. Thus, CBMs can conceivably help serve one of the other goals of arms control, avoiding war, by providing a kind of deterrent against it or final firebreaks in its path.

In theory, CBMs should also prove useful in crisis de-escalation and war termination, where communication and verification are both at a premium but confidence may be lacking because of intervening events. The objective in both cases would be to disengage from positions and actions previously taken, of course, but it would also consist of doing so in such a way as to minimize possibilities for reigniting the conflict of interest that originally sparked the crisis or the war. Part and parcel of the objective, in other words, is a smooth transition back from the 'war' side toward the 'peace' end of the spectrum depicted in Figure 1.1. CBMs for communication and consultation could help initiate that process and, as de-escalation developed, other CBMs could come into play (e.g. data exchanges, notification of force redeployments, verification provisions) as part of a wholesale reversal of the build-up previously undertaken.

CBM limitations

In addressing the arms control goals ascribed to them above, the biggest problems that CBMs have to overcome might best be understood by identifying the most likely ways in which such goals might be thwarted. This involves asking how peace might be broken, crises arise, and wars occur. Once again, a spectrum of possibilities presents itself, one bounded in this case by two polar answers to the question of how war might come about: through actions that are, in varying degrees, unpremeditated, on the one hand; or, on the other, through a variety of premeditated positions and moves. Both polar types and various gradations between them are illustrated in generic and highly summary fashion in Figure 1.2.

Unpremeditated			Premeditated
Accident (human or mechanical)	Misunderstanding	Miscalculation (e.g. preemption vs suspected first-strike)	Calculation (e.g. bolt-from-blue)

Figure 1.2 A causes of war spectrum

Included on the unpremeditated side of this spectrum are causes of war that range from accidents involving human or mechanical errors through misunderstandings of the kind alluded to in the discussion of how objectives associated with 'transparency' measures can contribute to the goals of arms control. Represented on the other side of the spectrum are causes of war – a perceived need to preempt against a suspected first strike or to maximize the element of surprise in a calculated attack – that are more or less premeditated. Crises escalating and conflicts erupting as a result of the actions of third parties, so-called 'catalytic' wars, would probably lie in the middle of the spectrum because they can arise on either side, through premeditation on the part of one of the major adversaries or from independent actions of third parties with whom a major adversary had strong ties.

This spectrum of possibilities raises a key question for CBMs: which side of the spectrum are such measures operating on at any given time during a transition from peace, to crisis, to potential war? Information and communication measures, for example, might contribute most effectively to the prevention of 'accidental' wars by keeping open lines of communication and opportunities for consultation throughout a crisis, thus helping to clarify ambiguities and intentions in the event of a genuine accident and to forestall possibilities for further escalation. Such CBMs might work to minimize false positive signals of impending attack by keeping additional sources of information flowing.

The very same measures, however, might be singularly ineffective in the face of a bolt-from-the-blue attack of the kind represented at the extreme right on the spectrum. Indeed, CBMs could prove to be worse than ineffective in this case because the very information exchanges and communication lines that they provide could conceivably be used as channels for deceptive information. Indeed, there is a danger that the whole pattern of compliance on one side is an elaborate sham aimed at lulling the other side into a false sense of confidence. A determined opponent might be manipulating CBMs unscrupulously to help mask a hostile intent, thus creating false negative indicators of a potential attack that would increase the element of surprise once the attack came. This would tend to increase the chances for a successful attack, rather than reduce them as intended with CBMs.

Two well-known models of conflict in this century help illustrate the main theoretical problem: how to find CBMs whose false positive signals are minimal and whose false negative aspects are equally low across the range of circumstances in which they might be employed – from peace, to crisis, to war, and even beyond.

One model draws on the First World War to portray a conflict that emerges and broadens through a series of escalatory steps. In the historic case, these steps started with a lone terrorist act in the Balkans; this provoked an international crisis; it soon escalated to include all the European powers and, ultimately, the United States as well. Whether or not the analogy is entirely correct, this model is often called upon to represent a war that comes about largely by miscalculation (e.g. the Germans overreacted to Russian mobilization efforts and failed to count seriously enough on Belgian resistance or British intervention), if not exactly by misunderstanding or accident.

The other model, of course, derives from the Second World War experience. It features an escalatory path from crisis to international conflict that is calculated, deliberate, and cloaked in as much secrecy as can possibly be maintained. The relentless land-grabs charted by Germany under Hitler, as well as by Japan under its militaristic leaders in the 1930s and early 1940s, provide the historical examples for this model. It portrays escalation as the product not so much of miscalculation (although there was clearly some of that on both sides) as of premeditation and surprise.

The First World War model serves as a case study for and prime example of those 'false positive' signals of hostile intent noted earlier. The argument in this case is that competing mobilization systems of both the Russians and the Germans (but of the Russians in particular) communicated superficially correct but erroneous information in 1914 about the degree of at least one side's interest in actually going to war. On the basis of this 'false positive' information, the other side also mobilized and then escalated by attacking. If crisis management tools could be found to reduce the likelihood of false positives, therefore, such tools could make a significant contribution to avoidance of this kind of war.

It can be argued that effective CBMs, especially the transparency measures among them, will contribute to the reduction of false positives as long as both sides continue to observe them throughout a crisis. Whatever other information political–military signalling during a crisis may be generating, clear and consistent compliance with established CBMs can send a strong message indicative of a fundamental willingness to keep the crisis in bounds and see it resolved peacefully in the end. CBMs alone may not solve the problem of false positives in a crisis, but their consistent observance by both sides can help. In the strategic force arena, for example, strict adherence to pre-notified test-launch schedules – with no additions to those schedules and possibly even some notified cancellations – could have a decidedly positive effect on preventing a crisis from escalating.

Even if the crisis does escalate, CBMs that have been complied with consistently throughout the crisis can continue to reduce false positives by providing a predictable pattern of military activities. This in itself could serve as a firebreak along the potential path to war and may even create a salutary climate for successful reversal of the original crisis build-up. Once such a reversal has been achieved and de-escalation of the crisis has begun, continued observation of exercise limits and advanced notification requirements for strategic or conventional forces should pay additional benefits in mutual trust and understanding. Good measures and good packages of measures that work effectively during the escalation of a crisis should work equally effectively during de-escalation of the crisis. Their context changes from one case to the other but not the individual and collective worth of the measures themselves.

In the Second World War model of a crisis building to conflict, of course, consistent implementation of established CBMs could prove disastrous. If one side is intent on launching a war, compliance with established CBMs might help that side conceal its intent and increase its chances for a successful surprise attack. If a broad strategy of deception by a cunning attacker included a pattern of CBM compliance, it could lull an otherwise wary defender into a false sense of confidence about the true nature of a crisis. Deceptive compliance with CBMs could conceivably help mask the attacker's true intent entirely or, more likely, so confuse the situation that the defender's attention is distracted from other, more telltale indicators of intent. Such dangers might be even greater on the de-escalatory side of a crisis than they might be on the escalatory side. Hitler, after all, cultivated just such a false sense of confidence among his opponents without the benefit of CBMs; he attacked Poland on 1 September 1939, for example, only after having created the impression that the hour of maximum danger had passed.

The defender's own continued compliance with CBMs in a crisis could even increase the risks. For example, a strategic force stand-down that was employed as a CBM might help dampen a crisis temporarily. If the Second World War model is operating, however, the potential defender might need to be alerting forces – not standing them down – in order to demonstrate readiness, resolve, continued vigilance and determination, all of which might help deter an impending conflict or, at least, better prepare the defender for it.

Transparency CBMs, therefore, do not help much and may even prove counterproductive in the Second World War model. Even in the First World War model they could prove problematical. If a state employs such measures to send signals of its continuing resolve, for example, as in the case of properly notifying (in order to call attention to) a large military exercise in the midst of a crisis, the result could be escalation, not de-escalation of the crisis.

More trustworthy indicators of actual intent might be continued observance of constraint measures throughout a crisis. This would especially be the case when such measures themselves limited military capabilities that were absolutely essential for going to war. If, for example, both sides had agreed in advance to keep all their ammunition (or their missiles) downloaded and under continuous observation by the other side in designated storage sites, and they maintained that constraint throughout the crisis, then one might have reasonable assurance that the First World War model applied and that there was a well-founded hope of controlling further escalation.

On the other hand, if the agreed constraints were not highly essential to a war effort, or not very easy to verify, or relatively simple to overcome – e.g. constraints on the presence of certain types of equipment or on unit readiness levels within specified regions along geographic frontiers – then the continued observance of such measures could provide 'false negative' signals of intent. Fixation upon constraints as indicators of a potential attacker's intent could blind potential defenders to other indicators (e.g. movements of forces or logistics not regulated by a CBM regime) that might be more instructive in the circumstances. Furthermore, a potential attacker might be able to avoid having to violate existing constraints, even those that significantly impair the ability to launch an attack, until the eleventh hour of a crisis and break them only as the first step in escalating to war itself.

Some combination of both transparency and constraint measures, supplemented by robust observation and inspection provisions, would appear to hedge best against the distinctive problems posed by both the First World War and Second World War models. In different ways, both transparency measures and constraints work the problems of false positive and false negative signals of intent, while inspection and observation measures help clarify ambiguities when, inevitably, these arise. Ultimately, it is the combination of all three types of measures, working together in synergy, that stand the best chance of providing the necessary clarification required – not any one type of measure alone.

But what happens during a crisis in which CBMs have lost their punch? Perhaps both sides have chosen to violate or otherwise ignore them, yet the consequence is not war but, simply, a further, deeper crisis? Perhaps violation of a CBM regime has precipitated the actual 'crisis' itself. One could argue that Hitler's remilitarization of the Rhineland in 1936 conclusively violated (in the sense of finally overthrowing the last vestiges of) a CBM regime dating from the Treaty of Versailles, thus germinating an international crisis in Europe that escalated gradually but relentlessly over the next five years toward all-out war. What more, if anything, can CBMs then be expected to contribute to the situation? For that matter, what can they possibly contribute once a crisis has peaked and both sides are looking – or one side is not looking, as in Hitler's case – for mutual ways to de-escalate?

Most of these questions will be addressed in the third section of this chapter, which deals further with the potential contribution of CBMs to crisis management – in particular, to crisis de-escalation – even if they have been dispensed with or violated during a crisis. At this point, however, it should be observed that CBMs probably cannot carry the entire burden of such management alone. Without corroboration from other intelligence indicators, they really should not be counted on to distinguish definitively between 'false positive' and 'false negative' signals of intent, as discussed in conjunction with the First World War and Second World War models of escalation. It was noted earlier in this chapter that, by themselves, CBMs can hardly be relied on to carry major peacetime responsibilities (e.g. to provide an arms control alternative to, or in the absence of, force reductions). It should come as no surprise now to learn that they simply cannot be expected to bear the additional burdens of crisis management on their own.

1.3 THE HISTORICAL EVOLUTION OF CBM THEORY

What we now call CBMs probably owe their origins, at least in part, to the European military practice of inviting observers from various states to military exercises, which dates back to the years prior to the First World War, if not earlier. Similar measures emerged after that war in the context of the Versailles Treaty's attempt to control a defeated Germany.[2] Among other things, that treaty provided for demilitarization of the Rhineland (a type of constraint) and on-site inspections announced six days in advance (an access measure).

Following the Second World War, military liaison missions between and among the four victorious Allied powers were established, ostensibly to improve relationships (build confidence) between the forces of those Allies that were occupying Germany. With the onset of the Cold War, these missions soon turned into military intelligence-gathering devices (access measures) for all parties involved. In the 1950s and 1960s, forerunners of more modern-day CBMs were proposed at the Surprise Attack Conference held in Geneva during 1958 and to the Eighteen Nation Disarmament Committee in 1962.[3] Two US proposals during this period were actually instituted in the form of the hotline's direct communication links between national command authorities in Washington and Moscow (a communications CBM) and the agreement to ban nuclear testing in the atmosphere (a constraint measure), both of which were agreed to in 1963.

First-generation CBMs

CBMs as we now know them were born during the period of detente in US–Soviet relations that characterized the first half of the 1970s. This was a period of considerable, if short-lived, progress in both strategic nuclear and conventional arms control efforts. SALT I and the ABM treaty in the early 1970s were followed by the Vladivostok Agreement in 1975, which raised expectations that yet another strategic arms treaty (SALT II) would be concluded before the end of the decade.

Fueling further expectations of progress in arms control, the United States and the USSR signed, in succession: an Agreement on Measures to Reduce the Risk of Outbreak of Nuclear War in 1971, which provides for immediate notification of an accidental, unauthorized, or unexplained nuclear detonation; the Incidents at Sea Agreement of 1972, which attempts to decrease the potential for ship-to-ship harassment (e.g. simulated attacks) during peacetime; and, in 1973, a declaratory Agreement on the Prevention of Nuclear War, which provides for immediate and urgent consultations in times of crisis. In 1973, moreover, negotiations aimed at reducing both NATO and Warsaw Pact conventional force structures in Central Europe commenced in Vienna, while preparations were well underway for a new Conference on Security and Cooperation in Europe (CSCE) with participation by all European states (except Albania) plus the United States and Canada.

This latter context (CSCE) witnessed the birth of the first generation of CBMs, properly so called. They were designed primarily for conventional forces in Europe. However, their arrival on the international scene was not genuinely welcomed by the superpowers, who placed whatever real hopes they might have had for conventional arms control in Europe on the MBFR negotiations in Vienna.[4] Instead, CBMs were the favored child of neutral and non-aligned European states. These states resented their exclusion from the alliance-oriented Vienna negotiations and insisted on inserting something more than declarations of principles into the 'security' component of CSCE.

The result of these and other international interests and negotiating pressures was the 'Document on Confidence Building Measures' in the Helsinki Final Act of 1975. It contained a variety of CBMs involving:

- notification in advance (21 days) of
  - major military maneuvers (beyond 25 000 troops);
  - other maneuvers (below 25 000 troops);
  - major military movements (undefined);
- invitation of observers to major military maneuvers.

In terms of the different types of CBMs discussed above, these CBMs were heavily weighted toward transparency measures, given the predominance of notification provisions. Although the provision for invitation of observers was discretionary on the part of the state conducting the maneuvers, its inclusion in the package represented a nod, at least, in the direction of access measures.

The theory behind these measures was not the one associated with contemporary arms control efforts such as MBFR. Throughout the 1970s, in fact, the United States consistently refused to consider CBMs in the general category of arms control. Their purpose was not to limit the capabilities or otherwise control the military forces that states had in being, it was argued, much less reduce their numbers. Nor were there any verification provisions attached to these measures. Instead, as indicated in the Final Act and elsewhere, CBMs were aimed at increasing 'openness', reducing the secrecy with which military matters were traditionally surrounded (particularly in Eastern Europe), and improving the predictability of military activities in general.

In a word that was to become emblematic of this rationale in years to come, promoting greater 'transparency' with regard to military affairs in Europe was to be the main purpose of CBMs. Greater transparency, in turn, was expected to reduce the mutual suspicion that secrecy tends to breed as well as reflect. In theory, this would then lessen the chances that war might come about as a result of misunderstanding or miscalculation.

According to this theory, increasing the transparency or openness of military activities in Europe might even lessen fears that a surprise attack could occur or that military exercises could be used successfully for political intimidation. When explained in terms of a hierarchy of arms control objectives, therefore, CBMs could be said to promote the immediate objective of increasing transparency. This would then promote higher-level arms control objectives like reducing miscalculation and misunderstanding, which in turn would support even higher-level objectives such as preventing war and preserving peace.[5]

But there were few illusions about the ability of CBMs to promote these higher-level arms control objectives any time soon, especially among the superpowers and their allies. The absence of any specific verification provisions for the Helsinki measures, their non-binding character as voluntary *political* – as opposed to mandatory *legal* – measures, and even their lack of definitional rigor (e.g. the term 'major military movement' was left completely undefined) effectively undercut any hopes that the Helsinki CBMs might actually go beyond the goal of simply promoting greater military transparency.

Nuclear force analogues

Relevant analogues in the strategic nuclear arena to the first-generation of conventional force CBMs might include, for example, notification in advance of test launches of ballistic missiles and the invitation of observers from the other side to witness such events. If notification far in advance of the event proved difficult to achieve, the Helsinki experience would suggest that notification of strategic nuclear exercises just before or soon after their commencement could be substituted. In this case, any provision for the invitation of observers would also be obviated. By May 1988, in fact, the United States and the Soviet Union had agreed to notify each other, 'no less than twenty-four hours in advance, of the planned date, launch area, and area of impact for any launch of a strategic ballistic missile', whether an intercontinental ballistic missile (ICBM) or a submarine-launched ballistic missile (SLBM). The agreement did not provide for observers to be present at the launches.[6]

The Helsinki CBMs tend to suggest that some grading of strategic activities might be possible. As in the case of major military maneuvers of ground forces that exceed 25 000 troops, some threshold could be established for strategic nuclear forces – say, any exercise involving more than one missile-launch. Such exercises might be singled out for special treatment, as major maneuvers were in the Final Act. They could be subjected to notification further in advance of their occurrence and to observer requirements, while other exercises because they are smaller (and presumably less threatening) are held to less stringent standards – for example, notification 'no later than twenty-four hours' in advance and no provision for observers, as in the current US–Soviet agreement on single missile-launches.

The theory behind employing such measures in the nuclear world would be the same as it is for similar measures in the conventional force arena. If one is on the other side, knowing in advance about such activities as test launches of nuclear delivery systems – especially simultaneous multiple launches of such systems – removes some of the apprehension that is bound to be associated with such events. Having observers invited to the launches should lower this level of apprehension further. Even simply being informed at the initiative of the side conducting a strategic nuclear exercise that it is about to happen or has just occurred would probably have a calming effect.

According to the theory of increasing transparency, the mere fact that the side conducting a potentially threatening activity tells the other side about it tends to reduce likely anxiety levels. Is this a good thing, or could such measures be used to promote a false sense of confidence in situations where greater apprehension might be warranted – for example, if the notification of an exercise, even the invitation of observers to it, were a clever prelude to a surprise attack? Critics of early CBM theory were quick to raise this question and to diminish the potential utility of such measures as a result of negative answers to it. The dual effect of CBMs in promoting transparency – i.e. they can reduce apprehensiveness but, in the process, can conceivably build 'false' confidence – was a theoretical problem that the first generation of CBMs could not solve.

Second-generation C(S)BMs

A new generation of CBMs grew out of the attempt to solve this and other problems. Born in the wake of the Soviet invasion of Afghanistan in 1979, as well as Soviet threats to Poland in the early 1980s, the new measures were both an outgrowth of and a reaction to the virtual disappearance of detente in East–West relations. It was one thing to worry about false confidence being generated by CBMs in a period of declining tensions and increasing arms control. It was quite another matter to contemplate this problem as tensions were mounting and CBMs were being used, as they were by the Soviet Union *vis-à-vis* Poland in 1981, to magnify the signals of political intimidation that were clearly being sent by Soviet force deployments.[7]

Furthermore, because of the precipitate decline of detente, the early 1980s were temporarily bereft of traditional arms control efforts. SALT II was suspended, the START talks took long to unfold, the Soviets initially refused INF negotiations, and things slowed to even less than their customary snail's pace in MBFR. On this barren landscape, two outcroppings appeared that were later to yield substantial fruit. One was the effort by several US Senators (Sam Nunn, John Warner, Henry Jackson) to ease tensions that were apparent within the United States (e.g. in the nuclear-freeze movement) as well as in Europe over interruption of the superpower dialogue. They proposed negotiation with the Soviets of new crisis-management tools to include, if feasible, nuclear risk reduction centers manned simultaneously and continuously by both sides. Such proposals ultimately resulted in new American–Soviet agreements to add a facsimile transmission capability to the hotline (signed in 1984) and to establish nuclear risk reduction centers in Washington and Moscow (signed in 1987) primarily to exchange the information and notifications required under other agreements on arms control or confidence-building measures.[8]

The other effort that grew and developed in the arms control wasteland of the early 1980s was the attempt to negotiate a new and improved set of CBMs for conventional forces in Europe. This effort reached fruition in the Stockholm Document on Confidence and Security Building Measures of 1986. The addition of 'security' to the title of CBMs in that document, thereby making them 'CSBMs', signified that new objectives had been devised for such measures. In the language of the document, which took over six years to negotiate (not only in Stockholm itself but also at the Madrid review meeting of CSCE, where agreement even to hold the Stockholm talks took three years to reach), the new measures were to be more 'militarily significant, binding, and verifiable' than their predecessors. They were to have more politico-military 'bite', hence a greater 'security' component, as protective compensation for the sharp downturn in East–West relations that was occurring at the time.

As negotiated in Stockholm, the new CSBMs consisted of the following *mandatory* measures – i.e. they were no longer subject to a participating state's discretionary choice as to whether or not, or to what degree, to observe them, in any category:

- notification in advance of major military exercises or 'concentrations' of force (whether movements or maneuvers) involving lower thresholds than those for previous CBMs (e.g. 17 000 versus 25 000 troops);
- notification upon commencement of the activity of certain other exercises required to be notified in advance;
- publication a year in advance of annual calendars of all military activities subject to prior notification;
- invitation of observers to all exercises or concentrations required to be notified in advance;
- on-site inspection by challenge, subject to a limit of three on any one country's territory per year;
- constraints on the ability to conduct large-scale exercises that have not been notified one (40 000+ troops) or two years (70 000+ troops) in advance.

In terms of the different types of measures discussed in section 1.3 above, this package, while still focused on transparency measures for improved information and notification, was more heavily weighted toward access measures (non-discretionary observation and inspection provisions) than its Helsinki predecessor. It even made a first step in the direction of constraint measures.

The theory behind these 'CSBMs' was no longer that of transparency *per se*. Transparency was still an immediate objective, of course, one which figured prominently in the Stockholm Document's various notification requirements. Moreover, the negotiations in Stockholm featured at least one serious proposal to create a multinational consultative mechanism for the face-to-face exchange of information. One hope for this proposal was that it might evolve into a crisis management center for Europe along the lines that Senators Nunn and Warner were proposing for the United States and Soviet Union. In the spirit of the times, some suggested that CSBMs themselves might be better understood as tools for the management of crises that otherwise might escalate to nuclear conflict; thus, they too should be considered 'nuclear risk reduction' measures.[9]

In addition to proposals for special consultative mechanisms, which were ultimately unsuccessful at Stockholm, and to proposals for notification of specified activities in advance, which were adopted, other requirements were included in the Stockholm Document to insure that any information provided as a result of increased transparency (through the annual calendar requirement, for example, or the lower thresholds) could be trusted. The aim for the new CSBMs was to help guarantee that seeing was indeed tantamount to believing. As noted above, this had demonstrably not been the case for CBMs.

The new objective for CSBMs, therefore, included not only prevention of war by misunderstanding or miscalculation (hence, the need for greater transparency) but also a reduction in the possibilities for surprise attack and even, if possible, in the ability to use military forces for the purpose of political intimidation (as the Soviets had in Poland). Key to success for the new measures lay in their provision of independent means for verification of compliance and intent. A potential attacker could still attempt to mask preparations for war and maintain opportunities for surprise by continuing to comply with the CSBM regime to the last possible moment. The hope was, however, that such continuing compliance with the notification requirements would force a degradation in attack preparations and that, in any event, such preparations would be detected through measures providing for observation and on-site inspection. If an attacker were to refuse to permit such observations or inspections in hopes of preserving secrecy, that refusal itself would send a warning signal to the defender.

In theory, the new measures sought to prevent war both by increasing the transparency of military activities in general and by creating a telltale double-bind for the potential attacker, should increased transparency alone fail to provide the defender with accurate information. The objective was a worthy one and the Stockholm CSBMs came surprisingly close to achieving it. Their potential for success hinged on the Stockholm Document's verification measure, which for the first time provided for on-site inspections to be invoked at the discretion of the inspecting side. However, the number of such inspections that the Stockholm Document permits on any given state's territory in any given year – three – is probably too low to help guarantee that a potential surprise-attacker will ever be faced with the double-bind. The number of such inspections may even be too small to help prevent misunderstanding or miscalculation, although nothing prevents a state from waiving its rights, upping the quota, and permitting additional inspections on its territory in the interests of clarifying an ambiguous situation and preserving the peace. (In a crisis, this would itself be a kind of confidence-building measure.)

Furthermore, it is not clear that Stockholm's notification thresholds themselves are low enough to complicate a determined attackers' planning for surprise. It is conceivable that such an attacker could artfully make all the preparations necessary within the calendar and notification requirements established, endure several on-site inspections without detection of the hidden intent, and go on to launch a surprise attack successfully – the more so, because of overt, up-to-the-last-minute compliance with the CSBM regime. Such compliance may not enable a potential attacker to mask other indicators of hostile intent as well, but it might help confuse a defender's attempt to assess the full significance of these other indicators.

Although such a scenario is conceivable, it is probably highly unlikely because the risks of random detection are too great. CSBMs measurably improved on CBMs in this regard, and attempts to improve them further – e.g. by expanding information exchanges, improving access quotas, lowering thresholds for notifications, and establishing a risk reduction center for Europe – are likely to be achieved at the CSBM negotiations, which have taken place in parallel with the Conventional Armed Forces in Europe (CFE) talks in Vienna. Nevertheless, CSBMs are not as foolproof as one would like, given the stakes involved, nor do they have much positive effect on reducing the uses of force for political intimidation.

No-notice alert measures of significant size can still be called with impunity in a crisis, thus adding to rather than dampening the potential for escalation.[10]

Nuclear force analogues

Relevant analogues in the nuclear world to second-generation CSBMs could include annual calendars, exchanged a year or more in advance, of planned strategic force exercises that are otherwise subject to notification (either in advance or at their outset, as discussed above). One would expect that all strategic missile test launches might be listed on such calendars but, beyond that, it is hard to say what thresholds for other activities might be set. For example, might all strategic submarine deployments – to include going on and coming off patrols – be encompassed in calendar requirements? Might not only the exercises but also the (re)deployment of strategic aircraft be included as well?

All activities listed on the calendar would be subject to reconfirmation via a separate notification process that would take effect the closer one got to the actual event. As part of this process, observers could be invited to certain exercises – e.g. all land-based ballistic missile launches – as a matter of right. Furthermore, each side would have the right to a certain number of random challenge inspections on the other side's territory every year for the purpose of monitoring compliance with CSBMs for nuclear forces more thoroughly. These inspections could conceivably be limited to land-based strategic facilities and might include rights to inspect launch facilities, air bases, and ports – even silos, aircraft loads, or submarine tubes, if both parties could agree to make such assets available for inspection.

CSBMs in a strategic context could also attempt to constrain the ability of both sides to conduct certain military activities. The Stockholm Document sought to do this for conventional forces by prohibiting (in effect) exercises between 40 000 and 70 000 troops that were not notified one year and two years, respectively, in advance. A comparable CSBM for strategic forces might, for example, rule out mixed forces exercises – i.e. air, land, and sea, or any combination of the two – that were not planned and placed on an annual calendar at least one or two years in advance. Another possibility might be to require that all test launch azimuths and target location be pre-announced well in advance (e.g. via an annual calendar) and to prohibit any additions, corrections, or changes other than cancellation of the test entirely.[11]

Third-generation C(S)BMs

In the area of East–West military competition, the world of the late 1980s appeared to be a kinder and gentler place than it had been in any other decade since the Second World War. Detente-like conditions had returned to the fore, the arms control industry was booming again, and prospects for peace and prosperity being at the head of everyone's agenda for Europe had never been brighter. In particular, the limits of the possible in conventional arms control appeared to be infinitely expandable, at least for the near term.

Into this world, where so many new things seemed feasible that were out of the question before, a new generation of CBMs were introduced. These measures would seek to set limits or 'constraints' on conventional military forces that were much tighter and more direct than any witnessed thus far. Instead of trying to limit military exercises indirectly, as the Stockholm Document did with calendar notification requirements of up to two years in advance, the new measures would simply and directly ban the specified activities. If exercises above a certain threshold were a problem, then exercises at those levels would be prohibited. If high readiness levels among units were the issue, then constraint measures would dictate what the acceptable levels should be, in effect, by defining and prohibiting certain unacceptable levels. If the problem involved deployment of particular forces in certain areas or so-called 'keep-out' zones, then these too could be drawn up, tailored specifically to the forces at issue, and subjected directly to a ban on deployments there.

Constraints of this type have been proposed in the context of negotiations on CFE. To accompany the force reductions to parity that it is advocating in those negotiations, NATO has put forward a package of proposals that includes measures for information exchange, stabilization, and verification. Most of these measures resemble CSBMs in the ways that they are intended to operate. For example, the NATO package includes a requirement that call-ups of 40 000 or more reservists within the CFE treaty area should be notified to all parties 42 days in advance; a system of inspections that aims to allow all parties to the treaty to inspect each other's forces and activities at virtually any time; and a quintessential transparency measure, namely, a call for each side to disclose the exact location of its military units as well as the quantity and types of its treaty-limited equipment.

This same NATO package, however, also includes constraint measures of the type described above. The package contains provisions for placing various types of military equipment (e.g. tanks, artillery, armored troop carriers, and bridging equipment) in monitored storage sites and for limiting the amount of such equipment that can be removed from storage at any given time. It also bars signatories of the treaty from conducting military exercises in excess of 40 000 troops or 800 main battle-tanks more than once every two years. In addition, NATO would require CSBM-like notification a year in advance of such exercises being conducted and notification 42 days in advance for any movement of permitted equipment out of the storage sites.[12]

In terms of the types of measures discussed in section 1.1, therefore, the NATO proposals are robust and balanced across the board. There are proposals in every category, including some of the most demanding information and inspection provisions yet seen in arms control. In addition, there are real and direct limits – i.e. constraints – on the use of the forces that were to remain after CFE reductions.

There is no reason in theory, however, why constraint measures cannot be negotiated independently, whether or not they are accompanied by arms reduction agreements. In fact, in the absence of such agreements, certain types of constraints (e.g. strict limits on the movement of forces outside of their garrisons) might provide some substitute for force reductions. When combined with effective verification measures, such as the 'small army of inspectors' that NATO is expecting to have visiting Warsaw Pact military units 'at short notice, with no right of refusal', constraints on conventional forces could add significantly to the warning-time available in advance of a conflict.[13]

Constraint measures deal more forthrightly and directly with the theoretical problem that CSBMs attempt to solve via the synergistic effect of notification and inspection measures. Recall from the discussion above that such measures, in combination, are intended to confront a potential attacker with the problem of a double-bind. Constraints sharpen that bind by establishing prohibitions on military activities that are significant, more straightforward to define, and relatively easy to verify. Any violations of those prohibitions, therefore, are grounds for serious and immediate concern.

Robust verification measures, like the on-site inspection regime that NATO is proposing for CFE, add confidence to the value of the information afforded by constraints, as in the case of CSBMs. But in the case of constraints, the prohibitions involved are clearer and more direct, with fewer loopholes. CSBM notification requirements provide their own built-in exceptions – e.g. alert exercises, even those at the same thresholds required for notification in advance, can be called on a moment's notice, with only notification upon initiation of the alert being necessary, at the discretion of the side conducting the exercises. In theory, constraint measures allow for no such exceptions, or if they do, they are of the scope and magnitude reportedly envisaged in the current NATO proposal, wherein any nation 'that believes "extraordinary events" endanger its "supreme interests" may withdraw from the proposed conventional arms-control treaty after giving three months' notice.'[14]

Nuclear force analogues

Analogues to constraints on conventional force activities for strategic nuclear forces are relatively easy to suggest, but potentially hard to swallow, one suspects. Prohibitions on exercises involving multiple rocket launches, or launches in a certain direction (e.g. north–south, as opposed to east–west), or with depressed trajectories are several possibilities for land-based strategic missile forces. Mixed force exercises – i.e. air, ground, and sea forces, variously combined – might also be banned outright, rather than limited more indirectly through annual calendar notification provisions of the kind discussed above in connection with the Stockholm Document's CSBMs.

Other possibilities might include prohibitions on concealment of strategic nuclear force exercises. The United States and the Soviet Union, for example, might agree on the kind and extent of telemetry information that they would both pledge not to encrypt during a missile launch. In addition, the two sides might agree that strategic ballistic missile test launches could only be conducted from designated test sites, in effect banning any launches in peacetime or in a crisis from any other sites. Going further, both parties might conceivably agree to maintain, in both peacetime and crisis, various sanctuaries for each side's strategic submarines and corresponding keep-out zones for the other side's anti-submarine warfare assets. Such measures could provide firebreaks in a crisis that otherwise seemed out of control, even a crisis that had already erupted into a conflict.[15]

1.4 C(S)BMs AND CRISIS DE-ESCALATION

Thus far in this chapter, CBMs and the theories behind them have been presented as mechanisms that might be able to help prevent development of, or manage as it develops, an international crisis. The preceding discussion, therefore, has been oriented mainly toward the 'peace' side of the arms-control spectrum presented in section I and couched primarily in terms of the contributions that various measures might make at the front end of a crisis. The dominant questions addressed have been how to prevent needless crises from arising or escalating in the first place and how to help discern true intentions in a crisis that cannot be avoided because of a fundamental conflict of interests (as in the Second World War model discussed above).

It remains to ask whether and how different types of CBMs, but especially those involving the nuclear force analogues noted above, might contribute to crisis de-escalation and possibly even war termination. In this context, it would seem to make a fundamental difference whether a CBM regime has been in existence and continuously observed throughout the transition from peace to crisis escalation and beyond, or whether the regime has been violated in whole or in part at any time during the transition, thus requiring reestablishment of former measures or creation of new ones on an *ad hoc* basis.

In the best case, the integrity of a CBM regime would endure and, ideally, furnish signs that certain restraints, at least, are still being maintained despite the crisis. One would hope that, somehow, such signs might even help defuse the crisis and direct it toward the path of de-escalation. In less than ideal circumstances, a CBM regime might survive the crisis intact but have little influence on its development or resolution; nevertheless, if the regime survived the ordeal, CBMs might play a welcome role in de-escalation. Where they had no influence before, the measures might find themselves awash in a wellspring of interest because of their potential utility in the changed circumstances. Even if certain measures within the regime (e.g. notification provisions) had been violated during a crisis, others that were more militarily significant or important to crisis management (e.g. constraint measures) might have been complied with unfailingly. Such continued compliance might help set the stage for successful resolution of the crisis, perhaps by maintaining a baseline of CBM activity that remains trustworthy (e.g. because of continued compliance with constraints) and capable of expanding to include other measures – even measures previously violated (e.g. disregarded notification requirements).

When adherence to an existing CBM regime is maintained throughout a crisis build-up, as in the best case, it would seem that all the different types of measures discussed above would be able to contribute positively to de-escalation of the crisis. Communication via hotlines or risk reduction centers could serve to notify the other side of changes in force dispositions or activities. To confirm what was actually taking place, transparency measures might establish procedures for going off alert, which could include notification procedures for the standing down of forces as well as additional data exchanges. These might be supplemented by monitoring devices at strategic nuclear force bases, silos, or elsewhere and by access measures providing for observers or inspectors of stand-down operations at these locations. Uninterrupted adherence to constraint measures, such as limits on the number, direction, or force mix of test launches or exercises would clearly help, as a kind of earnest for each side's desire to maintain at least some controls over an escalation. If they were continuously monitored by access measures of one type or another, constraints could also help guard against possibilities for a surprise attack, especially at a time when it might least be expected (e.g. once the peak of the crisis seems to have passed) and an unsuspecting defender might be most vulnerable (e.g. as it was standing down its forces).

A robust regime of measures, like the third-generation proposals discussed above, would be more ideally suited for this role than individual measures by themselves or less robust first-generation (transparency-oriented) or second-generation (access intensive) packages of measures. But even with less than robust measures, when it comes to finding messengers of intent in times of crisis, there is still an advantage inherent in relying on CBMs that have already been established and operating for some time. Such measures, imperfect as they may be, may simply pose fewer risks than those that might result from trying to invent new measures on the spot. At a minimum, there is a language, a track record, and some shared understanding of what existing measures are intended to convey that is cultivated during a peacetime experience with them. There may not be any such shared experiences for *ad hoc* measures, and the intensity of a crisis may not provide sufficient time to establish a mutually understood basis for implementing, much less interpreting, them properly.

The hotline between the superpowers, after all, is not simply a communications link consisting of receivers and transmitters but, rather, established procedures – even agreed-upon formats – for their use. In much the same way, previously-established C(S)BMs are part of the established communicative structures of international life, forged through long years of negotiation and experience. Improved or even acceptable substitutes for them may prove impossible to invent, introduce, or gain mutual acceptance for on the fly, least of all in the midst of a crisis.

But even in the best case, where all previously-established C(S)BMs are being complied with throughout a crisis, there may be an inherent limit to what such measures can contribute to de-escalation of the crisis. After all, if the C(S)BMs have been working properly all along, then the crisis itself must have arisen over other (non-CBM) issues. It seems unlikely, therefore, that C(S)BMs themselves can somehow bring about a settlement of those issues. Only in a case where violation of a C(S)BM had provoked or fueled the crisis would compliance with the C(S)BMs appear to promise a settlement.

In a crisis where C(S)BMs have been and continue to be complied with, 'more of the same' is simply not a very promising recipe for de-escalation of the crisis. The best that C(S)BMs can hope to contribute in such circumstances are: a baseline, or rules of the road for ongoing military activities, as discussed above; facilities (e.g. the hotline or other communication means) for continuing crisis management and the pursuit of de-escalation; and some breathing space for the exploration and development of initiatives (other than CBMs) that could produce a satisfactory resolution of the crisis short of war. This last contribution – C(S)BMs' potential help in 'buying time' for crisis de-escalation to begin – may be the most important one of all.

In the worst case, not only the existing regime of CBMs but also individual measures may have been violated or otherwise dispensed with in the course of a crisis. Does this mean that the further usefulness of these CBMs in that same crisis is finished, for either escalation or de-escalation control, or might they still play some helpful role? The re-emergence of compliance with an existing set of CBMs that had been violated earlier in a crisis by one side or the other would certainly send an interesting signal. It might be a sign of willingness to de-escalate, it might represent an attempt to set limits to the crisis (and, thus, keep it from getting out of hand), or it could be a trick. In any event, such a move to reintroduce the old measures would command a certain degree of attention, particularly in view of the immediately preceding record of non-compliance with those measures.

If, for example, one side or the other started notifying military exercises or test launches that it had failed to notify before during a crisis, the other side would at least have to sit up and take notice. As an attention-getter, therefore, reintroduction of familiar measures and patterns of implementation that have lapsed might help communicate whatever message is intended. It might even communicate that message more effectively, one might argue, than other signals invented on the spur of the moment, in the political–military 'fog' of the crisis.

Nevertheless, while the fact of such messages might stand out clearly, their content would be inherently – even dangerously – ambiguous. Unilateral restoration of agreements previously broken still carry the legacy of having been broken in the first place. The Second World War model of intentionality during a crisis always remains in our minds for its sober reminder that a deceptive ploy could be involved, rather than a genuinely de-escalatory signal or step. Hence, refurbished CBMs are not to be trusted in the same ways that they might have been previously. Advance notification of a major upcoming launch or exercise during a crisis, after a period in which such announcements had not been forthcoming, should breed suspicion as well as heightened attention. The effect may be to focus the attention on the activity thus notified but the proof of its significance as an indicator of intent would depend on what happens next, as a result of the notification and other (CBM and non-CBM) indicators.

Reintroduction of individual measures or an entire package of CBMs that had been violated or suspended during a crisis could conceivably help trigger a process of de-escalation. Such measures, however, probably cannot and should not be trusted to carry the burden alone, at least not in the 'reintroduction' mode. The alternative is a resort to *ad hoc* measures (e.g. notification of force redeployments to the rear, where no requirement for such notification existed previously). As noted above, any approach based on *ad hoc* measures is also fraught with risks, although in this case, if established CBMs can no longer be trusted, there really may be no alternative.

For purposes of crisis de-escalation, in fact, it may never be prudent to write any CBM option off entirely, despite the problems and pitfalls inherent in using either CBMs that have been violated or *ad hoc* measures. Crisis de-escalation, after all, almost by definition implies a search for CBMs – for some kinds of trustworthy footholds that enable opponents to climb carefully and safely back down an escalatory ladder. Once the search for such footholds has begun on both sides, even *ad hoc* or previously violated measures can prove helpful. Such measures themselves may not be trustworthy enough to help initiate the search; something else – a political settlement of issues fueling the crisis, or a ceasefire halting a conventional conflict – may have to stop it from escalating further and start it moving in the opposite direction.

Once a crisis begins to turn down a de-escalatory path, however, the careful, intelligent use of even previously violated C(S)BMs could provide useful mechanisms to advance the process. There really are very few, more trustworthy, military communications devices available. This realization alone should give pause to any temptations by one side or the other to violate established CBMs in a crisis: at a minimum, it might lead to a determination by both sides to maintain compliance with at least some CBMs throughout a crisis. Continued compliance with such measures, or at least some of them (e.g. a commitment to consult in the event of any nuclear explosion, even during a conflict), still affords the best chance of making a positive contribution to crisis management, to avoiding war, and to furthering – if not initiating – the de-escalatory process.

NOTES

1. The current NATO proposals and the joint draft text at the negotiations in Vienna, Austria, to conclude a treaty on Conventional Armed Forces in Europe (CFE) include provisions both for reducing forces (e.g. tanks, artillery, and armored fighting vehicles) and for regulating their operations (e.g. mandatory exchanges of information, measures requiring pre-notification of various military activities, and mechanisms for verification of the entire arms control agreement). See the British American Security Information Council, 'BASIC Reports from Vienna: A regular update on the CFE and CSBM Negotiations from the British American Security Information Council', Washington and London, 21 September 1989.
2. Volker Kunzendorff, *Verification in Conventional Arms Control*, Adelphi Paper No. 245 (London: International Institute for Strategic Studies, Winter, 1989), pp. 14–15.
3. John Borawski, *From the Atlantic to the Urals: Negotiating Arms Control at the Stockholm Conference* (Washington and New York: Pergamon-Brassey's, 1988), pp. 4–5.
4. It is not clear that either the US or the USSR harbored any real hopes for arms control 'results' from MBFR. The US wanted to avoid unilateral withdrawals of US troops from Europe, which Senate Majority Leader Mike Mansfield was proposing at the time; the USSR wanted the CSCE for political and economic reasons. MBFR was the price for both.
5. Johan Jorgen Holst and Karen Melander, 'European Security and Confidence-building Measures', in Christopf Bertram (ed.), *Arms Control and Military Forces* (London: International Institute for Strategic Studies, 1980), pp. 223–31.
6. United States Arms Control and Disarmament Agency, *Arms Control and Disarmament Agreements: Texts and Histories of the Negotiations* (Washington, DC: ACDA, 1990), p. 457.
7. Borawski, pp. 29, 58–59.
8. ACDA, pp. 336–44.
9. James E. Goodby, *Risk Reduction: A Second Track for Arms Control* (Washington, DC: American Association for the Advancement of Science, 1987).

10. For further analyses of various CSBM proposals launched at the Stockholm talks, see Y. Ben-Horin et al., *Building Confidence and Security in Europe: The Potential Role of Confidence- and Security-Building Measures* R-3431-USDP (Santa Monica: The RAND Corporation, December 1986) and J. Kahan et al., *Testing the Effects of Confidence- and Security-Building Measures in a Crisis* R-3517-USDP (Santa Monica: The RAND Corporation, December 1987).
11. Thomas Hirschfeld at RAND deserves special thanks for his review of an early draft of this chapter; in that review, he suggested a number of possible strategic nuclear analogues for CBMs, some of which are represented here and elsewhere in the chapter.
12. British American Security Information Council.
13. John J. Fialka, 'NATO Proposes Plan for Big Reductions in Conventional Arms, Troops in Europe', *Wall Street Journal,* 22 September 1989, p. 10.
14. Ibid., p. 10. See also the non-circumvention provision in Section V of the British American Security Information Council, p. 7.
15. For further discussion of possible sanctuary proposals, see Alan J. Vick, 'Building Confidence During Peace and War', *Defense Analysis,* Vol. 5, no. 2, 1989, pp. 104–5.

2 A Soviet View

Sergei Y. Tikhonov

2.1 INTRODUCTION

During the past several years, the international situation has changed greatly. Efforts to maintain strategic stability have replaced the desire for strategic superiority. Equally important, new thinking in the Soviet Union has greatly accelerated the political warming between the superpowers. As a result of these developments, the Soviet Union and the United States have come to the conclusion that a nuclear war cannot be won and should never be fought. These events have drastically reduced the probability of the deliberate use of nuclear or conventional weapons.

However, the risk of a military crisis and its consequences still exist. Indeed, the risk of a nuclear exchange is still possible. What has changed, however, is that in the current international climate, a crisis or war may result unintentionally because of misperceptions, misunderstanding, accident, or technical fault. While the probability of this is admittedly small, it remains far greater than that of deliberate conflict.

The purpose of this chapter, therefore, is twofold. First, it identifies potential sources of unintended crises and conflicts and recommends appropriate confidence-building measures. Second, it addresses CBMs and their potential roles in nuclear crisis de-escalation.

The second section discusses deterrence and the continued risk of war. The third further explores sources of unintended conflict. The fourth section outlines the roles of CBMs, including a Soviet view of the usefulness of such measures, and it describes previous Soviet CBM proposals. The fifth section explores CBMs and crisis avoidance. The final section suggests CBMs that may be useful in crisis de-escalation and war termination.

2.2 DETERRENCE AND THE RISK OF WAR

Effectiveness of deterrence

During the cold war, the two main goals of all military and political doctrines, concepts and plans were first, to deter the potential adversary and, second, to win if deterrence failed. The ability to emerge victorious from a nuclear conflict was not only suggested by military planners, but expressed publicly. In 1980, for example, then Vice-President George Bush said that it was possible to win such a war if 'you have a survivability of command and control, survivability of industrial potential, protection of a percentage of your citizens, and you have a capability that inflicts more damage on the opposition than it can inflict on you. That's the way you can have a winner.'[1]

Although the Soviet Union never officially accepted the possibility of successfully waging a limited or protracted nuclear war, some Soviet statements, as well as the Soviet force posture in the 1970s, did not help to clarify the Soviet position.[2] The development of highly-accurate ICBMs convinced many Americans that the Soviet Union not only accepted the possibility of successfully waging nuclear war, but suggested Soviet preemption in crises was highly likely.

Today the situation has changed. We are witnessing enormous political, military, economic, and ideological changes in the world, especially in the Soviet Union and Eastern Europe, and the relations between East and West have improved substantially. The level of military rivalry has been drastically reduced, approaches to the elimination of nuclear and conventional weapons have been accomplished, and the political climate in the world has become much warmer. Today even skeptics believe neither in the 'evil empire' nor in the possibility of 'burying' the other.

The strategic balance and stability that has developed over the past two decades has led many politicians, military men, and scholars to emphasize the stability benefits of deterrence. As Soviet Foreign Minister Eduard Shevardnadze noted, 'We give due credit to that doctrine, recognizing that for a fairly long period of time, it was of some use in maintaining peace.' However, he further argued, 'The new times call for a new policy, because nuclear deterrence inevitably perpetuates the totality of confrontational relations among states.'[3]

The structure of deterrence, depending as it does on the potential for deliberately creating a nuclear holocaust, contains within it all the elements for bringing about a non-deliberate nuclear disaster. Moreover, and particularly worrisome, is the concern that nuclear weapons modernization has increased the danger of an unintended or accidental launch of nuclear weapons.

Many American and Soviet scholars share this concern. Richard Ned Lebow writes, 'The history of Soviet–American relations indicates, however, that armaments, threats, and attempts to portray the use of nuclear weapons as rational policy can help provoke the very kinds of conflicts deterrence is designed to prevent.'[4] Similarly, Soviet scholars have argued that 'the concept of parity (even if calculated with qualitative indexes) and the concept of strategic stability (on which estimates of the likelihood of war are based) have begun to be at variance, whereas in the past they more or less coincided. Thus a paradox takes shape: the threat of premeditated nuclear aggression is decreasing but the threat of war may be increasing'.[5] This ironic, discomforting, and dangerous result of the advancement of technology is often ignored by the advocates of deterrence policy.

Technical aspects of deterrence

The modernization of nuclear weapons during the last two decades has not contributed to crisis stability. The increased accuracy of systems, the introduction of stealth technology, and the reduced flight-times of SLBMs and SLCMs have sharply limited the decision-making process, increased the vulnerability of ICBMs and command and control facilities, raised fears of a preemptive strike, and led to the necessity of maintaining strategic nuclear forces on a high alert status. This concept of 'enhanced readiness' or 'deterrence by readiness', although effective, increases the risk of an accident or a faulty launch of nuclear weapons.

The modernization of early warning systems is intended to improve the capability of detection of any launch of an adversary's missiles and to decrease the quantity of false alarms, i.e.

to improve the capability of recognizing missiles from other objects. These goals are dependent, and their effects are, to some extent, contradictory. As we increase the sensitivity of early warning systems, we simultaneously increase the likelihood of false alarms. These are especially dangerous in conjunction with launch on warning (LOW) policies. LOW substantially increases the risk of accidental launch because of technical errors or faulty human estimates, which often occur in limited decision-making periods. More important, the probability of such mishaps is not a constant value; instead, it increases as weapons are modernized.

The modernization of command and control facilities also does not counter the effects of modernized weapons, nor does it decrease the likelihood of nuclear outbreak. As early warning systems are modernized, the human factor in the command and control loop decreases in importance, and the launch of forces becomes almost exclusively tied to early warning detectors and computers. In combination with short flight-times, such state of the art equipment can lead to disastrous consequences.

In both countries, the launch of nuclear weapons depends on several common interconnected elements in the command and control loop. The most sensitive elements are: information received by the political and military leadership and its interpretation, forces available for retaliation, organizational input, and technical facilities. Errors, mishaps, or faulty human estimates in any part of this loop, especially likely in crises, can lead to unintended use of nuclear weapons and to nuclear war. Ashton Carter has noted that 'an inquiry into accidental initiation of nuclear war must focus not on the first detonation, but on the first decision to order the organized use of nuclear weapons'.[6] It should be emphasized that information alone – that can be false – about the suspected launch of nuclear weapons in a crisis can lead to immediate retaliation and to nuclear war.

Growing awareness and concern of this situation has accelerated efforts at crisis prevention, nuclear risk reduction, and the introduction of CBMs to prevent the unintended or accidental use of nuclear weapons. According to some western scholars, the continuous use of the deterrence will sooner or later lead to nuclear conflict.[7] In short, these researchers have concluded that unintended, undeliberate, or accidental nuclear war is not only possible, but mathematically inevitable in the long term. Moreover, the probability of nuclear war in crises will drastically increase.

2.3 SOURCES OF UNINTENDED CRISES

Crisis environment

The danger of military conflict and nuclear war will remain as long as military blocs and nuclear weapons exist. But how does this danger look nowadays? Changes in the Soviet Union and Eastern Europe have eliminated the possibility of a deliberate military conflict between the two nuclear superpowers or the two military blocs. Even in much more difficult periods, the superpowers did not use military forces against each other; today, fears of the danger of deliberate war are quite unnecessary. While we cannot forecast the future social–political order in the East European countries, there is no doubt that it will not be Stalinist orthodox communism. If, as the Soviets have proposed, the two military blocs are transformed into political organizations, the probability of war will decrease further. But, as noted above, the risks of war through accidents, misperception, and actions of third parties will persist.

To develop and implement CBMs that could help to decrease the likelihood of inadvertent military conflict, it is necessary to briefly analyze possible sources of conflict.[8] The reasons that lead to unintended military conflict and the use of nuclear weapons can be placed in two categories: technical and human.

Technical reasons include: faults and mishaps with early warning systems, data proceeding systems, C^3I, nuclear weapons and their guidance systems, launchers, strategic defenses, and the effects of EMP and meteorological conditions.

Human reasons include: misperceptions and misunderstanding of activities of adversaries or third parties, including nuclear terrorism, mistakes in the decision-making process, unauthorized launch of nuclear weapons (especially SLBMs and SLCMs), and uncontrolled escalation of military actions in local conflicts.

The maximum likelihood of unintended or mistaken launch of nuclear weapons exists because of technical reasons in 'vertically-integrated' (early warning systems and communication) systems and because of human factors in 'horizontally-integrated' (command and control of nuclear weapons) systems.

Danger areas

Variants on the use of nuclear weapons, excluding the deliberate decision of the government of any country, include accidental launching, unauthorized use, launching by mistake, launching by third parties, and nuclear terrorism.

Accidental launch

The accidental launch of nuclear weapons may occur for technical reasons, notably in the vertical integration of the C^3I systems. In his often-cited 1986 report to Congress,[9] Bruce Blair wrote that the United States might launch ICBMs if it had warning about Soviet nuclear attack from both satellite infrared sensors and ground radars. But Blair also noted that the launch of nuclear weapons could occur even if signals were received from only one type of sensor.

A single technical mishap in any section of the C^3I system is unlikely to trigger the launch of nuclear weapons. But one cannot rule out a series of mistakes overlapping or following each other with a short interval that does not allow enough time to correct the previous false alarm signal before the coming of the next one.

Early warning systems and computer analysis of signals may, in fact, multiply mistakes. For instance, first-level mistakes in the NORAD system, requiring conferences on 'discovering the missiles', occur on average *twice every three days*. Second-level mishaps, requiring a conference of military–political leadership on the 'assessment of the threat', occur three to four times a year.[10] Fortunately, these have all been correctly assessed as false signals. Yet, this fact should not give grounds for optimism, all the more so in combination with the launch-on-warning concept.

Unauthorized launch

Can nuclear weapons really be used without a corresponding

sanction by political leaders or military commanders? In the Soviet Union, all types of nuclear weapons are under strict control, supplied with PALs (computer and mechanical devices that must be unblocked by a special electronic code) before their employment. This includes the launch of SLBMs, which are under strict negative control.[11]

In the United States, the situation is different. In addition to the President, several persons can launch nuclear arms. In contrast to army and air force weapons, navy nuclear warheads and bombs, including anti-submarine and air defense weapons, are not supplied with PALs.

Unauthorized launch can also occur even with the President's sanction.[12] For example, concerns existed during the Watergate era that President Nixon might order the launch of weapons. In the Soviet Union, the likelihood has been lower due to collective decision-making on launching nuclear weapons. However, the introduction of US-style Presidential powers may change this.

Launching by mistake

Launching by mistake can occur because of overstated assessments of the adversary threat or mistakes in the decision-making process. Former US Defense Secretary McNamara has warned that while cool and rationally-thinking political and military leaders will not use nuclear weapons first, crises do not promote cool, well-informed, or rational thinking.[13]

The possibility of a human mistake leading to the launch of nuclear weapons is exacerbated by the horizontal integration of the C^3I system in both the United States and the Soviet Union, but this is only part of the problem. Early warning and nuclear weapons control systems of one side are connected with those of the other under the action–reaction principle. In practice, the functioning of such an integral system will be a great deal more complicated than in theory. Consequently, the risk of misinterpreting the enemy's actions is also growing.

Launching by third parties and nuclear terrorism

Nuclear weapons in third countries make their accidental or unsanctioned use more likely for reasons beyond those mentioned above. First, uncontrolled escalation in regional conflicts, especially in the Middle East, can lead to unintended use of nuclear weapons. In Europe, British and French nuclear weapons are more vulnerable and less guarded against accidental or unauthorized use, and the risks of superpower nuclear use, especially in political or military conflict, are not trivial.

As more countries obtain nuclear weapons, the likelihood of their unintended use increases. Even more certain, an increase in the number of countries possessing nuclear weapons increases the probability that they will be used as instruments of terror and misinterpreted by the United States or the Soviet Union as acts of superpower aggression.

2.4 ROLES OF CBMs

The importance of structural arms control

CBMs are an increasingly useful tool in reducing the risk of war, but they do not diminish the importance of structural arms control. Today, the total liquidation of nuclear weapons would be the most fundamental long-term measure for avoiding any nuclear crisis and unintended war.

We cannot and should not view structural and operational arms control as separate entities. Rather, structural and operational arms control should be pursued simultaneously, and in the long term will contribute to the common goal of reducing the risk of nuclear war. As a first step in structural arms control talks, the Soviet Union and the United States should stop the production, testing, and deployment of nuclear weapons. The primary goal here is to stop the deployment of new and potentially destabilizing weapons, not to consider confidence-building measures that might reduce the danger once the weapons were deployed.[14] Other nuclear countries should join them in this process. However, in the long term, nuclear disarmament should remain our goal. Until this occurs, the Soviet goal remains mutual deterrence at the lowest force levels consistent with stability. This goal requires invulnerable forces capable of responding to attacks and inflicting unacceptable damage.

At the USA–Canada Institute, a number of studies has been undertaken to determine optimum nuclear force structures at lower force levels. Strategic force reductions of 50, 75, and 95 per cent have been explored.[15] The studies have consistently shown that under 50 and 75 per cent reductions, the main elements of nuclear forces should be single-warhead mobile ICBMs and SSBNs. The studies have also emphasized geographic bans on anti-submarine warfare activities and have advocated drastic reductions in the share of launchers having a large number of warheads with hard target kill capabilities.

Under 95 per cent reductions, the studies argue that the most optimum nuclear structure should consist of 600 mobile single-warhead ICBMs that can be launched along relatively predictable trajectories, enhancing strategic stability. The study concluded that SSBNs should not be included in force structure because of their 'loose' command and control arrangements.

A key aspect of reducing force vulnerability is the bilateral transformation from silo-based to mobile ICBMs and the simultaneous mutual liquidation of counterforce weapons, weapons with short flight-times, and 'invisible' weapons, such as SLCMs and stealth bombers. A ban on stealth research and testing with a simultaneous ban on SLCMs (nuclear and conventional – in order to eliminate verification problems) would play a substantial role in maintaining strategic stability on the highest possible level. This measure would limit the capability for a first strike, yet reserve the potential for retaliation.

A ban on space weapons (including the deployment of SDI) should occur to prevent the undermining of strategic stability. Defensive systems, in combination with offensive nuclear weapons, can create an unpredictable and unmanageable system. Used in conjunction with nuclear weapons, defensive systems can create an illusion of invulnerability, reducing the nuclear threshold. Limited defensive systems under strict quantitative restrictions (like that around Moscow) could serve as safeguards against nuclear terrorists and should be encouraged.

Finally, the Soviet Union supports the installation of self-destructive devices on nuclear warheads.[16] Verification problems exist, especially fears that electronic codes could be discovered by others; nevertheless, the positive effects of this step seem much more important than the negative ones.

Structural arms-control efforts should not be limited to nuclear forces. Restructuring conventional forces in Europe to make surprise attack and offensive operations more difficult is an equally important short-term goal.[17] As surprise-attack operations are made more difficult, the defensive capabilities of conventional forces should be strengthened.

These actions are being considered in European conventional arms talks. CFE agreement should eliminate weapons and facilities used in offensive operations, such as bridging and armored equipment. Limits on troops, tanks, defensive systems, and other weapons in three 50-kilometer corridors on either side of the East–West border in Central Europe (as was proposed by scholars of the USA–Moscow Institute) would undoubtedly enhance stability and mutual confidence.

Unilateral measures can also play an important role in structural arms control efforts. For example, President Gorbachev recently announced that the Soviet Union has decided to unilaterally liquidate some sea-launched weapons in the Baltic. As a first step, the Soviet Union has already withdrawn two SSBNs. By 1991, the remaining four Golf-class SSBNs and their stockpiles of nuclear missiles were liquidated.[18]

CBM benefits and costs

Attempts to prevent unintended nuclear war remain largely outside the traditional arms-control agenda. Traditional arms-control has emphasized quantitative restrictions on arms, but problems involving the unintended use of nuclear weapons have first of all a *qualitative* character, not a *quantitative* one. As such, the likelihood of unintended use depends more on the nature of the weapons, types of launchers, and C^3I systems, and less on the number of weapons. Moreover, quantitative limitations on nuclear weapons, short of their total liquidation, may not drastically influence the likelihood of unintended nuclear war. Fruitful structural arms-control negotiations may enhance crisis stability and may influence perceptions, but they cannot decrease the likelihood of technical faults in C^3I and early warning systems. It is therefore useful to pay more attention to issues of crisis prevention, accidental nuclear launches, and confidence-building measures rather than settle for strategic stability through quantitative restrictions.

Confidence-building measures is a broad term. Generally speaking, actions in any field that serve to increase confidence, mutual understanding, eliminate fears, or establish cooperation (in politics, military affairs, the economy, science, etc.) are

CBMs. These interactions create a global system that can broadly influence relations between particular countries. For instance, economic CBMs (e.g. the creation of joint ventures) can improve the political climate and provide economic opportunities, but they can also indirectly influence the military behavior of countries. Far too little attention has been focused on these non-military CBMs.

The most critical CBMs involve military forces. Military CBMs have similar characteristics and include information exchange and the explanation of military activities and military–political doctrines and strategies. Exchange of military personnel (from Ministers down to soldiers; a good example is the exchange of students between the Soviet military academy and West Point), invitation to military maneuvers, and the establishment of joint risk-reduction centers are other examples. CBMs do not signify disarmament, but they can do much to stabilize the strategic situation, enhance stability, and improve conditions for agreements on arms control reductions.

CBMs might be called 'stabilizing' or 'risk-reduction' measures and deal primarily with military operations rather than capabilities. As US Ambassador James E. Goodby has noted, CBMs promote 'short-term stability during periods of intense and possibly turbulent international confrontation';[19] however, CBMs (especially CBMs designed to avoid crisis) can promote long-term stability and are also very useful in times of detente and peace.

A subset of military CBMs are measures that establish restrictions on or ban certain types of military operations. Most of them broadly serve to prevent or reduce the probability of military conflict beginning from the unintended use of weapons to deliberate military actions.

Military CBMs can be divided into four main categories:

- CBMs that avoid accidental crises
- CBMs that avoid deliberate crises
- CBMs that facilitate alerted force de-escalation
- CBMs that terminate war.

The first two categories are fairly self-explanatory. CBMs that prevent accidental crises often focus on technical failures that can lead to crises, such as failures of early-warning systems. CBMs that prevent deliberate military crises are typically broader in scope, ranging from restrictions on military operations (e.g. limits on alert levels, geographic force restrictions, etc.) to measures that diminish the motivations for surprise attacks (e.g. notification of large-scale maneuvers, challenge on-site inspection of suspicious activities, etc.). De-escalatory CBMs represent special de-escalatory mechanisms to be implemented after alert levels have been increased. The final category of CBMs is a set of 'restoration measures' that depend on the status and nature of the conflict.

Historical aspects

The United States and the Soviet Union have established several agreements to reduce the risk of nuclear war. Most attention has been given to the hotline and to nuclear risk reduction centers in Moscow and Washington. Important measures involving conventional forces have also been established.

The main steps towards more mutual confidence at the conventional level were made in Helsinki and Stockholm. The Helsinki Agreement contained several voluntary provisions described earlier in this volume. The Helsinki CBMs were, however, too narrow to provide a full picture about the real military posture in Europe and contained only limited verification provisions. CBMs established at Stockholm had more of an operational character.

Some Soviet CBMs proposals at the end of the 1960s did not entirely reflect the military–political realities and to some extent were one-sided. Despite their positive sense in general, proposals to establish geographic limits on nuclear-armed bombers, nuclear-armed aircraft carriers, and SSBNs disproportionately served Soviet security interests since Soviet strategic forces consisted mainly of ICBMs, and US forces consisted mainly of SSBNs and bombers.

Nevertheless, several Soviet proposals seemed reasonable and might have been accepted had the Nixon administration been more flexible. For example, the notification of mass take-offs of aircraft (from airfields or aircraft carriers), cooperation to prevent provocative attack by third parties, and the renouncement of the first use of nuclear weapons could have substantially reduced the risk of unintended nuclear war.

2.5 CBMs AND CRISIS AVOIDANCE

Crisis management has two basic imperatives: crisis avoidance where possible, and crisis termination at the earliest and lowest level.[20] We believe that the greatest benefits are to be found in crisis avoidance. This is not to diminish the importance of crisis management; however, crisis management is unpredictable and complex, and the consequences of failed crisis management are enormous. Declaratory CBMs, the establishment of and the expansion of the objectives of risk-reduction centers (RRCs), information exchange, cooperative technical solutions, and operational restrictions can all play an important role in crisis avoidance.

Declaratory CBMs and continued improvements in political relations play perhaps the most critical roles in crisis avoidance.[21] Recent initiatives have greatly reduced the probability of crises.

First, President Gorbachev has advocated the transformation of the Warsaw Pact from a military–political organization into a purely political–military one.[22] While some may dismiss this as rhetoric, it is important to note that this declaration can create a climate in which other more substantive confidence-building measures can be considered. The Warsaw Pact's Political Consultative Committee has similarly advocated a new summit meeting of 35 European states (a 'new' Helsinki) to determine a new, more cooperative European security order.[23]

Second, in accordance with the new principles of foreign policy, Marshal Akhromeyev has emphasized the new united military doctrine of the Warsaw Pact. The Soviet Union and its allies have declared their defensive purpose, indicating that that they would never attack anyone first. The Warsaw Pact has repeated its pledge not to use nuclear weapons first.[24]

The importance of the no first-use pledge should not be understated. The Soviet Union is prepared to mutually renounce the first use of nuclear weapons even if a crisis situation led to the limited use of conventional weapons. Similarly, it has advocated no first use of nuclear weapons until confirmation of the first nuclear impact on its own territory.

The United States has usually treated this issue as little more than Soviet propaganda since a no first-use pledge does not affect the capability for a surprise attack. Theoretically, there is some logic to this argument. But this argument is hollow since both sides have come to the conclusion that there could not be any winner in nuclear exchange regardless of which side strikes first. Moreover, a no first-use pledge (that could be expanded to include conventional weapons) would increase mutual confidence, especially since it would greatly decrease the likelihood of accidental nuclear war resulting from early-warning system failure.

The establishment of RRCs has greatly reduced the danger of unintended war. US Senators Sam Nunn and John Warner certainly had both crisis avoidance and crisis management in mind in creating RRCs. But the centers' most important contributions are the around-the-clock maintenance of communications, facilities, and personnel for *crisis avoidance*.[25] RRCs could, and should take on additional responsibilities, enhancing stability during peacetime and preventing and terminating potential crises at early levels. Centers could facilitate the exchange of information about military maneuvers and nuclear tests, and the exchange of information in case of threats from third parties. The members of the Warsaw Pact's Political Consultative Committee have advocated the creation of similar military risk-reduction centers in Europe.[26]

RRCs could also work in connection and cooperation with the International Space Organization, Delhi Six and with the United Nations. The Soviet Union supports the creation of a multilateral risk reduction center based at the UN, as well as reviving the UN Military Staff Committee. In the future, it would seem very useful to create a network of risk-reduction centers. This network could replace NATO and WTO, serving as a stabilizing axis in post-1992 Europe.

RRCs will facilitate the sharing of information, but the Soviet Union welcomes the greater sharing of information, particularly President Bush's 'open skies' initiative. In addition, the Soviet Union has called for opening up land, the seas and outer space to inspection. It is reasonable for the open-skies concept to be applied to all members of military blocs and to all countries with military bases.[27]

The Soviet Union also supports the notification of strategic force activities and the explanation of their objectives. For example, the flushing of large numbers of SSBNs from their ports, or the take-off of strategic bombers from airfields should be notified in advance and perhaps executed by means of

RRCs. Research from the USA–Canada Institute, under the auspices of Dr Alexander Konovalov, has proposed 'advanced' information-exchange CSBMs, including permanent air surveillance in sensitive zones based on the open-sky concept, and the permanent inspection of offensively-oriented units.

Improvements in C^3I reliability would also serve as useful CBMs, particularly in avoiding unintended conflict. The development and deployment of an international early-warning system independent of national technical means and a subsequent agreement to transmit information to all nuclear countries would greatly reduce the probability of unintended conflict both in peacetime and during crises. The International Foundation of Scientists, led by Evgeniy Velikhov, recommends a slightly different approach. Velikhov has proposed the installation of US-controlled sensors in the Soviet Union and Soviet-controlled sensors in the US. These sensors could inform each side whether missiles had indeed been launched by the other side.

Bilateral changes in the command structure, especially the subordination of tactical nuclear weapons, should also be pursued. In particular, the control of tactical nuclear weapons should be taken out of the conventional forces structure and put under the direct subordination of military–political leadership, as is the case with most strategic forces.[28]

Operational restrictions are also needed to avoid crises. For example, keeping a certain agreed percentage of subs in ports by both sides would lower fears about surprise attack from another side and would enhance crisis stability. The idea of keeping a certain amount of nuclear submarines and bombers in ports and bases meets strong opposition from military circles of both countries. The main old-thinking argument is that such a step can make them more vulnerable and increase the incentives to strike first. This, however, does not correspond with the statement and common sense that nuclear war could not be won.

Operational bans, such as the Warsaw Pact proposals to establish nuclear-free corridor, chemical-free zones, and zones of confidence and cooperation along the East–West border, also seem timely and helpful in avoiding crises. These geographic zones could be expanded as relations continue to improve.

Additional crisis-avoiding CBMs in the conventional field should be pursued. Dr Alexander Konovalov has proposed operational restrictions, including strict limits on offensive forces in areas of direct contact between WTO and NATO, the saturation of these zones with defensive-oriented barrier forces, and the redeployment of offensive-oriented units and categories of weapons out of borderline zones.

Finally, reducing the risks of conflict by third-party involvement should be accomplished by strengthening the non-proliferation regime, thereby reducing the risk of use of nuclear weapons by third parties and involvement of other nuclear powers.

2.6 CBMs, CRISIS DE-ESCALATION, AND WAR-TERMINATION

Despite more than four decades of living with nuclear weapons and several US–Soviet crises, no mechanism exists for reducing nuclear force alert levels. Crises have shown us that political measures are required first for crisis resolution; however, de-escalation mechanisms can greatly reduce the risk of unintended war. As Soviet–US relations continue to improve, operational arms control issues, including ways to reduce nuclear and conventional force alert levels in crises, should be addressed.

In general, de-escalation and war-termination CBMs should be treated as management instruments designed to reduce the pressures from decision-making in crisis and war. CBMs should provide breathing room and slow the decision-making process.

In an unintended military crisis (e.g. one started in the absence of any apparent political dispute), the first de-escalatory measure should be undertaken by the side that initiated the crisis. For instance, if a nuclear submarine accidentally appeared in foreign waters or a hostile aircraft entered foreign airspace, explanations for such actions should be communicated immediately via the hotline or risk-reduction centers. Multiple events, especially if occurring in a short time-period, would probably lead to increased alert levels and might begin an escalatory spiral. It is important that large-scale retaliatory alert measures are avoided.

De-escalation from deliberate increases in alert levels will, of course, occur only after a political resolution to the crisis has been achieved, and then it should occur gradually and on a bilateral basis. The weapons most destabilizing in a crisis should be stood down first: SSBNs, and then counterforce ICBMs. Other measures discussed in this volume would also be useful. Aircraft-free zones, submarine keep-out zones, ASW free zones, and other de-escalatory measures involving troops seem useful in crisis de-escalation.

Unilateral de-escalatory steps are likely to be very important. Even modest unilateral steps, such as insignificant, yet visible decreases in alert rates, could significantly reduce tensions and could serve as 'signals' of confidence. Some danger exists that unilateral steps could be interpreted as weakness, and this could paradoxically lead to crisis re-escalation.

It is difficult to imagine the construction of detailed de-escalatory CBMs during a crisis. Confidence would be lacking, as would the political will for cooperative measures. But the main directions of de-escalatory steps could be elaborated in peacetime through arms-control negotiations. Bilateral (or multilateral) talks should occur immediately after the first military actions (conventional or nuclear) have been undertaken. Hotline and nuclear risk-reduction centers could arrange the exchange of the most urgent information. The role of the UN and its contribution should increase dramatically.

War-termination CBMs are more difficult to construct. They are very delicate measures, and it is very difficult, if not impossible, to establish them in advance for a number of reasons. Their character will depend on the stage of the conflict, damages and losses suffered, the status of communication facilities, perceived opportunities of winning, and many other factors. De-escalation from conventional war is plausible, but the opportunities after a nuclear conflict are limited and perhaps non-existent. Moreover, the transition from conventional to nuclear war may be rapid and unavoidable, also limiting war-termination measures. Because of this, an agreement renouncing the first use of nuclear weapons could play a very positive role.

Mechanism for mutual security

The advent of new thinking in the Soviet Union and the political warming between the superpowers have drastically reduced the probability of the deliberate use of nuclear or conventional weapons. However, the risk of an unintended war remains unacceptably high, and both structural and operational arms control measures should be pursued vigorously in arms-control negotiations. Crisis management must be improved, but more important, crisis avoidance must be our primary goal.

A new security order, including a new approach to international security issues, must also be found. Political, economic, cultural, and other CBMs are critical components of this new order. As Soviet scholar Sergei Rogov has written, 'It is necessary to overcome the inheritance of the "cold war" and to begin the building of the new structure of relations between our two.'[29]

This structure must include new Soviet and US thinking on security issues. In particular, as Andrei Kokoshin of the USA–Canada Institute noted in US Congressional testimony, approaches to security issues in the nuclear age must include mechanisms, including CBMs, for *mutual* rather than individual security.[30] If we fail to adopt this new approach, we will continue to run the risk of unintended nuclear war and its disastrous consequences.

NOTES

1. Robert McNamara, *Blundering into Disaster* (New York: Pantheon Books, 1986), p. 137.
2. The 1976 Communist Party Congress noted, for example, that 'detente does not abolish and cannot abolish or change the laws of class struggle' and that the struggle between the ideologies offered 'no place for neutralism and compromises'. 'Material 25 s'ezda KPSS', Moscow, 1976, pp. 33, 74.
3. Eduard Shevardnadze, 'Is Perestroika a Soviet Version of the New Deal?', *Washington Post,* 8 October 1989.
4. Richard N. Lebow, 'Extended Deterrence: Military Fact or Political Fiction', in Eric H. Arnett (ed.), *New Technology for Security & Arms Control Threats & Promise* (Washington, DC: American Association for the Advancement of Science, 1989), p. 57.
5. Vitaly Zhurkin, Sergei Karaganov, Andrei Kortunov, 'Reasonable Sufficiency – or how to break the vicious circle', *New Times,* 12 October 1987, p. 13.

6. Ashton B. Carter, 'Sources of Error and Uncertainty', in Ashton B. Carter, John D. Steinbruner, Charles A. Zraket (eds), *Managing Nuclear Operations* (Washington, DC: The Brookings Institution, 1987), p. 613.
7. D. Babst, R. Aldridge (eds), 'The Nuclear Time Bomb: Assessing Accidental War Dangers Through Use of Analytical Models', Peace Research Institute, Dundas, Ontario, Canada, 1986.
8. CBMs can also help to reduce the risks of *deliberate* conflict. Avoiding *any* war in Europe (accidental or deliberate) is critical because of the combination of its high population density and its high number of nuclear power-stations and chemical plants. Even conventional war in Europe would lead to environmental consequences equal to those following nuclear war, as our experience with Chernobyl has painfully demonstrated.
9. Blair's report is summarized in D. Babst, R. Aldridge, D. Krieger, *Nuclear Insecurity: the Growing Disparity Between Security and the Danger of Inadvertent Nuclear War,* Technical Report N2, Nuclear Age Peace Foundation, Santa Barbara, 1986.
10. G. Blair, J. Marian, A. Grant, 'No One is Responsible (An Assessment of Software Reliability in Nuclear Weapons Systems)', Department of Computing, University of Lancaster, Bailrigg, Lancaster, 1986.
11. Aleksei Arbatov, 'Strategic Stability: Limiting Competition in Nuclear Arms', in Graham T. Allison and William L. Ury with Bruce J. Allyn (eds), *Windows of Opportunity: from Cold War to Peaceful Competitions in U.S.–Soviet Relations* (Cambridge, Massachusetts, Ballinger Publishing Company, 1989), p. 246.
12. One can argue whether this use of nuclear weapons would be considered unauthorized. However, in this madman scenario, the launch of weapons would certainly not be considered intentional.
13. McNamara, p. 76.
14. Bruce J. Allyn, 'Toward a Common Framework: Avoiding Inadvertent War and Crisis', in Allison, et al., p. 201 notes that 'proposing measures to reduce the risk of inadvertent war while deploying new weapons systems is like putting your feet simultaneously on the brake and the accelerator'.
15. 'Strategic Stability under the Conditions of Radical Nuclear Arms Reductions', Report on a Study, Committee of Soviet Scientists for Peace, Against the Nuclear Threat, Moscow, April 1987.
16. This has also been suggested by McNamara, p. 110.
17. See A. A. Kokoshin, A. A. Konovalov, V. V. Larionov, V. A. Mazing, *Voprosy obespecheniya stabilnosti pri radicalnyh sokrazcheniyah vooruzhennyh sil i obychnyh vooruzheniy v Europe,* Committee of Soviet Scientists for Peace and Against the Nuclear Threat, Moscow, April 1989, for a detailed discussion.
18. 'Vystuplenie M. S. Gorbacheva', *Pravda,* 27 October 1989.
19. James E. Goodby, 'Risk Reduction, a Second Track for Arms Control', AAAS Annual Meeting Symposium, May 1985, pp. 4, 5.
20. D. M. Snow, *Soviet–American Security Relations in the 1990s* (Lexington MA: Lexington Books, 1989), p. 13.
21. As noted earlier, structural arms-control efforts and their contribution

to crisis-avoidance should not be understated. The Soviet Union and its allies have proposed several quantitative measures involving forces in Europe, including asymmetric arms reductions and the simultaneous liquidation of the Warsaw Pact and NATO. Research by Dr Alexander Konovalov of the USA–Canada Institute has proposed several measures that could significantly reduce the risks from future crises in Europe. The research suggests a range of quantitative limits on offensive forces, such as reducing the share of mobile strike units and the number of tanks per ground unit.

22. 'Vystuplenie M. S. Gorbacheva,' *Pravda*, 2 August 1989.
23. 'Kommyunike sovezchaniya PKK', *Pravda*, 9 July 1989.
24. S. Akhromeev, 'SSSR-za diolog i sotrudnichestvo. A SSHA?', *Pravda*, 30 October 1989.
25. Sam Nunn, 'Risk Reduction and Crisis Prevention', in John Borowski (ed.), *Avoiding War in the Nuclear Age: confidence-building measures for crisis stability* (Boulder: Westview, 1986), p. 170.
26. The benefits from centers are somewhat limited. In particular, centers cannot substitute for political and military CBMs that reduce the risk of misperceptions. Nor can the centers substitute for the hotline or for meetings between military and political leaders during a crisis. Mikhail Mil'shtein, 'Developing Risk Reduction Institutions and Procedures: Soviet View', in Allison, et al., p. 95.
27. Yuriy Zhukov, 'Otkrytoe Nebo', *Pravda*, 2 November 1989.
28. A. A. Kokoshin, V. V. Larionov, *About the Level and the Character of the 'Minimum Nuclear Deterrence' in Europe* (Moscow: Committee of Soviet Scientists for Peace and Against the Nuclear Threat, Institute of the USA and Canada, 1989). Kokoshin and Larionov argue that this would raise the threshold of use of these weapons and would have a great politico-psychological significance.
29. Sergei Rokov, 'SSSR i SSHA: poisk vzaimnoi bezopasnosti', Za Rubezhom, no. 35, 25–31 August 1989.
30. 'Kokoshin Briefs US House Committee', *Defense & Disarmament Alternatives*, Vol. 2, no. 4, April 1989.

3 Some Lessons from Twentieth-century Crises and Wars

Philip J. Romero

3.1 INTRODUCTION

Several times over the past generation, the dominant perspective of students of the military dimensions of crisis management has shifted. In the late 1950s, Wohlstetter's 'Delicate Balance of Terror' pointed out the instabilities (i.e. incentives for an adversary to preempt in a crisis) inherent in nuclear force structures that were soft and highly-concentrated in peacetime. Kahn's attempt to develop a taxonomy of escalation (the so-called 'escalation ladder') in the mid-1960s dealt with the use of military forces as communications devices, transmitting finely-tuned messages regarding the importance a nation assigned to the stakes in a particular crisis and the level of violence it was willing to undertake to achieve its objectives.

Gradual escalation and highly-discriminating use of military signals had their heyday in the 1962 Cuban Missile Crisis, at least in the minds of many of the crisis managers. Vietnam demonstrated the difficulties: 'misperceptions' (as coined by Jervis) could gum up the works – the message the transmitter intended to send might be different from that which the recipient understood. Besides fundamental cultural or political blindness, Allison pointed out two other reasons why the channel might be so garbled. First, compromises among factions in the sending country's cabinet would dilute the clarity of the message (log-rolling so that several military services participate), and the competing 'hawks' and 'doves' in the receiver's cabinet might choose to interpret the signal differently. Second, military forces – indeed the operational elements of any large organization – are blunt instruments; they implement political instructions in terms of standard rules and procedures, and so may depart in critical details from the leadership's wishes (often because these wishes were not disseminated to military commanders, or even fully recognized by the political leaders themselves).

This recognition of frictions in the discriminating use of military force spawned an interest in the early 1980s in 'command and control' – the systems and procedures by which military forces are directed. One of the early concerns pertained to the vulnerability of the command structure: if an attacker could kill the national leadership or sever their links to their forces, he could complete a nuclear attack with little risk of prompt retaliation. Other than improving the survivability of the command chain and its communications links, the only means of buttressing deterrence would be to pre-delegate authority to use nuclear weapons to a larger group of commanders – risking the opposite danger, unauthorized nuclear use.

The common thread running through the evolution of crisis-management scholarship in the 1980s was the recognition that the *details* of military plans and procedures could have a profound impact on the prospects for unintended escalation. Posen illustrated how certain operational plans for conducting conventional war could 'inadvertent(ly)' threaten Soviet nuclear assets. Sagan's historical research manifested the ignorance of many senior decision-makers concerning alerting procedures; he also catalogued several instances in which US military activity, prudent in terms of its own narrow objectives, inadvertently posed an increased risk of escalation (either by threatening the Soviets or by creating circumstances that resembled a Soviet attack).

The pace of research into past risks of inadvertent escalation will largely be set by the declassification of military records, so more incidents like those revealed by Sagan may be uncovered, but it seems unlikely that any will be as sensational. A more profitable research question can be found by returning to the roots of the discipline, and asking a question analogous to that addressed by Wohlstetter. He noted that a nuclear force structure that had been designed for peacetime efficiency and positive control was vulnerable to preemptive attack and thus introduced instability in a crisis. Can activity intended to de-escalate, such as the implementation of CBMs, instead invite escalation?

This paper draws from several past crises and wars to outline some propositions concerning the risks (real and merely apparent) inherent in de-escalatory measures:

Nuclear crises: Suez/Hungary 1956, Cuba 1962, the Middle East 1973

Conventional wars: Russo-Finnish 1939–40, Korea 1950–53, the Middle East 1973[1]

Two types of de-escalations will be discussed: the reduction in a force's preparedness in a crisis to engage in combat operations, and the diminution or cessation of combat operations in wartime.

These propositions are based on an unscientific sample, for the most part using secondary sources, so their generality cannot be claimed. (In any event, proving generality based on comparative history is virtually impossible, because it is impractical to be comprehensive, and because the simplifications necessary to achieve a usable categorization scheme will never satisfy specialists.) The intent is to provoke and shape work that is more eclectic in its approach, recognizing the tensions between protecting national interests and avoiding war, and cognizant of the range of purposes that military forces must simultaneously fulfill in a crisis.

3.2 THE THREE USES OF MILITARY FORCES IN CRISIS BARGAINING

Forces can be used for three distinct purposes in an international dispute: (1) they can gain leverage by creating a material military advantage; (2) they can force the adversary to act more quickly or more slowly than he otherwise would; (3) they can signal concern or commitment (in the same way that diplomatic actions or public statements can). When the leadership's intent is to de-escalate, forces can be ordered to reduce levels of activity or alert rates in order to visibly yield an available advantage (what this chapter will term the 'main arena'); or they can suspend or reduce the pace of confrontational symbolic activity (maneuvers, tests, etc., which will be termed the 'collateral arena'). Naturally, different force elements can concurrently perform escalatory and de-escalatory acts, either because the leadership wishes to hedge or because of imperfect control.

The next few sections will outline in capsule form specific instances of each of these activities, and their consequences.

The main arena of military competition in crises: the balance of forces

Manipulating alert rates in nuclear crises

Because both the United States and the Soviet Union have only a fraction of their intercontinental nuclear weapons available for use 'day-to-day' – varying from as high as 95 per cent of American land-based missiles to as low as perhaps 10 per cent of Soviet bombers – the act of mobilizing those forces can have a dramatic effect on the nuclear balance.[2] By the same token, a reduction in one side's alert level prior to a reciprocal reduction in the opponent's can be equally dramatic.

However, alerts cannot be maintained indefinitely. As discussed in Chapter 5, alerts are costly, and physically risky. Increasing the number of nuclear weapons platforms that can be directed to their target with very little warning (e.g. 15–20 minutes) means reducing crews' rest, training and maintenance. All these things will, in time, mean more mistakes and accidents. Calculations of the results of hypothetical nuclear exchanges usually use the 'day-to-day' and the 'fully-generated' alert rates as boundary conditions. In a crisis, the actual alert rate could be between these if forces are executed while still generating. If the alert continues for longer than the force's ability to sustain at that level, the alert rate will decline, possibly to below the day-to-day level:

> Protracted alert could eventually cause mission capability to drop below peacetime levels, owing to suspension of major maintenance and training, and to fatigue. The initial improvement over peacetime readiness cannot be sustained indefinitely. Eventually, readiness will gravitate toward an equilibrium point [that] may even fall below normal steady-state activity.[3]

The fundamental question from the perspective of those who decide upon and maintain the alert is thus: 'How long will it need to be maintained?' If the prediction is proved wrong, the decision-maker is faced with a choice: stand some forces down now (presumably while the crisis is still underway), or 'borrow' from post-crisis resources to keep the alert going.

Needless to say, there are severe constraints on the decision-maker's flexibility. If he feels that the probability of war is at all high, he will be very reluctant to stand down forces. Even if not, he may not wish to reveal weakness (if the adversary correctly diagnoses the reason for the stand-down) or appear conciliatory. If the alert is extended long enough, he will eventually lose much of his discretion, as accidents and malfunctions ground aircraft and jeopardize systems' mission capability – and probably add to domestic and international pressures to be conciliatory. Crisis-managers might worry about an enemy's exploitation of such constraints and consider preempting before capability degrades too far. Looking ahead from an earlier point in the crisis, 'military establishments might exert pressure to act while at the peak of their mobilization'.[4]

Consequently, a decision to go to a moderate-level, more sustainable alert may actually 'build confidence' in the sense that it would pose a less urgent deadline than a maximal alert. A mobilization that brought nuclear forces to, say 80 per cent alert rates might be seen as much more than twice as escalatory as a 40 per cent alert. The record of US crisis alerts highlights the pressures posed by uncertainty about crises' duration, and the difficulty in gaining leverage through intermediate-sized alerts.

1956: Suez and Hungary crises SAC was alerted in November in response to Soviet threats against England and France for their assault against the Suez Canal. KC-97 tankers were first concentrated in mid-November into task forces and dispersed to bases in the northeastern US, Newfoundland, Labrador, and Greenland. Eight B-52s flew non-stop around the periphery of North America (i.e. several thousand miles parallel to the Soviet Arctic coast). Two wings of B-47s and one of B-36s were deployed overseas.[5] SACEUR General Alfred Gruenther reported that Soviet attacks on either Britain or France would mean the destruction of the Soviet Union 'as surely as night follows day'.[6]

SAC ran over 1000 Power House and Road Block training sorties up to the periphery of the Soviet Union.[7] Quite a number of them, apparently, actually penetrated Soviet airspace, according to a 1987 interview with retired CINCSAC LeMay:

> There was a time in the 1950s when we could have won a war against Russia. It would have cost us essentially the accident rate of the flying time, because their defenses were pretty weak. One time in the 1950s we flew all of the reconnaissance aircraft that SAC possessed over Vladivostok at high noon ... no resistance at all.[8]

While LeMay does not specify the date, there was no other point in the 1950s when SAC had as much encouragement from President Eisenhower to display its capability as during the Suez crisis.

SAC's operations lasted for about a month.[9] There is no numerical information on SAC's alert rate, but in the alert associated with Lebanon in 1958, SAC's alert rate was about 40 per cent.[10] Presumably it was at least as high during Suez.[11]

1962: Cuban crisis[12] The nuclear alert over offensive weapons in Cuba lasted from 22 October to 21 November. Politically, the most intense days of the crisis were from 24 October, when the first ships approached the quarantine line, to 28 October, when Khrushchev agreed to withdraw the offending weapons. SAC had begun taking preparatory action on 20 October, went to DEFCON 3 at the time of Kennedy's announcement of the quarantine on 22 October and peaked (in terms of the number of alert weapons) on 4 November.[13]

The alert was sustained, and intensified, after 28 October over the issue of the withdrawal of IL-28 medium bombers that had been introduced into Cuba as part of the summer build-up. Unlike the SS-4 missiles, these bombers were to be turned over to the Cuban air force and were considered by Castro to be Cuban property. Castro did not agree to release them – and never agreed to international inspection as proposed by the United States – until 19 November: Kennedy announced the settlement in a press conference on 20 November.

The timing of US military forces' generation only roughly corresponds to the diplomatic pressure being put on the Soviets. As mentioned, SAC was still adding launchers and weapons to its force (through the conversion of test ICBMs into operational ones, and the repair of aircraft that had been stood down for extended maintenance) until early November.[14] Conventional forces arrayed for an airstrike or invasion of Cuba reached their peak of availability on 15 November, and were estimated to be available for roughly thirty days.[15] Minutemen missiles that had been converted from test and training roles to operational status on an emergency basis in late October remained on alert at least through 22 November.[16] By contrast, NORAD air defense forces began returning from dispersal bases as early as 17 November.[17]

The point behind this array of dates is that (a) the crisis, at least insofar as influenced by the US nuclear alert, lasted much longer than the proverbial thirteen days; (b) the generation process was not, and probably could not be, closely timed to the diplomatic situation. Although the greatest increase in force availability came between 20 October and 23 October, at least modest numbers of weapons continued to be generated for two more weeks. Standing-down of forces may not have been entirely deliberate: it is hard to explain the cancellation of air defense dispersal while the international dispute over bomber aircraft continued. There may, in fact, have been a substantial disconnection between the availability of US conventional forces poised to attack Cuba and that of its nuclear forces: the former were estimated as maintaining their availability for thirty days (i.e. till mid-December), while SAC's time horizon extended only until the end of November.[18]

During the crisis, SAC moved from roughly a 40 per cent ground alert rate to over 80 per cent in 20–22 October,[19] peaking at 89 per cent on 4 November, and maintained a 'one-eighth' airborne alert by its B-52 force.[20] SLBMs similarly went from 46 per cent to nearly 100 per cent. ICBMs' day-to-day alert rate was roughly 85 per cent, and increased to close to 100 per cent.[21]

It is difficult to speculate on how long US force could have maintained such a high posture – indeed, doing so for over a month was a remarkable achievement. The crews pulling airborne alert were flying one roughly 24-hour sortie every six to eight days, with much of the remaining time spent on ground alert.[22] No training was undertaken during the month, aside from whatever was possible collateral to airborne alert sorties – which would have been extremely limited given the importance of these aircrafts' combat mission. Preventative maintenance was impossible, and it is likely that some platforms or weapons were cannibalized to keep others mission-capable. It appears that normal operations would call for an aircraft to be down up to 50 per cent of the time, and a crew 25 per cent, for maintenance and rest.[23] Certainly much less than this was possible at the high alert rates sustained in the crisis. In early November, CINCSAC Power informed the JCS that on 15 November, roughly three weeks after the start of the alert, he intended to resume low levels of training, reducing the alert rate for SAC bombers from nearly 90 per cent to roughly 80 per cent, a rate he felt could be maintained without serious degradation for 30 days.[24] There is no evidence that he implemented this plan; it appears the full alert was maintained until the stand-down on 20 November.

At some point, possibly as early as late November, alert rates would have had to decline. If LeMay's proposal had been adopted, the drop would have been modest. Beyond the 30-day mark he expected substantial degradation. Clearly, over a long crisis concerns about the force's endurance could have constrained the leadership's flexibility in diplomacy and might provide arguments for preemption in either country.

1973: War in the Middle East Preparations by the Soviets to airlift two or more airborne divisions into the Middle East to intervene in the Arab–Israeli war prompted the United States to declare a symbolic alert on the night of 24 October. DEFCON 3 was chosen because [according to Kissinger] 'we all agreed that any increase . . . would have to go to at least DEFCON 3 before the Soviets would notice it.'[25] The military actions most relevant to the local crisis were the dispatch of an additional aircraft carrier to the Eastern Mediterranean and the alert of the 82nd Airborne division.

Some SAC tankers were dispersed, and the B-52Ds that had remained on Guam since the bombing campaign in Vietnam had ended in August were redeployed to continental US bases. Undoubtedly, there was some increase in the ground alert rate, perhaps to 70 per cent.[26] The nuclear alert lasted no more than 36 hours – Soviet hesitancy to deploy their forces in the face of the American alert had become clear within hours[27] – and stand-down was rapid. The conventional naval confrontation, however, was much more intense, as noted below.

Implications The 1973 alert, like the 1960 alert described in Sagan 1985, was arguably a 'symbolic' alert, intended to convey concern, without serious expectation of war. It will be discussed briefly below in the section on uses of military forces as communications media.

In the 1962 and 1956 cases, US nuclear forces were brought to their maximum level of alert and kept there until American objectives had been fulfilled. There was no need for gradual de-escalation in order to signal a willingness to compromise: the Soviets, being grossly inferior in numbers of available weapons, never counter-escalated. The sole partial exception was the cessation of NORAD's dispersal on 17 November, three days before the nuclear alert was cancelled.

The 1962 case in particular highlights the constraints on the leadership's flexibility to gradually escalate or de-escalate. While a less-than-maximum alert would serve two useful purposes– signalling restraint and maintaining the ability to increase pressure if necessary – uncertainty about the probability of war, and its imminence, discourages this. If a crisis were to lead to war the next day, a leader would be derelict not to have fully mobilized his forces – and it sometimes can be plausibly argued that such a mobilization, which establishes superiority or denies it to the opponent, may actually reduce incentives to initiate a war. On the other hand, in a long crisis, operations are much more labor- or spare parts-intensive than they are on a day-to-day basis, and this risks the problems discussed above. Not surprisingly, leaders tend to emphasize the immediate challenge and defer concern about the hypothetical problem of alert endurance until it happens. The record thus far seems to support this approach: the longest recorded alert of one month in October/November 1962 was achieved without degradation, and could have been maintained considerably longer according to CINCSAC.[28] In future crises, both sides will have forces that are less dependent on mobilization than those of 1962, which will probably further mitigate endurance concerns.[29]

Manipulating the pace of combat operations to achieve war termination (or to improve the terms of a settlement)

This section briefly summarizes salient aspects of three cases. It assumes substantial knowledge of the 1973 October War and the Korean War. The Russo-Finnish War is discussed briefly.[30]

Russo-Finnish (Winter) War, 1939–40 The bargaining over the stakes in the Russo-Finnish War really began in April 1938. The Soviet government approached the Finnish government in secret to begin negotiations aimed at making border readjustments to improve the security of both countries. Leningrad, the second city in the Soviet Union, was a scant twenty miles from the Finnish border, and Stalin was interested in acquiring additional depth in Karelia. (The situation had existed since Finland's independence in 1918, but the cause for Soviet concern was growing Finnish–German amity and the perennial Soviet concern with a German attack through Finland.) As a secondary objective, Stalin wanted a permanent Soviet base in the mouth of the Gulf of Finland to protect Leningrad from Baltic threats; the best candidate was the Finnish port of Hanko (near Helsinki). In exchange, the Finns were offered an area in Lapland several times the size of the area the Soviets asked for in Karelia; this area had long been the preoccupation of Finnish nationalists interested in reuniting with ethnic Finns. After several personal appeals by Stalin and eighteen months of negotiations in which the Soviets showed no flexibility as to their aim – protecting Leningrad and the Baltic coast against the Germans – but substantial flexibility as to how they could achieve their aims (i.e. several islands in the Baltic would do), they attacked Finland on 30 November 1939.

The political course of the brief war and its eventual termination in March 1940 cannot be understood without an awareness of the political perspectives and objectives of the two parties before the war broke out. This chapter is not the place for a narrative case study, but a few insights should be noted. First, it is clear that the Soviets did not want to go to war and attempted to show some flexibility in order to achieve their goals without having to fight. The Soviets were not well-prepared to fight, as evidenced by their initial limitation to resources in the Leningrad Military District. (When the early offensives failed, units from several other military districts were sent in, and ultimately fully half of the Red Army in the European USSR was fighting the Finns.) Second, despite the most unequivocally negative assessment of Finland's military prospects from General Mannerheim, the chief of the defense staff, Finnish leaders refused to budge in the prewar negotiations, being certain that any concessions to the USSR would be only the first of many. This rigidity persisted even after the Nazi–Soviet pact eliminated any prospect of German military aid, and after the British, French and American governments had made clear their reluctance to support the Finns and thus alienate the Soviets.

This willfulness was encouraged by the results of the early fighting in December 1939 and January 1940, in which the tiny Finnish army achieved remarkable success at stopping Soviet offensives against the Lagoda and Mannerheim Lines. The army was bolstered in part by the Soviet decision to form a Finnish Communist 'government-in-exile' and to recognize its legitimacy within days after crossing the frontier. (There was a delay before this decision was announced, suggesting that the Soviets still hoped to revert to negotiations without significant bloodshed. In fact, the Soviet-backed Finnish 'volunteer' units were never committed to combat; this was likely another figleaf held out to the Finns.) But the early successes quickly disappeared, and the Finns agreed to negotiate an end to the war in early March, when the second Finnish city, Vilpuri, was nearly surrounded, and promised French and British aid evaporated. At that time, the Soviets dispensed with their 'loyalist' government and tacitly renewed their recognition of the Finnish government.

The stakes in the termination talks, which lasted several weeks in February and March and were conducted in Stockholm between the Soviet ambassador to Sweden and various Finnish emissaries (including the Foreign Minister and the President), were only moderately larger in scope than the initial Soviet demands of the previous year. Finland was given a 'take-it-or-leave-it offer' in the form of a draft peace treaty in which she ceded much of Karelia and the area of Lapland north of Lake Onega, a sizable part of the narrow 'waist' in the North, rights in the Rybachiy Peninsula and the Petsamo naval base on the Barents Sea, a lease on the Hanko base, and several islands in the Gulf of Finland. Of the territories that had been the locale of combat, only fractions had fallen into Soviet hands, and only in the few weeks preceding the treaty. However, in those weeks, the imminence of their defeat had finally impressed itself upon the Finnish leadership, and the absence of other than moral support from the West became manifest. Soviet pressure on the battlefield increased. In one instance around Vilpuri, the local Soviet commander launched a major offensive in the waning hours of the war in an attempt to capture the city so that his divisions, and not the diplomats, would receive the credit.

The Soviets thus offered a number of concessions to avoid the war, and to end it quickly after it began. The end-game in late February and early March resembles nothing so much as a race. The Finns tried to hold out until the illusory Allied help arrived, and after the sham was exposed, they tried to achieve a ceasefire before they suffered total defeat. When the Soviets were suffering humiliations on the battlefield, they were eager to settle on generous terms; once victory finally became certain, they maintained the pressure on the ground and escalated their demands to take advantage of their dearly-won leverage.

Terminating the Korean War, 1951–53 On at least two occasions offensive operations played an explicit part in inducing concessions during the long 'termination phase' of the Korean War. In early 1951, in one of the most remarkable revivals in military history, new UN Commander Matthew Ridgeway halted his forces from the headlong retreat southward in the wake of the Chinese intervention in late 1950 and pressed a counterattack, returning the battleline to roughly the 38th parallel. The Chinese, hard-pressed and at the end of long lines of communication, accepted President Truman's offer to negotiate a settlement, which had likewise been made when UN forces were still on the defensive. Thus each side had to suffer a reversal as a precondition of negotiations.

The UN offensive brought the Chinese to the negotiating table, but arguably they were there to buy time rather than to end the war equitably. As they prepared defensive positions exceeding those of the Western Front in the First World War and increased their frontline strength by over 50 per cent, there was a dispute within the UN leadership over the wisdom of halting large-scale offensives. In time, the Chinese defenses were so well-reinforced that even the UN's offensive adherents acknowledged that the military gains would not compensate for the casualties that would be suffered. Ridgeway's perspective on planning for further offensives underscored his desire to force concessions rather than achieve significant operational victories: his goal was 'to kill Chinese', not to gain territorial advantages.

Two years later, in the early summer of 1953, the United Nations and Chinese had finally agreed on the most troublesome issue – prisoner-of-war repatriation – and were prepared to end the war. Syngman Rhee, the President of the Republic of Korea, would accept nothing less than reunification, wanted the UN to go on the offensive, and by unilaterally releasing Chinese and North Korean prisoners under his jurisdiction, tried to scuttle the agreement. The Chinese responded with the first major offensive since the summer of 1951, directed exclusively at South Korean units. This forced Rhee to concede.

In each instance, an offensive act forced a recalcitrant party to participate in a joint de-escalation. The lesson is that a credible offensive threat is often necessary to create a conciliatory atmosphere.

Cementing a ceasefire in the 1973 Arab–Israeli War In the endgame of the October war, the Israeli army raced the United Nations and Henry Kissinger to try to establish the strongest bargaining position in the postwar settlement. The details of the abortive ceasefire attempts and the Israeli encirclement of Egypt's Third Army on the west bank of the Suez Canal are thoroughly treated in Dupuy[31] (for the military aspects) and Kissinger[32] (for the diplomatic ones).

Israeli behavior resembles that of participants in many other wars. The feature that distinguishes the 1973 war is the existence of superpower 'sponsors' of each belligerent, who put limits on the asymmetry permissible in the war military and diplomatic outcome. Consequently, most 'confidence building' took the form of concessions offered privately to intermediaries (primarily Kissinger) in settlement negotiations – the audience being each belligerent's sponsor at least as much as the co-belligerent. Nevertheless, some military concessions were significant in facilitating the disengagement and ultimate settlement talks – such as Israeli willingness to allow sustenance to reach the Third Army, and Sadat's offer to keep very few Egyptian forces (much less than a division-equivalent) on the east bank of the canal.

3.3 THE COLLATERAL ARENA: USE OF FORCES TO CONVEY CONCERN

In the 1960s-era escalation and 'signalling' literature, military forces were treated as if they were a rheostat: nations were assumed to understand the level of concern indicated by each of a wide range of military actions, and a participant in a crisis could simply choose the set of actions that accurately expressed his level of concern and commitment (allowing for incentives to bluff). Later, researchers recognized that decision-makers often prefer to remain ambiguous about their precise interests, and that large organizations lack the nimbleness to support finely-tuned signalling. Given these impediments, the issue for designers of confidence-building measures is: 'Have force activities been used to send signals of a desire to reduce tensions, and has the recipient noticed them?'

Restraints on military activities

Confidence-building bulked large in American crisis behavior in 1962, but with very substantial, probably inadvertent, exceptions. The United States restrained several activities that would otherwise have been standard components of its alert repertoire (or had been conducted as part of normal peacetime activities). After a High-Altitude Sampling Program U-2 strayed over the Chutoski Peninsula on 26 October, further flights were cancelled.[33] Several sources, all of them retrospective and possibly incestuous, state that the 15 US Jupiter missiles in Turkey were ordered by Kennedy *not* to be alerted. Forces in EUCOM were kept at a lower level of alert than DEFCON 3.[34] The naval quarantine was generally handled with considerable restraint, notwithstanding later civilian criticism.[35] Finally and ironically, the airborne alert of SAC aircraft was actually less threatening militarily than a ground alert; the expected number surviving a Soviet strike was presumably increased, lessening any US incentive to preempt (while the alert could be maintained), and the overall availability of B-52s was probably lower than if they had been restricted to ground alert.[36]

At the same time, several activities, all of which may have been unknown to the ExComm, could not have helped ease the crisis. Sagan reports that an Atlas ICBM was test-launched from Vandenberg AFB on 26 October, after press notification.[37] There are at least two unconfirmed reports that force status or war-plan information was transmitted by unencoded radio messages.[38] Lastly, there were four nuclear weapons tests during the crisis, including three (Calamity on 27 October, Kingfish on 1 November, and Tightrope on 4 November) at medium or high altitudes (15 to 59 miles).[39]

For the Soviets' part, they conducted eleven atomic tests during the crisis, including two at high altitude (on 28 October and 11 November), which may have damaged one or more satellites.[40] Additionally, Khrushchev announced a Warsaw Pact alert on 24 October (the day the quarantine went into effect), repeating his claim on 12 December to have alerted forces.[41] There is, however, no evidence that any significant Soviet or Pact alerting activity actually took place. In a sense, this could be considered a two-track confidence-building measure: Khrushchev showed restraint to his crisis adversary while playing the hawkish role before the Communist bloc.

In the 1973 crisis, by far the greatest provocation came from the deployment of Soviet naval forces in positions to take quick offensive action against three US aircraft carriers, which had 'closed ranks for self-protection southeast of Crete. An advance Soviet unit in each formation trailed its quarry and passed targeting information to cruise missile platforms bringing up the rear. For eight days [presumably 25 October to 2 November], they maintained continuous high readiness to engage U.S. forces in battle.'[42]

In sum, while neither side gave up a material military advantage to de-escalate any of these crises, they were each willing to restrain military activities that would not affect the nuclear balance, but which could add to tensions (although with many provocative acts slipping through the cracks) to allow the essential disputes to be resolved diplomatically. In 1956, the United States deliberately kept up the nuclear pressure, but by 1962 it showed more restraint about minor activities than is sometimes recognized. The Soviets were less restrained in 1962 than is generally acknowledged, and by 1973 they had taken a leaf from the US book with respect to the exploitation of leverage from the threat of naval tactical nuclear weapons.

Do political leaders notice restraint?

A crucial premise of military 'signalling' is that the leadership of the country that receives the signal must understand the significance of changes in military posture. If political leaders are not especially interested in or sensitive to the details of the military situation in a crisis, then they will neither gain confidence from 'confidence-building' nor be provoked by 'provocative' acts.

Clearly the experience of 1962, the richest crisis in terms of duration and extensiveness of 'signals', suggests that such sensitivity is rather overestimated. This can be summarized by two propositions.

(1) '*At the highest level, the diplomatic drives out the military.*' In 1962, ExComm members were inconsistent in their view of the increase in theoretical Soviet capability offered by the Cuban missiles (citing estimates from 40 to 100 per cent), and showed great confusion about the extent of time pressures posed by preparation of the SS-4 sites (believing the deadline was anywhere from 'six hours to two weeks').[43] No one questioned McNamara's assessment that the Cuban missiles had little military significance, a view he acknowledged contradicted that of the Joint Chiefs.[44] Similarly, there is no evidence that the ExComm showed any concern about the Soviet high-altitude tests. Diplomatic challenges were more salient than military ones; Kennedy, for example, felt that Soviet proposals were causing him to lose the initiative,[45] and several ExComm participants have confirmed that time pressures were felt more strongly regarding maintaining the diplomatic initiative than over military questions.[46]

(2) '*Political leaders abhor thinking about military contingencies.*' On 27 October, the darkest day of the 1962 crisis, when it appeared that the Soviets might continue preparing the missiles sites in spite of the quarantine and US low-altitude reconnaissance aircraft were taking heavy fire, McNamara attempted to stimulate the ExComm to consider options in the event that Khrushchev did not withdraw the missiles. The committee completely misunderstood him and was unwilling to think contingently.[47] McNamara even acknowledges his own unwillingness to do so at one point.[48] Similarly in 1973, the participants in the WSAG's (Nixon's version of the ExComm) deliberations recalled

that they would have been willing to take further military action than the DEFCON 3 alert if the Soviets did not call off their intervention in the Middle East, but that no specifics were discussed.[49]

The prevailing impression gained from a review of the published information regarding decision-making in these two crises is of the surprisingly small attention paid to the *military* significance of one's own and one's adversary's military activities. While at first glance this does not bode well for confidence-building, it may actually be positive: measures may receive similar weight whether they involve relinquishment of real military advantage or mere symbolism. Since leaders will have a much easier time constraining or initiating symbolic acts than those the military believes are vital to their crisis mission, these are the fruitful area for development.

3.4 CONCLUSIONS: THE ROLE OF FORCE ACTIVITIES IN STABILIZING CRISES

The wrong kind of confidence-building – ceding an advantage to encourage reciprocal concessions – can be very costly, and politically risky, but the right kind – symbolic restraints on military activities that would otherwise be a 'normal' part of the crisis checklist – can have modest benefits at little, if any, cost.

The idealized escalation/de-escalation paradigm – where leaders have a tight rein on their forces, carefully consider the 'messages' they wish to send, and recognize 'messages' in the activities of the opponent's forces – is wildly at variance with historical fact. Control is always quite loose; but leaders, being experienced pragmatists, recognize this and generally discount a great deal of adversary activities that a theorist might consider 'provocative' – such as the US ICBM test-launch or the Soviet exoatmospheric tests in 1962. In all likelihood, they overdiscount and pay little attention to all but the most urgently threatening military (as opposed to the political) aspects of forces' activities. The Soviets have shown more restraint than the United States in the main arena – alert rates, that directly affect the military balance – while showing less with collateral military activities.

The record also casts doubt on both the wisdom and the feasibility of gradualism, on the way up or down the 'escalation ladder'. When the United States has raised its nuclear forces' alert levels, it has generally done so abruptly, usually pre-emptively, and has maintained that level until the crisis concluded. (Several times it maintained the alert after the public 'crisis' had passed.) This has been possible in part because American objectives have been achievable in no more than one month of heightened alert. Confidence-building might be less discretionary if a long alert required reduction to stave off total failure of any important force element.

Future research should emphasize metrics of cost and benefit of symbolic military confidence-building, to make them commensurable with CBMs that affect the military balance directly. The author has asserted that symbolic measures have near-zero costs, but this should be framed more rigorously.

If practitioners remember to maintain the distinction between CBMs that affect capability and those that do not – instead of assuming fully rational crisis partners who will discount the latter category – then it will be seen that political control of collateral or 'symbolic' military acts has substantial precedent, and if no stunning successes, certainly no failures.

NOTES

1. Note that this paper addresses both nuclear crisis de-escalation (involving the United States and the Soviet Union) and conventional war/ceasefire aspects (involving Israel and Arab nations) in the 1973 conflict.
2. Analysts use the convention of an 'alert rate': the fraction of forces of a given type available within some short period (usually 15 or 20 minutes). At the time of the Cuban crisis, for example, the day-to-day alert rate for SAC bombers was about 40 per cent, whereas just under 90 per cent were available at the peak of the alert on 4 November. Raymond Garthoff, *Reflections on the Cuban Missile Crisis*, 2nd ed. (Washington, DC: The Brooking Institution, 1989), p. 62, and J. C. Hopkins and Sheldon A. Goldberg, *Development of the Strategic Air Command*, Office of the Historian, HQ Strategic Air Command, 21 March 1976, p. 97.
3. Bruce G. Blair, 'Alerting in Crisis and Conventional War', in Ashton B. Carter, John D. Steinbruner, and Charles A. Zraket (eds), *Managing Nuclear Operations* (Washington, DC: Brookings Institution, 1987), p. 106.
4. Ibid., p. 106.

5. Norman Polmar (ed.), *Strategic Air Command* (Annapolis: Nautical and Aviation Publishing Company of America, 1979), p. 56.
6. John Prados, *The Soviet Estimate,* (New York: Dial Press, 1982), p. 55.
7. Ibid., p. 55.
8. Richard H. Kohn and Joseph P. Harahan (eds), 'U.S. Strategic Air Power, 1948–1962: Excerpts from an Interview with Generals Curtis E. LeMay, Leon W. Johnson, David A. Burchinal, and Jack J. Catton', *International Security,* Vol. 12, no. 4, Spring 1988, pp. 78–95.
9. Polmar, p. 45.
10. This figure is derived from Polmar's assertion that SAC generated over 1100 aircraft (bombers and tankers), at a time when there were approximately 2700 bombers and tankers in the force. Ibid., p. 56.
11. Responding to the Soviet ICBM threat, SAC stipulated a goal of 33 per cent day-to-day alert in 1957, and achieved it in May 1960. In March 1961, President Kennedy called for SAC to achieve a 50 per cent alert rate, which was accomplished in July 1961. The SIOP-62 briefing to President Kennedy shows an alert rate of 48 per cent. This was to be the highest peacetime alert rate in SAC history. Scott D. Sagan, 'SIOP-62: The Nuclear War Plan Briefing to President Kennedy', *International Security,* Vol. 12, no. 1, Summer 1987, pp. 22–51. Also see Polmar, pp. 49, 60, 73.
12. Scott D. Sagan, 'Accidents at the Brink: the Operational Dimension of Crisis Stability', unpublished paper, February 1989, provides an excellent compilation of aggregate information about SAC's alert level during the Cuban crisis.
13. Information on the timing of the US nuclear alert comes from several sources, including Polmar, pp. 80–1, Sagan 1989, p. 12, Garthoff, p. 208, and Scott D. Sagan, 'Nuclear Alerts and Crisis Management', *International Security,* Vol. 9, no. 4, Spring 1985, p. 108, fn 20.
14. No information was found regarding nuclear alert levels after the 'peak' of 4–5 November. Availability was probably nearly as high until stand-down began on 20 November.
15. Dan Caldwell (ed.), 'Department of Defense Operations During the Cuban Crisis: a report by Adam Yarmolinsky to the Secretary of Defense', *Naval War College Review* Vol. 32, July–August 1979, p. 93.
16. Sagan 1989, p. 19.
17. Ibid., p. 26.
18. General Power several times provided the JCS with a rolling estimate of SAC's ability to sustain its alert. In each case, the horizon was roughly two weeks. The messages did not apparently discuss the consequences beyond these time horizons. Interviews.
19. Sagan 1989, p. 12 reports that the alert rate increased by 50 per cent. This should be interpreted as 50 per cent of the total bomber force, not a 50 per cent increase over the day-to-day alert rate of roughly 40 per cent. Figures in Garthoff indicate that the rate went from 39 per cent on 19 October to 86 per cent on 24 October, peaking at 89 per cent on 4 November.
20. In the late 1950s, SAC had instituted a program of airborne alert training, which by the time it was announced in January 1961, had

flown 6000 sorties, or an average of 8 per day. Richard K. Betts, *Nuclear Blackmail and the Nuclear Balance* (Washington, DC: Brookings Institution, 1987), p. 103, states that by the summer of 1961, twelve B-52s were kept on station continuously. Sagan 1989, p. 12, reports that 66 sorties were flown per day, peaking at 75 on 4 November. At 22.5 hours per sortie (derived from Sagan 1989, p. 12), this indicates that 9.7 per cent to 11 per cent of the B-52s were on airborne alert. (Space aircraft set aside to replace aborts might account for the 'one-eighth' designation.) Burchinal in Kohn and Harahan, p. 93, refers to a 'one-third airborne alert', but this appears to be an error. Also see Polmar, p. 76.

21. Day-to-day alert rates for SLBMs and ICBMs from Sagan 1987, p. 25 and Prados, p. 121. The ICBM estimate is roughly between the 92 per cent rate reported for SIOP-62 and the 75 per cent rate reported for SIOP-63. Presumably alert rates declined as newer systems (Minutemen) were phased into the force.
22. This may actually understate the strain on elite crews, who pulled primary responsibility for airborne alert. Interviews.
23. This speculation is based on Polmar, p. 55: 'alert operations [in peacetime] logically fell into a four-cycle arrangement: ground alert duty, flight planning, flying, and a day off'. If each part of the cycle is assumed to be of the same duration, and if aircraft maintenance is possible only during the flight planning and rest portions, this yields the estimates in the text.
24. 'Interview with General Power', SAC Historian's Office, 15 November 1962. (I am grateful to Scott Sagan for providing this material.)
25. Quoted in Betts, p. 124.
26. The ground alert rate had been formally reduced to 40 per cent beginning in 1967 due to the requirements to support the Vietnam air campaign, Polmar, p. 107. Betts speculates that the alert rate would today increase from about one-third to two-thirds at DEFCON 3. If we interpret him as meaning that the non-alert rate would fall by 50 per cent, then the 1973 alert rate would have gone from roughly 40 per cent to 40 per cent + (0.5 times 60 per cent) = 70 per cent.
27. Barry M. Blechman and Douglas M. Hart, 'The Political Utility of Nuclear Weapons: The 1973 Middle East Crisis', *International Security*, Vol. 7, no. 1, Summer 1982, p. 137.
28. See note 17. The 'Summary Record of ExComm Meeting No. 24', 12 Nov. 1962, shows that McNamara was kept informed concerning SAC's sustainability on alert. (I am grateful to Scott Sagan for supplying this document.)
29. Both Paul Bracken, *The Command and Control of Nuclear Forces* (New Haven: Yale University Press, 1983) and Sagan have pointed out that a narrow interval of vulnerability could still occur if SAC bombers were ever launched under Positive Control, then recalled. Those aircraft would be off alert for the few minutes or hour necessary to refuel them and change aircrews (if available), and vulnerable to attack – a strategic version of the problem faced by aircraft carrier commanders in the Pacific carrier battles of the Second World War. On 8 December 1941, American B-17s in the Philippines were caught by the Japanese after

earlier being 'flushed' on news of the attack on Pearl Harbor. See Herman Kahn, *On Thermonuclear War,* (Princeton: Princeton University Press, 1960).

30. For more detailed information on the Russo-Finnish War, see Anthony Upton, *Finland 1939–1940,* (Newark, DE: University of Delaware Press, 1974).
31. Trevor Dupuy, *Elusive Victory: The Arab-Israeli Wars,* (New York, Hippocrene, 1974).
32. Henry Kissinger, *Years of Upheaval* (Boston: Little, Brown, 1982).
33. See Sagan 1985, pp. 118–21.
34. Blair, p. 78.
35. For example, several of the reports of submarines being 'forced to surface' refer to the tailing of diesel submarines that were required to surface to recharge their batteries every 24 hours or so.
36. The early cancellation of NORAD's dispersal on 17 November could also be construed as a CBM, albeit probably not a deliberate one (since the Cuban IL-28s were the principal issue under dispute at the time). At the civilian level, the Cabinet – and their spouses – stayed in Washington. Kennedy asked his wife to leave the city, but she refused. David Detzer, *The Brink* (New York: Thomas Crowell, 1979) reports on pp. 207–8 that contingency evacuation plans did *not* include spouses.
37. Scott D. Sagan, *Moving Targets: Nuclear Strategy and National Security,* (Princeton: Princeton University Press, 1989), p. 146. There is no evidence that higher echelons were aware of this launch through public affairs channels.
38. Sagan 1985 was the first to report that General Power, CINCSAC during the 1962 crisis, deliberately sent a generation report in the clear. Michel Tatu, *Power in the Kremlin* (trans.), (New York, Viking, 1969), p. 264 asserts that 'Polaris submarines throughout the seven seas exchanged with their bases unencoded messages about targeting.'
39. Chuck Hansen, *U.S. Nuclear Weapons: The Secret History* (New York: Crown, 1988), pp. 84 and 88.
40. Thomas B. Cohran, William M. Arkin, Robert S. Norris, and Jeffrey I. Sands *Soviet Nuclear Weapons,* Nuclear Weapons Databook, Vol. IV (New York: Harper and Row, 1989), p. 353.
41. Sagan 1985, p. 129.
42. Blair, p. 95.
43. Marc Trachtenberg, 'The Influence of Nuclear Weapons in the Cuban Missile Crisis', *International Security,* Vol. 10, no. 1, Summer 1985, p. 169.
44. Ibid., p. 184.
45. Ibid., p. 198.
46. David A. Welch and James G. Blight, 'The Eleventh Hour of the Cuban Missile Crisis: an Introduction to the ExComm Transcripts', *International Security,* Vol. 12, no. 3, Winter, 1987/88, p. 34.
47. Ibid., pp. 72–3, and 78.
48. Ibid., p. 56.
49. Blechman and Hart, p. 151.

4 Behavioral Factors in Nuclear Crisis De-escalation

Paul K. Davis and Barry Wolf

4.1 INTRODUCTION

Hypotheses

This chapter[1] dealing with problems that might be encountered in nuclear de-escalation is built around certain precepts consistent with a larger research agenda:

- Behavioral factors could be crucial to the success or failure of de-escalation efforts during a nuclear crisis or conflict.
- Contextual details – especially the people involved and the manner in which the situation developed – would matter greatly.
- The likelihood of success could be significantly increased by anticipating possible behavioral problems and taking measures to avoid or mitigate them.
- Models of human decision-making and related simulations can be unusually valuable in anticipating, understanding, and dealing with such problems, but such models must consider a wide range of possible contexts.

By behavioral factors we mean, for example, the mindsets, fears, and perceptions of decision-makers, along with their styles, under stress, for both decision-making and action. We do not in any way intend to demean the significance of such 'objective factors' as how the war is going or, in crisis, the extent to which one side or the other has clear-cut and usable military superiority, but the focus here is on behavioral issues because they have generally been given short shrift in government work, despite a considerable academic literature noting behavioral problems, including problems affecting war decisions. Jervis, Lebow, Stein,

Axelrod, and George are among those who have studied these issues in some depth.[2]

Previous research

The approach taken here is based on previous work on first-strike stability, work seeking to understand in the natural terms of real-world human decision-making how a decision to launch a massive first strike might actually come about.[3] That work, in turn, drew upon theoretical efforts to build knowledge-based models of human decision-making in crisis and conflict.[4] Such models have been developed and exercised to some extent as part of the research program of the RAND Strategy Assessment Center. They are seen primarily as mechanisms to improve the rigor and clarity of discussion rather than as reliably predictive tools. Further, the insights one gains from them are akin to the insights one gains from successful war-gaming in that there is no objective way to be certain the insights are 'correct', instead, one must be satisfied knowing that certain arguments and images are clearly wrong and that others 'feel right' and meet certain minimum conditions of plausibility and logic. An essential part of the approach is recognizing the need to have *alternative* models of superpower behavior, since individual decision-makers vary a great deal in terms of values, motives, style, and psychological attributes.

Departing briefly from this conservative assessment, let us say that building and exercising the models in simulations has upon occasion had major effects on the thinking of ourselves and colleagues, although, in retrospect, such revised thinking can and should be justified without depending on the models *per se*.[5] Indeed, the revised views often seem, *in retrospect*, highly intuitive. This type of experience, including the occasional discontinuous shifts in intuition, is familiar to technical people who have worked with other kinds of simulation dealing with classes of issues that people generally handle poorly because of fundamental cognitive limitations.[6]

4.2 SCOPE AND APPROACH

To narrow our discussion, let us focus on crisis and conflict scenarios that have not involved a large-scale nuclear exchange and in which, from a God's-eye view, both or all participants seek initially not only nuclear de-escalation but a termination of hostilities. This excludes the important instances in which one or more parties are actually using an apparent de-escalation process to gain military advantages. The authors emphasize that they are excluding the process of deceptive de-escalation not because they take it lightly, but because the subject is substantial enough to warrant full treatment on another occasion. We also exclude interesting scenarios envisioning a future world in which substantial strategic defenses exist. Finally, we can do little more here than identify some of the many behavioral factors that could be importantly at work. Thus, the purpose is to be provocative, not comprehensive, and to encourage others to take seriously the value of formal decision-modeling as a tool for improving prospects for effective crisis management.

4.3 A FRAMEWORK FOR DISCUSSION

A model of human decision-making

Let us provide first some background on a modeling approach we have been taking to help illuminate *human* decision-making. There are at least three basic aspects of the approach:

- A *process model of decision-making* (Fig. 1).
- *Hierarchies of variables* constructed so that high-level decisions can be considered to be dependent on only a small number of variables, although each of those variables may in turn depend on subordinate variables, through many levels of hierarchy.
- *Decision rules* of the form 'If <condition 1> and <condition 2> Then <judgment or decision 1> and <judgment or decision 2>.' A trivial rule might be 'If strategic-warning is High Then Let Force-order be strategic-alert.'

This approach uses concepts from artificial intelligence, but also reflects a strongly analytic orientation. Whereas in many artificial intelligence programs the emphasis is on having a computer language that can make sense of a bundle of discrete rules collected from 'experts', the approach taken here is to build a clearcut cause–effect model.[7] This model's rules are motivated by logic and analysis, because there are no experts who could provide comprehensive rules on the many situations we wish to contemplate. To be sure, however, we draw heavily on history, experience from serious political–military war-gaming, and the expressed views of policymakers.

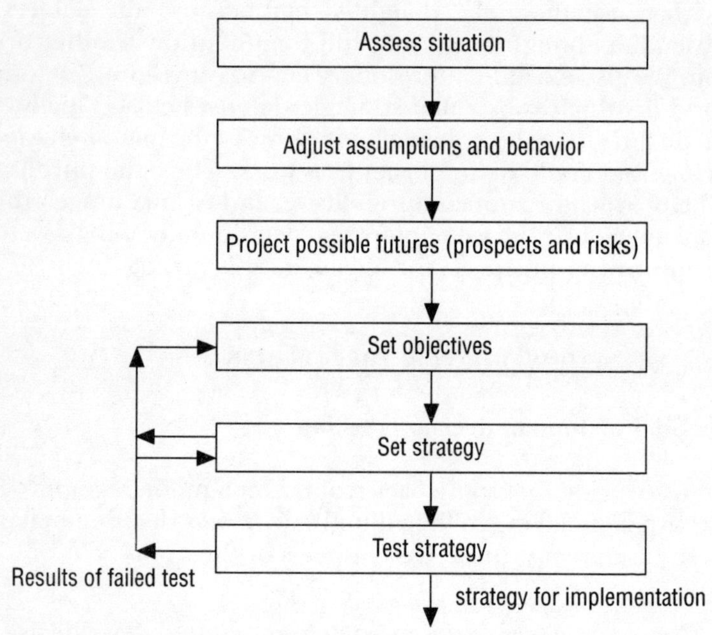

Figure 4.1 A process model of decision-making

A fault tree for failure of de-escalation

Distinguishable failure modes

Figure 4.1 suggests the technical superstructure of the decision-making models. The approach has advantages in many respects, including correspondence with more qualitative concepts of decision-making to be found in the literature, but it has the disadvantage that certain interesting issues are treated in diverse portions of the model. For example, there are rules affecting the ultimate decisions about whether to escalate or de-escalate in each of the modules indicated, starting with situation assessment. It is therefore useful in some cases to stand back and see if we can pull the concepts at work into one structure, even though the model is not itself constructed according to this structure.[8] Figure 4.2 illustrates one useful method for doing so. It involves a 'fault tree' – i.e. a tree-like diagram showing the various ways a 'fault' can occur; the 'fault' in this case (at least from the world's point of view) is a first-strike decision. Although developed for other purposes,[9] this tree is highly relevant to the topic of nuclear de-escalation, because in the event that the sides were attempting de-escalation, the principal concern would be that one or more sides would reverse the process and launch a massive first strike.

The fault tree embodies much of the conceptualization underlying the decision rules in the formal and computerized version of the model, although the structure and syntax is different. In the fault tree diagram, the ideas 'Opponent is almost certain to go first imminently' and 'Cost of going second is very high' contribute to the conclusion 'We must preempt.' Were these concepts to be recast into decision rules, the result would be along these lines (although there might be further subtleties in the detailed rules):

If the opponent is almost certain to go first imminently and
If the cost of going second is very high,
Then
We must preempt.

Such decision rules can potentially capture the gist and some of the nuances of real-world decision-maker thought in crisis. These rules, like the fault tree diagram, can be used to capture both 'hard' and 'soft' factors, the former being relatively well-defined and perhaps even quantifiable, and the latter being more fuzzy (e.g. the belief that the opponent is 'crazy').

Dangerous ideas

A key feature of Figure 4.2 is the concept of 'dangerous ideas' that might be accepted by decision-makers, ideas leading them to launch a first strike. In this depiction, a first strike is more likely an act of desperation than an act of tactics. Note that most of the dangerous ideas could be stimulated or exacerbated by 'soft' factors such as personalities, fears, and mindsets. For

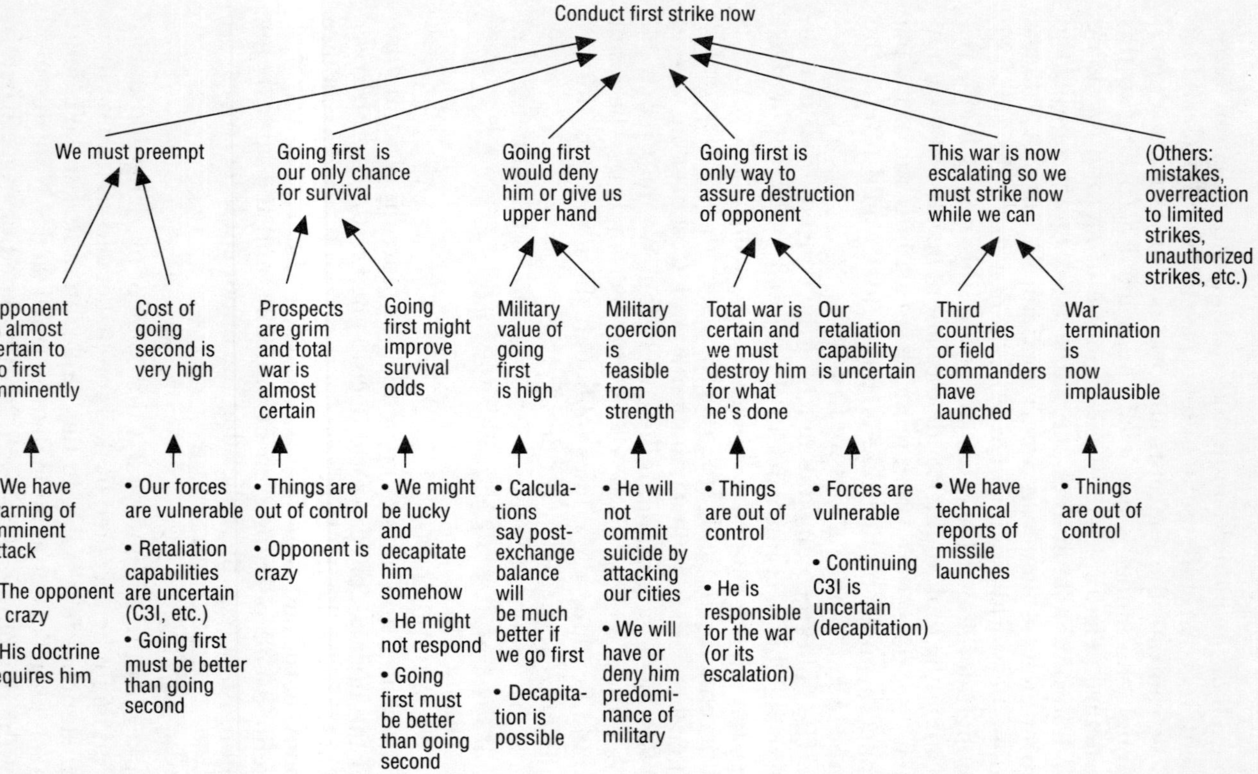

Figure 4.2 A fault tree for the failure of de-escalation

example, a highly unfavorable image of an opponent could add credence to a warning of imminent attack, thereby making a 'preemptive' strike more likely. Although the tree is intended to be rather general, it is useful in this discussion of nuclear de-escalation to make an overlapping but somewhat different list of dangerous ideas phrased in terms particularly suitable to the de-escalation challenge. Figure 4.3 illustrates some of the items we consider interesting and plausible. These items are divided into two broad categories: (1) Notions about the opponent or circumstances; and (2) Notions about consequences.

Some of the ideas noted in Figure 4.3 are familiar to those who have thought about termination. What may be more novel, however, is framing the problem in these terms. That is, framing the problem as being *fundamentally* the challenge of assuring that such dangerous ideas do not inappropriately arise and find acceptance. We use the modifier 'inappropriately' here, because in a real-world conflict there might be truth in some of the ideas. For example, it is hardly uncommon in the history of mankind for one antagonist to doublecross the other in the course of war-termination efforts. Further, it is hardly difficult to imagine that one leader or the other in a superpower stand-down might recognize that the outcome, after war-termination, would be a fundamental and unacceptable change in the geostrategic balance and/or that he personally would suffer intolerable consequences. Nonetheless, in this paper we are interested in cases where the nuclear de-escalation fails for bad reasons – e.g. misunderstandings and misconceptions.

Narrowing the focus: two key decision processes

By perusing even the incomplete list of dangerous ideas in Table 4.1 we can see that they are associated with many different parts of the decision process – i.e. some are the result of situation assessment, some are assessments of the opponent's intentions or the intentions of third countries, and so on. We cannot cover all of these issues here, so instead let us focus on two aspects of the problem where behavioral factors are particularly critical: assessing the opponent's intentions and framing the issues when conceiving or evaluating alternative courses of action.

Assessing the opponent

Although opponent-assessment plays virtually no role in standard strategic analysis, it has played a crucial role in many and perhaps most historical wars. The leader or leaders of one side regularly assess their antagonist's interests, intentions, fears, resolve, and strategic predilections, as well as their capabilities. Further, they may tailor their strategies to reflect these assessments, which may focus on opponent leaders or opponent nations (i.e., on some individuals or on a people collectively).[10]

Table 4.1 Some dangerous ideas undermining nuclear de-escalation

Notions about the opponent or circumstances

- We must preempt because he is about to launch a first strike:
  - He is crazy
  - His doctrine will require him to do so under these circumstances
  - He has doublecrossed us (me); he's not really standing down, but rather preparing for a strike
- We must *preempt,* because the other side is out of control:
  - They're not doing what he promised; their military is probably taking control, and they may not be cohesive either; they look like they are preparing a strike
- We will have to attack:
  - He is doublecrossing us (me) and trying to use the termination process to win the war conventionally and politically; it's only a matter of time until we will be back at it again unless we want to preemptively surrender I will have to attack:
  - By terminating we would be surrendering; it wasn't clear before, but it's clear now; if we continue to fight, he will recognize we are doublecrossing him and launch a first strike
  - If I don't act quickly, I will be overthrown
  - I don't have full control any more, and if my commanders start using nuclear weapons on their own, the lid will be off but we will be acting incohesively; better to do the best we can in a unified first strike
- We will have to attack:
  - Those damned — (a third country) — are about to launch a strike and the lid will then be off, even if he understands what's happening.

Notions about consequences

- The cost of going second rather than first is very high:
  - We might be able to decapitate him, causing him to quit, retaliate ineffectively, or simply collapse in paralysis
  - We might be able to disarm him or at least reduce his capabilities so drastically as to assure our own survival
  - We might be able to change the balance of forces so drastically as to coerce him into surrendering or ceasing his aggression and negotiating an acceptable outcome
  - Our decapitation is possible and would be catastrophic
  - The military cost of going second rather than first is high, even if we are assuredly able to retaliate
  - By virtue of a first strike, we might actually survive an attack if it were less than fully effective. Indeed, our only chance to survive is by conducting a first strike and hoping it is more effective than our confidence level indicates
- The worst that will happen is that he will respond in kind to our counterforce attack, and we will come out stronger in such an exchange. He wouldn't be dumb enough (or wouldn't have the guts) to escalate further.

Framing the issues when evaluating alternatives

Common sense, a quality that most policymakers possess to a considerable degree, would argue for thinking about nuclear escalation and de-escalation decisions in broad terms such as (a) nuclear war is a very bad idea; (b) general nuclear war would be an unmitigated catastrophe for all mankind; and (c) extraordinary measures should be taken to avoid general nuclear war. Even if these concepts were in tension with such objectives as assuring the survival, sovereignty, and independence of one's own and allied nations, the tradeoffs should – and would – probably not be made on the basis of detailed nuclear exchange calculations of the sort so comfortable to strategic analysts. However, the military–technical issues are not irrelevant and are in fact emphasized by the organizational processes that produce the staff expertise that might be called upon in time of crisis and conflict. Furthermore, the notion that going first is better than going second is a broad intuitive concept consistent with virtually all conflict experience. Nuclear war is unique here because the cost of preempting in an incorrect judgment that the opponent is about to launch is extremely high. Over the years, this uniqueness has been more 'obvious' to some people than to others. It is also striking to observe the degree to which the know-nothing cliché of 'use-it-or-lose-it' appears actually to apply to the thinking of many people who should know better.

This tendency to accept use-it-or-lose-it attitudes may be due in part to the manner in which issues and potential decisions are framed. Thus, while the United States has a massive strategic nuclear arsenal that could destroy the Soviet Union in a second strike launched after fully absorbing a Soviet first strike, many seem nonetheless to believe that it would somehow be crucial to launch our ICBMs before they were destroyed in their silos. Framing questions regarding second-strike capabilities in terms of absolute instead of relative damage done to an opponent might reduce pressure to launch silo-based ICBMs quickly.

In a period of intended nuclear de-escalation, it is plausible that decision-makers would frame the issues poorly and unwisely narrow the range of alternatives considered feasible. One can see this happening in some of the postulated dangerous ideas of Table 4.1. There is a problem in discussing these matters, because the result could easily be the conclusion that surrender would be better than incineration and that it would therefore be good policy to preemptively surrender rather than risk the failure of nuclear de-escalation. If we are to understand possible crisis decision-making, we must recognize that there are inherent and unavoidable inconsistencies between sound peacetime thinking – and related decisions about doctrine, deterrence, and strategy – and sound thinking when the world is at the nuclear precipice. Even at the precipice, however, it is unclear that we would want our leaders to flinch first in the cosmic game of Chicken. 'Flinching', in practice, might mean something like accepting war- termination under unfavorable circumstances such as Soviet occupation of Western Europe for decision-makers at the helm, such outcomes would be more than mere 'bitter pills'. As noted by Fred Iklé in his classic book on the subject, war-termination is *very* difficult without changes of government, perhaps accomplished with violence.[11]

Given such complexities, it would be no surprise if efforts at nuclear de-escalation proved to be failures.

4.4 SELECTED BEHAVIORAL FACTORS IN DECISION PROCESSES

With this background, then, let us now discuss briefly some of the cognitive factors that might bear on assessing one's opponent or framing issues. Once again, this discussion is merely illustrative of a vast problem area.

General cognitive processes

Based on a recent survey of the psychological literature, Table 4.2 identifies a number of well-documented human proclivities with particular bearing on the assessment of one's opponent and the framing of issues.

Table 4.2 Cognitive processes affecting attribution of hostile intent

- The overattribution of causality
- Overuse of vivid information*
- The belief that causes resemble effects
- Seeing linear trends
- Focusing on extreme examples within a group of data
- Attributing others' actions dispositionally rather than situationally*
- Failing to adjust probability estimates to the extent warranted by new events*
- Fitting events into schemas*
- Focusing on familiar or visualizable scenarios rather than more probable scenarios*
- Overweighting low-probability events

As some examples here, consider the following (items marked with an asterisk in Table 4.2):

1. *Fitting events into schemas.* Stalin refused to accept evidence of Hitler's imminent hostile intent before Operation Barbarossa, and even in the early days after it had begun. Strategic warning indicators were numerous. By contrast, Eden characterized Nasser's nationalization of the Suez Canal as matching a Hitlerite behavior pattern, which it did not, however contrary to British and French interests the action was.

2. *Failure to adjust probability estimates.* In 1973, the Israeli government failed to recognize the significance of Soviet withdrawal of dependants from certain Middle Eastern countries in 1973, just prior to the Yom Kippur war. Because previous alarms (not including such actions) had proven false but expensive, the Israeli government had raised the threshold for action too much, and therefore failed to acknowledge strong indicators.

3. *Overutilization of vivid or emotionally important information.* It has been reported that Brezhnev's decision to invade Afghanistan was seriously influenced and possibly triggered by the assassination of a prominent Afghan communist to whom Brezhnev had personal ties. Similarly, George Bush's final decision to invade Panama has been attributed, at least in part, to Panama's mistreatment of individual US citizens. The invasion might have occurred in any case, but the triggering event seemed to have been the murder of an officer and the mistreatment of another officer's wife.

4. *Focusing on easily visualized scenarios.* Lyndon Johnson continued to believe that the North Vietnamese would straightforwardly buckle under American military pressure – an apparently 'reasonable' expectation given the magnitude of that pressure.

5. *Seeing events dispositionally.* Throughout the eighteenth century, the British and French perceived each other as having generally aggressive intentions in North America, when in fact the sides' intentions were apparently rather limited.[12] Iran, in the aftermath of the *Vincennes*' shooting down of a passenger airliner, viewed the incident as so malevolent as to require revenge, which was apparently visited upon the US in the form of the bombing of the Pan American airliner over Scotland.

Effects of stress on cognition

In a similar vein, there are well-known effects of stress that could readily affect the assessment of the opponent's intentions as well as other important judgments.[13] Table 4.3 summarizes these effects.

Table 4.3 Effects of stress on cognition

- Thinking becomes rigidified, less abstract, and less tolerant of ambiguity
- The ability to separate trivial from dangerous events is reduced
- The adversary is visualized as much more threatening and effective than is realistically the case
- People begin to distrust their own judgment and are more easily swayed than usual
- Behavior becomes increasingly random
- People become less decisive or make decisions prematurely
- Memory, attention, and perception are impaired; error rates increase
- Problem solving flexibility decreases
- People become preoccupied with the immediate problem and downgrade long-term consequences
- People focus on the option that seems most likely to eliminate the threat which causes stress

Examples of the effects of stress on leaders' cognitions are legion. Stress may totally incapacitate a leader for a period of time, as was the case with Stalin in the week after the German invasion. Nehru, Nasser, Moltke, Ludendorff and Moshe Dayan are also alleged to have become incapacitated because of stress. While relatively minor short-term crises such as the Mayaguez incident do not seem to have stressed leaders significantly, more serious crises clearly have that potential even when war does not break out. There have been (contested) allegations that two members of Kennedy's ExComm were not functioning well during the Cuban Missile Crisis.

Even where stress does not result in complete dysfunction, the effects noted in Figure 4.5 may be manifested, with potentially dangerous results. Thus, Theodore Sorenson, a participant in the ExComm deliberations, has stated that on 27 October (the twelfth day of the crisis), 'we did show the effects of stress and fatigue, and the air strike *was* gaining strength, and its proponents were feeling more and more vigorous. The President was under *tremendous* pressure at this point'.[14] The pressure to remove the threat clearly was leading to a focus on an option that seemed capable of doing this.

Another potential stress-related problem in war-termination might be the sudden diminution in stress as a crisis appears to be terminating. Richard Nixon has written:

> The point of *greatest danger* is not in preparing to meet the crisis or fighting the battle; it occurs after the crisis or battle is over, regardless of whether it has resulted in victory or defeat. The individual is spent physically, emotionally and mentally. *He lets down.* Then if he is confronted with another battle, even a minor skirmish, he is prone to *drop his guard* and to err in his judgment.[15]

Anyone who has ever experienced a truly stressful event would agree with Nixon regarding the virtually involuntary fatigue and relaxation that occur as stress-aroused psycho-physiological systems return to normal. It is certainly conceivable that this would occur after a serious crisis or war appeared to be receding from its peak, and the ability of decision-makers to react appropriately to events might be hindered.

THE ROLE OF STAFFS AND SPECIAL ADVISORS

As our third example of psychological processes that might affect events, Table 4.4 summarizes some of the relevant attributes of high-level staffs and advisors. The effect of these phenomena could be to increase or decrease the perception of opponent hostility.

Table 4.4 Important attributes of staff and advisors

- General perception of how the world functions
- Perception of the adversary's personality, intentions, and doctrine
- Stressor resistance
- Group dynamics
- Knowledge, e.g. of military standard operating procedures, including especially the opponent's
- Psychological attributes of dominant members of the staff or advisory groups.

In scanning the attributes listed in Table 4.4, it is difficult not to think of the attitudes prevalent in the early Reagan administration when not only was the Soviet Union perceived as an 'evil empire' (an arguably valid description), but was also believed to be importantly superior in strategic forces (not a valid description). Nuclear war was apparently not unthinkable, and there was considerable top-level interest and participation in nuclear exercises. Factual knowledge about the strategic balance and forces was low.

Problems of this type are not unique to any party or administration. Anecdotes about the early Carter administration suggest a considerable level of ignorance among close Carter staffers and confidantes on military issues, particularly nuclear issues. They may not have been so anti-Soviet initially, and they certainly did not believe the military situation was so adverse as did the Reaganites, but it should come as no surprise that the confidantes of people elected to the Presidency do not start out their tours in the White House with much military sophistication: they have spent their careers being successful in entirely different domains.

Misperceptions of an opponent or a lack of knowledge (or possession of just enough knowledge to be dangerous) regarding strategic forces are potential exacerbating factors in a crisis. The perception that an opponent is intrinsically 'evil' may be a particular hindrance to crisis-termination efforts because the opponent's termination measures may simply fit into a schema of expected deceptions; this could make it difficult for the opponent to do anything that would be genuinely regarded as termination activities. On the other hand, it is important to remember that certain termination activities, e.g. reversing civil-defense evacuations, would carry sufficient credibility that they would tend to convince even those who held a strongly unfavorable image of an opponent that the opponent was sincere in his termination efforts.

A lack of knowledge about strategic forces would be particularly dangerous if decision-makers and their staff fixated on the military consequences of going second instead of going first in today's world (such a 'fixation' might make more sense in a world with some form of strategic defense). Both knowledge regarding strategic weapons and their effects and, as noted previously, the manner in which information regarding such matters as 'the cost of going second' were presented would be likely to influence the attitudes of decision-makers and their staffs toward termination measures which might have the effect of temporarily increasing force vulnerability. Once again, however, it is not sensible to blow these concerns out of proportion; the strong motivation that even semi-rational leaders would have to terminate a crisis or conflict short of a strategic nuclear exchange would tend to counterbalance military concerns of even the ignorant. It would be an exceptional circumstance if no one in the 'inner circles' reminded leaders forcefully that the force structures have been designed specifically so that *second*-strike attacks would be devastating and going first is unnecessary; and the consequences of going first in the mistaken belief that the opponent was about to strike would be 'immeasurable'.

4.5 DISCUSSION WITHIN FRAMEWORK OF MODEL

Decision-making and re-escalation: events, cognition, and decision

Some plausible events

We are all familiar with possible war scenarios, although the momentous events of the last year have rendered most of the old standbys obsolete. Here, let us imagine we have gone through some new not-implausible scenario in which, after serious conventional war, negotiations are successful in *initiating* a process of de-escalation intended to lead to war-termination. What are some of the things that might happen, and why? The purpose here is to engage in some divergent thinking and to suggest provocative possibilities, not to argue strongly for particular events. With that in mind, Table 4.5 describes some possible events that could disrupt the de-escalation and, possibly, lead to strategic nuclear conflict. As we go through them, consider that they might occur in any of many scenarios, except where otherwise noted. Again, the assumed context is that none of the parties is in fact planning nuclear use; they seek termination.

Table 4.5 Illustrated exacerbating events

- An assassination attempt on the President and Vice-President leaves the Vice-President critically wounded and the President slightly wounded. Arrests are made and the assassins are found to have been leftists who had traveled considerably in Europe during the 1970s and who had visited Cuba for extended periods of time.
- An SSBN fails to report back at its scheduled time. The assumption is that it has been sunk by enemy forces.
- HUMINT sources report that the French government is contemplating a 'demonstrative' use of nuclear weapons against the Soviet homeland, although no previous intelligence had indicated any French interest in such options even at a theoretical level.
- As terms of the initial agreement, the sides are beginning to stand down their nuclear forces, even to the extent of surfacing SSBNs, returning mobile ICBMs and bombers to their home bases, and reducing the alert level of those systems. Both sides' military leaders are unhappy about these procedures.
  - The US detects suspicious surface ships operating close to the US coastline. Some analysts believe they could be carrying nuclear SLCMs and may be effectively under Soviet control.
  - One of the national leaderships is briefed on a new and highly secret version of EMP weaponry that is expected to be able to severely disrupt communications and electronics more generally.

    There is heated discussion about whether the opponent has similar weapons and it is generally concluded that one must conclude that he does.
- One side pushes forward as hard as possible conventionally while pursuing the negotiations, seeking to maximize the strength of its military position at the end of hostilities.
- Some or all of the parties have initiated and continue to pursue vigorous civil-defense measures, including evacuation of leaders and urban residents. In the US case, this may take the form of spontaneous evacuation without government sanction, even in direct opposition to government preferences and promises. Soviet agents might observe that families of certain top-level officials are among those leaving the Washington area.
- Soviet naval vessels continue to harass US vessels despite the Soviet leadership's avowed intent to de-escalate.

Some plausible cognitions

If we return now to our discussion of how cognitive factors could affect our assessment of opponents and the way we would frame issues (see Tables 4.2 to 4.4), it is not difficult to postulate some bizarre and frightening sequences.

Let us start with the reasonable assumption that the leaderships involved in the conflict and trying to de-escalate hold generally unfavorable images of each other (this is typical of nations that have gone to war), and that the leaderships are moreover quite suspicious of each other's true intent in the current situation. If we then look at the events against this backdrop, it is easy to see how cognitive distortions could produce 'dangerous ideas' that could lead to re-escalation.

Consider first the assassination attempts. The well-documented tendency to over- and misattribute causality, coupled with the crisis atmosphere and the assassins' backgrounds, would encourage a belief that the assassinations were part of a comprehensive scheme to seize advantage at a critical time by destroying US leadership. The belief that causes and effects resemble each other (if the effect is great, the cause must be significant) would reinforce this. At the same time, the vividness of the information would make it difficult to consider baseline cases, i.e. the many assassinations or attempts that have *not* been sponsored by hostile nations. Given also a negative and stereotypically evil image of an opponent, these events would fit easily into a schema in which the bad opponent takes advantage of a United States that has let down its guard.

Similarly, many of the above-discussed cognitive processes would also come into play in regard to the SSBN's failure to report. Despite the fact that US SSBNs have historically been very hard to track because of their quietness, such 'baseline' data could likely be ignored because of the context in which the failure to report occurred. Instead, the tendency to overweight a low probability event (the sinking of a US SSBN), coupled with the over- and misattribution of causality and the tendency to fit events into visualizable, not probable, scenarios, would combine to make more seemingly reasonable the assumption that the SSBN had been sunk – and sunk moreover not as a result of some localized initiative, but as part of a cunning, coordinated plan to cripple US sea-based forces.

It is easy to see the 'dangerous ideas' that could arise as a result of these cognitive processes operating. Leaders might start to believe that a 'rational', if despised, opponent has been ousted, and that these events are symptomatic of hardliners or his military taking control. (This belief in and of itself fits a schema.) Or they might feel that the opponent, though still in control, has doublecrossed them, and is using the 'termination process' in a deceptive manner so that he can win by stealth what he could not win by strength. (Another schema.) Either of these beliefs could lead them to abandon the de-escalation process and renew hostilities. If the conflict level had previously been high, they might conclude – especially in view of the 'attack' on the SSBN – that the only thing left for the opponent to do was launch a first strike. If sufficiently convinced of this – and here stress and the narrowing of cognition could play a large part – than they might preempt.

Cognitive processes could interact with the other events to produce similar dangerous ideas. Human intelligence (HUMINT) reports regarding the French government's intention to make a demonstrative attack might be accepted despite the lack of previous French interest in such options.[16] The advantage that vivid information has over baseline information in competing for primacy during reasoning could once again be a factor here, as could the tendency to overweight low-probability events; images about the French or schemas regarding the part they might play in a confrontation could also play a role. If they truly believed the French were going to strike, then leaders under stress might become fatalistic and accept one of the most dangerous of the dangerous ideas: 'War is inevitable because a third party (in this case the French) will strike, and the attacked party will either not be able to determine who struck, won't care to determine who struck, or might have already instructed his forces to retaliate massively against all potential opponents. Therefore, we should strike while we are able.'

The reports of US evacuations could easily be viewed as evidence of US leadership intentions, and not activity at the grass-roots levels. Both the tendency to overattribute causality and the tendency to find resemblance between effects and causes ('this is a very significant action, therefore it could only have been ordered at the highest level') would militate in favor of the Soviets believing the US was about to re-escalate, if not preempt. The actions of the side that pushed hard conventionally might be seen as dispositional (they're evil) instead of situational (they're just trying to hedge out of fear the process will fail). The 'suspicious' ships operating near the US coastline might be seen as suspicious because of tendencies to misestimate causality, while the harassment by Soviet ships would less likely be seen to be a result of 'friction' of bureaucratic process than as a consequence of deliberate Soviet choice (overestimation of causality and effects resembling consequences). [The conclusion that the other side had new EMP weapons could be reached through the tendency to 'mirror-image', i.e. view the opponent as one does oneself.]

All of these events, if cognitively misinterpreted, could give rise to a fatalistic attitude that events are out of control and a renewal of hostilities inevitable, at which point seizing the initiative, even to the point of launching a preventive or preemptive strike, might seem wise. Figure 4.3 illustrates how these behavioral processes could interact to produce escalation rather than termination.

Two things must be noted. First, events would undoubtedly have a synergistic effect upon one another. The more of these events that occurred in a short time-period, the greater the likelihood that one or more of the above-stated 'dangerous ideas' would be accepted. The second point is in the nature of a caveat: cognitive misperceptions might, under the right circumstances, work to neutralize each other. For example, the tendency to accept the new intelligence regarding French intentions could be counterbalanced by the tendency not to revise old probability estimates in light of new information. Thus, cognitive fallacies will not necessarily have a completely negative effect: some might actually aid crisis-resolution. Nonetheless, things would undoubtedly be far less dangerous if we were not plagued with any of these cognitive limitations.

Exacerbating circumstances or policies

Although this speculative excursion has been only mildly structured, it is worth noting that a number of circumstances would tend to exacerbate any problems of the sort raised:

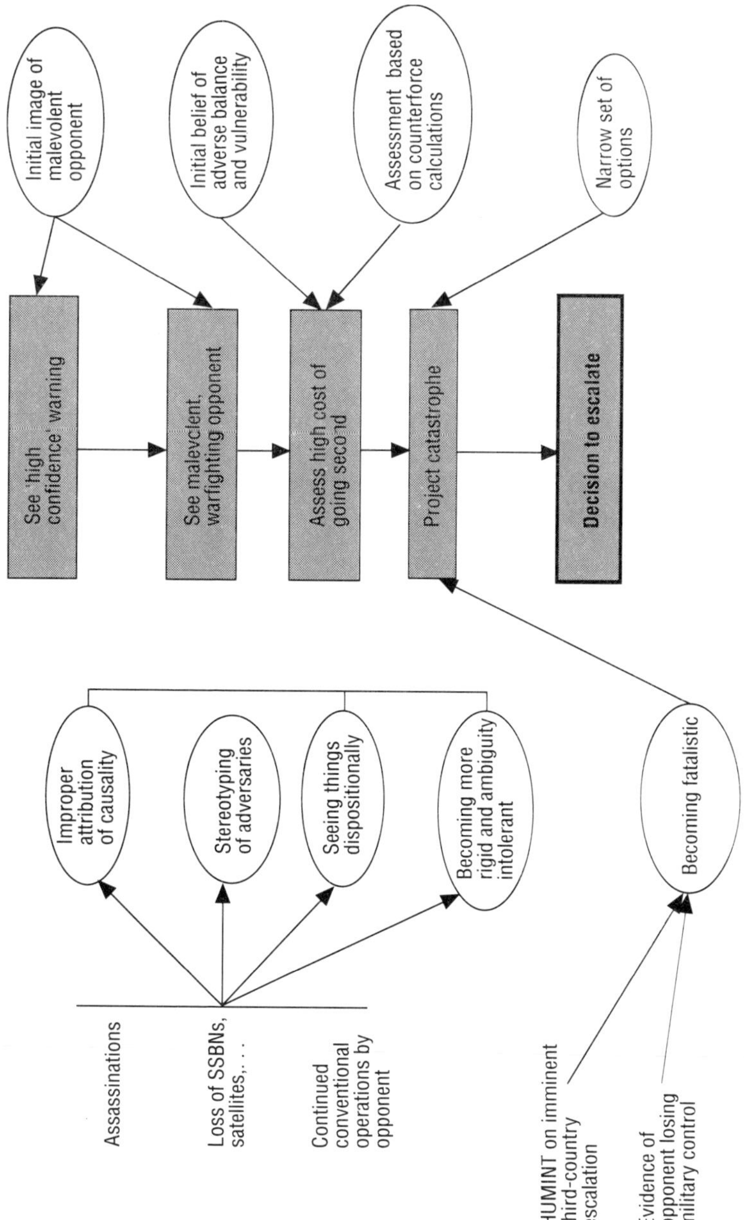

Figure 4.3 Interaction of events/behavioral factors affecting termination/escalation

- Circumstances in which one or both sides have deliberately increased its vulnerability to nuclear attack as part of the de-escalation process, to the extent that leaders perceive the cost of going second to be substantial
- Circumstances in which the parties are communicating only minimally and perhaps with inconsistent degrees of candor and truthfulness. In such instances, 'random' events could be seen as sinister and no alternative explanations might be offered. Unintendedly stereotypical (negative) images of the opponent would have a strong impact of each side's leadership and threatening operations would go unexplained.
- Circumstances in which national leaders start out with deep-seated beliefs in the evil intentions, and perhaps the lunacy, of their opponents
- Circumstances in which the promises of one or both sides' top leaders are contradicted by subsequent events, perhaps because leaders overestimated their control or the time required to achieve that control
- Circumstances in which national leaders start out with the belief that nuclear war can be fought and won, or at least that the other side believes that nuclear war can be fought or won.

Mitigating processes

Fortunately, there are often mitigating processes to protect us from the more negative features of our cognitive makeup. As some examples here, consider the following:

- Even if some of the threatening events occurred and a sober assessment of strategic warning assigned a high probability to an enemy first strike, a national leader convinced that his second-strike retaliatory capability was secure and that the 'value' of a first strike relative to a second strike was minimal would quite possibly hold out against the warnings and avoid pressure to 'preempt'.
- Even if a national leader had a deep and stereotyped image of his opponent as villainous and capable of nuclear war fighting, knowledge of his own retaliatory capability might compensate for his fears. Further, even a single person-to-person discussion (perhaps by video conferencing) might help correct the stereotyping tendency.[17]

– Even if a national leader and his immediate staff misinterpreted the behavior of the opponent's military forces, senior military officers familiar with standard operating procedures and doctrine more generally might, in these circumstances, be a calming influence.

Behavioral factors and de-escalatory CBMs

What then, might these behavioral factors and their effects in war-termination and crisis de-escalation suggest for de-escalatory CBMs described in other chapters? CBMs might interact with behavioral factors in both negative and positive ways.

CBMs that increase force vulnerability, such as the return of mobile ICBMs to garrisons or the return of some SSBNs to port, may do more harm than good. In particular, the implementation of these measures early in a terminating crisis followed by exacerbating circumstances – such as an opponent's refusal to follow through with a specified de-escalatory measure – could increase pressure to re-escalate or to preempt.

But other CBMs may be useful in light of these behavioral factors. For example, CBMs that help to 'lift' the fog of termination and to clarify intentions may be very useful. CBMs that establish rules of engagement in a chaotic military environment might convince leaders that things are not 'out of control' and thus mitigate pressures to launch a first strike. Similarly, CBMs that increase the sharing of information or the frequency of communications might mitigate the potential negative effects of infrequent or seemingly less than candid interchanges. Finally, CBMs may permit leaders to gain greater confidence that their opponent is not doublecrossing them and planning to re-escalate. CBMs that increase the transparency of military activities, such as the stationing of inspectors near an opponent's forces, might reduce these concerns.

Observations and conclusions about next steps

Our purpose in this chapter has been to stimulate thought rather than to provide answers and prescriptions. Nonetheless, several conclusions seem valid:

- Cognitive processes contribute to what Clausewitz called 'the fog of war', or, in this case, 'the fog of termination'.
- Negative feelings about opponents, combined with the tendency to view opponents dispositionally, can make it difficult for decision-makers to place themselves in the other leadership's shoes; this can result in dangerous misperceptions of opponent actions.
- Other common cognitive processes such as the over- and misestimation of causality, the overuse of vivid information at the expense of baseline information, and others discussed in this chapter, can also seriously impede efforts to terminate.
- Not all 'non-rational' cognitive processes would make de-escalation and termination harder; some could cancel each other out and others might favor successful termination.
- Other factors, such as staff expertise, and deliberate decision-making processes, could mitigate the bad effects of 'non-rational' cognitive processes.

The class of issues we have raised can be addressed to a considerable degree analytically. By becoming more conversant with the predictable classes of human reasoning error we can hope to introduce procedures and provide general educational backgrounds that would tend to mitigate these problems in the event of crisis. We see value in a new generation of standard texts, including texts for staffers charged in part with assuring that their bosses don't make classic blunders, improved briefing materials and procedures, improved decision aids, improved gaming and simulation, regular high-level discussions, improved communication facilities (surely the teletype that constitutes the hotline can be improved), and a host of other techniques. The biggest obstacle may actually be the lack of a felt need. After all, we have avoided nuclear war for nearly a half-century and there are no nuclear crises on the horizon, or even major conventional crises among the major powers. This, coupled with the extraordinary egos of high-level people, operate against efforts to do better. Nonetheless, the effort is important and worthwhile.

NOTES

1. This paper reflects work sponsored by the Carnegie Corporation. A similar paper was developed by one of us (Davis) for a related conference at Haverford College on 27–28 April 1990. That paper will be published by Greenwood Press in a book edited by Stephen Cimbala and Sidney Waldman. Some of the concepts discussed stem from earlier work sponsored by the Director of Net Assessment in the Office of the Secretary of Defense.
2. See, for example, Robert Jervis, R. N. Lebow, and J. G. Stein, *Psychology and Deterrence,* (Baltimore: Johns Hopkins University Press, 1985).
3. Paul K. Davis, *Studying First Strike Stability with Knowledge-Based Models of Human Decisionmaking,* The RAND Corporation and the RAND/UCLA Center for the Study of Soviet International Behavior, R-3689-CC, 1989.
4. Paul K. Davis, Steven C. Bankes, and James P. Kahan, *A New Methodology for Modeling National Command Level Decisionmaking in War Games and Simulations,* The RAND Corporation, R-3290-NA, 1986.
5. For examples, see Paul K. Davis, *Some Lessons Learned from Building Red Agents in the RAND Strategy Assessment System,* The RAND Corporation, N-3003-NA, 1989.
6. One of the most important examples of this is the human inability to deal well, *unaided,* with even relatively simple feedback phenomena. See, for example, Jay Forrester, *Urban Dynamics,* (Cambridge, Mass.: MIT Press, 1969), or any of Forrester's other books on System Dynamics. Many other examples arise in the literature on judgment and decision-making. See, for example, John D. Sterman, Modeling Managerial Behavior: "Misperceptions of Feedback in a Dynamic Decision Making Experiment," *Management Science,* Vol. 35, no. 3, March 1989.
7. Paul K. Davis, 'Applying Artificial Intelligence Techniques to Strategic Level Gaming and Simulations', in Maurice Elzas, et al. (eds), *Simulation in the Artificial Intelligence Era,* (Amsterdam: North-Holland, 1986). Also available as a RAND reprint Note, N-2752-RC, 1988.
8. The existing models are part of the RAND Strategy Assessment System (RSAS), which is used primarily for defense analysis and war-college educational activities. A given decision-making model involves about 15 000 lines of high-level computer code, the bulk of which is needed to explain simple things to the computer.
9. Paul K. Davis, *Studying First-strike Stability with Knowledge-Based Models of Human Decision Making,* The RAND Corporation, R-3689-CC, April 1989.
10. Examples include: Hitler's judgments about French and British non-action if he took over the Sudetenland; Japanese hopes, in deciding to attack Pearl Harbor and the Philippines, that the US would lack resolve for a long war; US expectations that North Vietnamese leaders would lack resolve to continue in the face of escalating use of American air power; Douglas MacArthur's judgment that the Chinese would not enter the Korean war; and, perhaps, Chinese misconceptions about US intentions as American forces swept into North Korea.
11. Fred C. Iklé, *Every War Must End,* (New York: Columbia University Press, 1971).

12. Robert Jervis, *Perception in Misperception in International Politics* (Princeton: Princeton University Press, 1976), pp. 24–5.
13. Alexander L. George, 'The Impact of Crisis-Induced Stress on Decision Making', in Frederic Solomon and Robert Q. Marston (eds), *The Medical Implications of Nuclear War* (Washington, DC: Institute of Medicine, National Academy of Sciences, National Academy Press, 1986).
14. James G. Blight and David A. Welch, *On the Brink: Americans and Soviets Examine the Cuban Missile Crisis* (New York: Hill and Perry, 1989), p. 50 (emphasis in original).
15. Richard M. Nixon, *Six Crises* (Garden City, NY: Doubleday, 1962), p. 37 (emphasis added).
16. The dangers of incorrect HUMINT are well known to students of intelligence. For example, during the Cuban Missile Crisis the premier Western spy in Moscow, Penkovsky, sent a message that the Soviets were preparing an attack. Remarkably, but fortunately, this message was not sent up the line to top decision-makers. As Raymond Garthoff observed to one of us (Davis) at a conference in which this paper was presented, it is quite plausible that this 'raw' intelligence could have made profound impact on deliberations. For details on the Crisis, see Raymond L. Garthoff, *Reflections on the Cuban Missile Crisis* (Washington, DC: The Brookings Institution, 1989).
17. This can backfire. Neville Chamberlain, for example, came away from discussions with Hitler convinced that the man, however difficult, could be dealt with. Chamberlain was strongly affected by a passionate desire to avoid a repeat of the Great War.

Part II

Nuclear Operations and De-escalatory Measures

5 De-escalatory Confidence-Building Measures and US Nuclear Operations

Glenn C. Buchan

Invulnerability is the best confidence building measure.

Andy Aldrin,
The RAND Corporation

5.1 INTRODUCTION

As long as the United States and other nations maintain nuclear arsenals, one or more nuclear powers might feel obliged to put their nuclear forces on alert in a serious crisis. It might result from a direct, serious confrontation between nuclear powers, such as the Cuban Missile Crisis. Alternatively, a nuclear power might alert its nuclear forces to 'demonstrate resolve' and influence the course of a peripheral conflict, as the United States did in the 1973 Middle East War. In either case, unless the nuclear powers involved actually do go to war, they eventually need to be able to stand down from their nuclear alerts in a safe, graceful way that does not exacerbate or actually precipitate a nuclear confrontation.

Fortunately, nuclear alerts have been rare to date and the parties have been able to stand down successfully. Still, the dangers inherent in the nuclear alerting process have long been of concern to nuclear strategists, who feared a modern analog to the mobilization race that contributed to the start of the First World War.[1] The obvious concern is that the process of alerting nuclear forces could develop a momentum and a logic of its own, producing escalatory pressures that would be difficult for policymakers either to control or to resist. The result could be a nuclear war that everyone would have preferred to avoid.

One possible approach to helping manage and de-escalate crises might be for nuclear powers to mutually agree upon a series of actions to return their nuclear forces to normal peacetime alert postures. Cooperation in de-escalating a crisis by instituting such stand-down measures might conceivably help foster the kind of mutual confidence between adversaries necessary to allow them to navigate their way out of a nuclear confrontation.

This analysis will examine the way the United States operates its strategic nuclear forces – how its alerting procedures work, what those alerting procedures accomplish, etc. – and the prospects for developing de-escalatory CBMs to defense nuclear confrontations. A fundamental premise is that the United States and the Soviet Union become involved in a crisis serious enough to alert their nuclear forces. The specific issues to be addressed include:

- Is alerting US forces likely to make things better or worse in a crisis? To what degree do alerted nuclear forces themselves contribute to the danger of the crisis? Are there ancillary actions during alert that might increase the risk of war?
- If there is a political settlement to the crisis, could stand-down measures reinforce the mutual confidence necessary to help the antagonists step away from the brink?
- Are there stand-down measures that would actually enhance crisis-stability and perhaps help promote a peaceful resolution of the conflict?

Problems with discussing US nuclear operations in a crisis

There are inherent difficulties in discussing how the United States would operate its forces in a crisis. They include classification, what I refer to as 'operational culture', and the inherent difficulties extrapolating from very limited historical evidence.

Classification

The details of US nuclear alert procedures and its war plan are necessarily classified and must remain so. The broadest features of alert procedures – dispersal, increased readiness, etc. – have long been discussed openly, but these descriptions are so general that they provide little useful basis for analysis and could actually be misleading. Recent descriptions of alert procedures at moderate levels of detail by Bruce Blair and others make it possible to at least discuss the subject in an open forum.[2] Still, 'the devil is in the details'; many operations that look straightforward in principle can be quite difficult in practice, and those kinds of difficulties can increase the risks inherent in alerts and generate instabilities in crisis situations. The amount of detailed information necessary to assess these risks fully is difficult to obtain even with access to the best sources available. Thus, any simplified assessment is likely to be somewhat suspect and will probably tend to understate the dangers of nuclear alerts. On the other hand, an analysis of this sort should look toward the future and be prescriptive, so weaknesses in assessing the current state of nuclear operational procedures may be somewhat mitigated.

Operational culture

If finding out what people are *supposed* to do during a nuclear alert is hard, assessing what they are actually *likely* to do is harder still. Even the most rigid plans leave some room for human interpretation. In fact, the most rigid plans are sometimes the ones most in need of a certain amount of human intervention and flexibility to make them work. Predicting how people will behave during a nuclear crisis adds an additional dimension of uncertainty to assessing the risks inherent in nuclear alerts. Operators will presumably act based on a set of beliefs about what their duty is, where their loyalties lie, and how they can most effectively fulfill their obligations as well as a set of perceptions about possible limitations of their equipment, reliability of their command structure, and the set of risks associated with being either too aggressive or not aggressive enough during a potential nuclear confrontation. This set of beliefs and perceptions of the operators is what I call 'operational culture'.

To illustrate, I would offer the following example. One of the advantages always claimed for manned bombers is that, in principle, they could be recalled after launch up to the time when they actually released their weapons. A question to ask, however, is whether bomber crews would really respond to such a recall order.[3] Moreover, would an antagonist *believe* that the bombers would turn back once launched? If not, he might take more aggressive action himself, thus precipitating the kind of spiraling escalation and crisis-instability that has given nuclear strategists and peace activists nightmares and has enriched the bank accounts of writers of cold war thrillers for decades.

Factors influencing op culture are all likely to change over time. Communications systems and nuclear safety devices are much better than they used to be. The bomber force need not be vulnerable for an extended period as it once would have been following a recall order. The Strategic Air Command of John T. Chain is a different organization than it was in the days of Curtis LeMay. The change in the international climate is even more dramatic, as recent events have underscored. All of the trends appear to reduce the danger of uncontrolled escalation evolving from a nuclear alert. Still, op culture will contrive to complicate discussions about how US nuclear forces operate in crises.

The limitations of historical analysis

The prudence with which the United States and the Soviet Union have behaved in avoiding confrontations that could have led to nuclear war has been the most durable historical lesson of the nuclear age. Still, there have been a few occasions when the United States raised the alert levels of its nuclear forces. The most famous – and the most dangerous – was, of course, the Cuban Missile Crisis. The US nuclear alert during the 1973 Middle East War was mildly dramatic, but much less dangerous.

Other somewhat quirky incidents have occurred along the way.[4] Scholars have extensively mined the public records of these incidents to glean insights about how nations behave during nuclear alerts and how the risks can be minimized. Indeed, there are potentially valuable lessons to be learned. However, the limited historical evidence must be sifted with care when trying to deduce how to manage future crises. Basic problems include limited data, anecdotal evidence, and *dated* evidence.

Because there have been so few nuclear crises, the total body of operational evidence is small. Much of it amounts to 'war stories' about things that went wrong. That is normal in military operations and such anecdotes usually lead to modifications in operational procedures to eliminate at least those particular problems in future operations. Of course, with so little actual experience to draw upon, no one can be overly sanguine that we have identified all of the 'bugs' in the system.

Technology has changed dramatically over the course of the nuclear age, and that significantly affects the value of historical evidence. Long gone, of course, are the days when planners had to worry about fueling ICBMs, spinning-up gyros, etc. before missiles could be launched and then having to act quickly before they started to break down. Also long gone are systems like the nuclear Genie air defense missile that caused alert problems in the past.[5] Warning systems are much better than they were, dramatically reducing the chances of some of the more spectacular false alarms that occurred in earlier times. Communications systems have improved significantly, thereby enhancing confidence in the ability of commanders to control nuclear forces. Nuclear safety devices on weapons are much better and their use is much more widespread. The United States depends much less on aircraft for reconnaissance than it used to. All of these things should make US forces less susceptible to failure than in the past and will minimize some of the identified risk. These changes in technology and operational procedures are going to make future confrontations look very different from those that occurred in the past.

5.2 WHY GO ON ALERT?

Going on alert makes military forces more ready to go to war. The rationale for going on alert can be military, political, or a combination of both.

What are the military objectives?

There are basically four military objectives of alerting US nuclear forces:

- reduce their vulnerability
- increase the number of weapons available to execute an attack
- increase the readiness of those forces to respond to orders to attack
- insure that commands to attack can be issued if necessary and can reach the majority of forces.

Alerts generally involve increasing the number of SSBNs at sea, increasing the number of bombers on alert and perhaps deploying some of them to other bases or placing some on airborne alert, and in the future, perhaps deploying mobile ICBMs away from their day-to-day garrison locations. Other likely actions involve preparing supporting systems – C^3 systems and selected conventional forces – for war. At high levels of alert, there could be active military actions to reduce the potential nuclear threat to the United States (e.g. ASW against enemy missile-launching submarines).

What are the political objectives?

Nuclear alerts get everybody's attention. Sometimes that is their objective. In the Cuban Missile Crisis, in addition to actually preparing for war, the United States clearly intended alerting its nuclear forces to send a political signal to the Soviets that it was serious about eliminating the Soviet missiles from Cuba and that it was willing and able to use nuclear weapons if necessary.[6] The sole purpose of the US nuclear alert during the 1973 Middle East War was to signal the Soviets that the United States strongly objected to their threat to introduce combat troops into Egypt.[7] Unlike the Cuban Missile Crisis, there was never any serious US intent to prepare for war, although the risk of uncontrolled escalation to a nuclear confrontation between the United States and the Soviet Union could never be ruled out entirely.[8]

What do US nuclear forces do in an alert?

Table 5.1 shows a notional future US strategic force that conforms to the restrictions imposed by the current version of the proposed START Treaty. This particular force was selected to include the widest possible range of future US strategic systems, such as the two mobile ICBMs – the rail-mobile Rail Garrison Peacekeeper and the road-mobile small ICBM (SICBM), to illustrate the richest mix of potential alert options. Given the United States' fiscal problems and the improved relations between the United States and the Soviet Union because of *perestroika*, the United States will almost certainly not actually deploy such a large, robust force. Still, its purposes and its size would have to be reduced substantially to alter the basic conclusions of the analysis.

Table 5.1 Notional future US strategic forces (START-constrained)

Weapon systems			
ICBMs	Number of platforms (Strategic Nuclear Delivery Vehicles) (SNDVs)	Weapons per delivery vehicle	Total number of actual weapons
Rail Garrison MX	50	10	500
Small ICBM	250	2	500
Minuteman Follow-On			
1-RV	300	1	300
2-RV	150	2	300
		ICBM Total Warheads	1600
SLBMs			
Trident D-5 (17 SSBNs)	408	8	3264
		Total Ballistic Missile Warheads	4864
Bombers			
B-52H (ALCM)	90	20	1800
B-1B (penetrator)	97	16	1552
B-2 (penetrator)	132	12	1584
B-52G (conventional)	100	—	
TOTAL BOMBER WEAPONS:			4936
TOTAL WEAPONS			9800

Table 5.2 shows the major actions that the United States might take in a crisis to alert its strategic nuclear forces and their associated C[3] systems. The alert measures vary considerably among the different force elements. There are also different levels of alert that policymakers can choose from.

Table 5.2 Major actions in a nuclear alert

ICBMs	SLBMs	Bombers and tankers	C^3
• Slight readiness increase of silo-based ICBMs and SICBMs	• Put more SSBNs at set	• Increased readiness	• Alert and disperse NCA successors
	• Increase readiness of SSBNs at sea	• Options – dispersal – airborne alert	• Disperse mobile command posts, satellite ground terminals, and relay aircraft
• Disperse Rail Garrison ICBMs	• Some re-positioning possible		
			• Options for delegation of command authority
			• Increased readiness of C^3 aircraft – options for airborne alert

ICBMs

Modern ICBMs, particularly those based in silos, are normally maintained at very high states of readiness. During a nuclear alert, the crews of silo-based ICBMs are warned to be prepared to launch their missiles if ordered to do so. Nothing else is really required.

The United States is considering deploying two different mobile ICBM systems, the Rail Garrison Peacekeeper[9] and the SICBM, colloquially known as 'Midgetman'. During a crisis, decision-makers can, if they choose, order Rail Garrison MX Peacekeeper to leave their garrisons and disperse along rail lines, thereby presumably making them more difficult for an enemy to locate and target.

SICBMs would operate quite differently. The missiles, mounted on truck-like vehicles called Hardened Mobile Launchers (HML),[10] could be based at existing Minuteman launch facilities, in which case they would be prepared to 'dash on warning' of an attack in progress and later 'hunker down' to harden themselves at appropriate locations away from their peacetime sites. Alternatively, HMLs might also be allowed to roam about on military reservations in the southwestern United States. During alerts, they could disperse over a larger area, move more often, or harden themselves as they saw fit.

In either case, nuclear alerts require relatively little change in routine SICBM operations, since their survival depends on their ability to react to tactical warning. They could probably be launched on receipt of tactical warning as well, although that would defeat the purpose of mobile basing.

SLBMs

Most of the United States' SSBN force is normally at sea. Of those about half are normally 'on station' (i.e. in appropriate locations to launch their missiles with their crews alerted).[11] The rest are 'in transit' to their patrol zones, presumably safe from attack but not ready to launch their SLBMs immediately.

During an alert, the most obvious action to take is to put the rest of the seaworthy SSBN force at sea. (There would probably always be a few SSBNs in port for major repairs that could not be generated in an alert.) At lower levels of alert, crews could be recalled from shore leave and the boats prepared to sail. In the case of Trident SSBNs with the new, larger D-5 missiles, it is conceivable that the SSBNs could be prepared to launch their missiles from port on warning of an attack if they had not had sufficient time to put to sea.

For the SSBNs at sea, some changes in activity in response to a nuclear alert are possible. The state of readiness of the SSBNs in transit could be increased so that they could fire their missiles more rapidly if necessary. Some SSBNs could be repositioned if necessary to improve the target coverage of their missiles.

Although not normally considered part of the United States' strategic nuclear strike force, SSNs armed with nuclear cruise missiles for land attack could, in principle, be diverted from their normal duties to be prepared to strike land targets if necessary. That would probably mean repositioning them close to an enemy's coasts in the proximity of key targets. Whether this would be the best use of SSNs in a crisis is unclear, but presumably the option could be exercised if it were important to do so.

Bombers and tankers

About one-third of the US bomber force is normally maintained on 'strip alert'.[12] That means that the aircraft are armed, fueled, serviced, and parked near runways on main operating bases and crews are 'housed' in a nearby alert facility, so the aircraft could take off in a matter of minutes. There are a number of intermediate steps that can be taken to increase the readiness of the alert bombers and tankers. These include:

- moving the crews into the aircraft
- starting the engines
- taxiing into position to take off.

If there is tactical warning of an attack, the Commander in Chief of SAC has the authority to launch the bombers to assure their survival, although they would still require direction from higher political authorities. This longstanding operational constraint has recently been reinforced by the installation of safety devices on bomber weapons.[13] Other conditions permit lower echelon commanders to launch bombers if their safety is in jeopardy.

During an extended crisis, there are additional options for alerting bombers. These include:

- placing more bombers and tankers on alert
- dispersing some bombers and tankers to other airfields which may not be targeted by an enemy
- placing some bombers and tankers on airborne alert.

C^3

Alerting the command and control network during an alert is at least as important as alerting the forces that it controls. In spite of the longstanding awareness in the professional community of the importance of C^3 and the vulnerabilities of the US system,[14] C^3 improvements have traditionally been given short shrift compared to weapon systems in the competition for budgets and attention. That neglect has created a set of potentially critical vulnerabilities which if exploited by an enemy, might cripple the C^3 network, perhaps to the point of preventing successful execution of a retaliatory strike.[15]

The danger is that an enemy might decide, particularly during a crisis in which all of his options appeared unpalatable, that an attack on the US C^3 structure was the best choice open to him. Similarly, if US policymakers believed their C^3 system to be vulnerable to attack or disruption, they might feel great pressure in a crisis to launch a nuclear attack with minimal or ambiguous provocation to avoid the risk of not being able to respond later – perhaps, the ultimate 'use or lose' situation. How real these vulnerabilities are now or ever were is open to debate,[16] but the *perception* of a problem could be as serious as the problem itself. That is the essence of crisis instability.

In recent years, the United States has taken significant steps to reduce the vulnerability of its strategic C^3 network.[17] Improvements have been made to virtually all communications networks. Mobile ground stations have been developed for satellites. C^3 aircraft have been improved. There have been comments in the open literature about additional alternate command posts to provide continuity of command if the fixed facilities were destroyed. There are now more tangible actions that the United States could take in a nuclear alert to reduce the potential vulnerability of its effectiveness. These include:

- alerting and dispersing Presidential successors to assure that the National Command Authority survives and can control nuclear forces

- dispersing mobile command posts, satellite ground terminals, and relay aircraft
- exercising options for delegating command authority over nuclear weapons to lower-level decision-makers
- increasing the readiness of C^3 aircraft, including periods of airborne alert if necessary.

As with the nuclear forces, there are various levels of alert for the C^3 network, so decision-makers have a range of options available.

Other forces

What other forces do during a crisis may be even more important than what strategic forces do in times of controlling escalation. Strategic forces are generally trying to stay out of harm's way. Other forces like fighter aircraft and attack submarines usually seek contact with the enemy. *Rules of engagement* become critical for such forces and these are largely determined by what else is happening at the time. For example, although a direct confrontation between the United States and the Soviet Union that begins at the strategic level cannot be ruled out, it is more probable that a strategic confrontation would evolve from a local crisis somewhere else in the world. Such crises could run the gamut from a third-party conflict, in which both the United States and the Soviet Union had interests, such as the 1973 Middle East War, to a major theater war in Europe in which Soviet and US military forces were directly engaged. Even in the Cuban Missile Crisis, which was essentially a strategic confrontation from the very beginning, from the US point of view, most of the forces that actually engaged each other – Soviet submarines and US ASW forces, US U-2 reconnaissance aircraft and Soviet and Cuban air defenses, US surface naval forces and Soviet transport vessels – were not really strategic forces by the usual definition. Thus, managing non-strategic forces is likely to be critical in preventing or controlling a serious strategic nuclear confrontation.

Controlling non-strategic forces poses several problems:

- Some rules of engagement for tactical forces that might reduce the risk of a strategic nuclear exchange could seriously impede the successful conduct of a theater war, which could itself make escalation to a strategic confrontation more likely.

- Considering the number and disparate nature of tactical forces, controlling them closely is inherently difficult, particularly if actual combat is occurring.
- Ambiguity is unavoidable in some cases even if rules of engagement call for avoiding certain types of provocative acts.

I will develop these points further in a subsequent section that discusses potential flash-points in a US–Soviet nuclear alert.

The complications that result from problems of managing non-strategic forces can affect not only the objective military situation, but also the perceptions of decision-makers on both sides, perhaps in asymmetrical ways. One side-effect of confrontations that involve alerting and actual use of non-strategic forces is the devaluation of many strategic warning indicators. Strategic warning depends on the identification of military activity that does not normally occur in peacetime. Naturally, if there is a war going on or even a serious crisis, there is going to be a lot of that kind of activity. That further complicates the problems of decision-makers in deciding what sort of nuclear alert measures might be appropriate at a particular time. Striking a prudent balance between protecting nuclear forces and avoiding unduly alarming or provoking the Soviets is complicated considerably by ongoing conventional force operations.

5.3 WHAT ARE THE CONSEQUENCES OF A US NUCLEAR ALERT FOR THE UNITED STATES AND THE SOVIET UNION?

Increasing the alert levels of US nuclear forces affects them in two ways: (1) it decreases their vulnerability to enemy attack; and (2) it increases their overall military effectiveness. The first clearly promotes stability in a crisis because it decreases the incentives of an enemy to attack US nuclear forces. The second might or might not be a concern depending on the nature of the threat that US nuclear forces might pose to the Soviet Union.

Vulnerability of US nuclear forces

Table 5.3 shows the impact of alerting US nuclear forces on their vulnerability to attack. When US forces are on day-to-day alert, most of the SSBN force is at sea and probably invulnerable. The one-third of the fleet that remains in port could not escape in time to survive an attack. Similarly, the 70 per cent of the bomber force that is not on alert would have no chance to escape a ballistic missile attack. The 30 per cent on strip alert have a chance to survive depending on how much warning they get and how rapidly they can respond. Traditional threats to the bomber force include:

- an SLBM attack, particularly a short-time-of-flight attack using depressed trajectory SLBMs (which the Soviets have never actually tested although they have been a theoretical possibility for decades)
- a cruise missile attack, especially an SLCM attack from a small number of submarines
- a commando attack against the aircraft on strip alert, probably followed by a ballistic missile attack.

Silo-based ICBMs can survive only if they are launched on receipt of tactical warning of an attack. Similarly, rail-mobile ICBMs in their garrisons would not have enough time to escape if an attack were in progress, so their survival would depend on launch under attack as well. Whether US decision-makers would have enough confidence in their tactical warning systems to make a nearly instantaneous decision remains problematical at best, particularly in a day-to-day situation where there is no reason to expect an attack. SICBM also depends on tactical warning for its survival. However, it need not launch; it only has to escape from its peacetime location and burrow into the ground to harden itself.

Many key elements of the C^3 system are vulnerable during peacetime. Only the strip alert aircraft might have a reasonable chance to escape to supplement the aircraft maintained on airborne alert. The fixed facilities would be destroyed and there probably would not be enough time to generate any alternate back-ups. Probably of greatest concern is the possibility of a 'decapitation' attack that might destroy the NCA and prevent attack orders from being issued.

Alerting the forces changes the picture dramatically:

- Virtually all SSBNs, except those in dry dock for major repairs, could be put at sea.
- Virtually all bombers and tankers, except 'hangar queens'

Table 5.3 Impact of alerts on strategic force vulnerability

	ICBMs	SLBMs	Bombers	C³
Day-to-day vulnerabilities	• Silos – vulnerable* • Rail Garrison – garrisons vulnerable* • SICBM**	• 33% of SSBNs in port vulnerable	• 70% non-alert bombers vulnerable • Alert bombers vulnerable to some precursor threats**	• Most command posts vulnerable*** • Radars vulnerable • Some fragile communications links and systems • Ground stations vulnerable
Alert vulnerabilities	• Silos* and SICBM** – tactical warning • Rail Garrison – location uncertainty • Logistics support • Crew fatigue	• Gradual attrition • Supplies	• Strip alert bombers – vulnerable to some attacks • Airborne bombers – accidents	• Most sensors remain vulnerable • Most capable (fixed) command facilities remain vulnerable

* Depend on launch under attack in response to tactical warning
** Must flush on tactical warning in order to survive
*** Some can flush on tactical warning

(i.e. aircraft perennially down for repairs) could be readied for action and be put on strip alert at main operating bases. Some could be dispersed or placed on airborne alert if desired.

- Rail Garrison ICBMs could be dispersed.
- Most mobile C^3 assets could be dispersed and arrangements made for delegation of authority for various command decisions.

In general, both the forces and their supporting C^3 systems are much less vulnerable to attack when alerted. Moreover, both commanders and operators are more likely to have a mindset that war could happen and they might be called upon to act than they would during normal day-to-day operations.

Vulnerabilities remain. Both personnel and machines are subject to fatigue, and logistics support for the alert force is a difficult problem unless the alert is brief. Sustained alerts are generally maintained at lower than peak-levels in any case, to minimize the wear and tear on the forces.

Silo-based ICBMs remain dependent on tactical warning to launch under attack to ensure their survivability. In a crisis with forces alerted, decision-makers are likely to feel more confident that warning of an attack is real and be less inhibited to launch ICBMs after receipt of such a warning. Paradoxically, the pressures to launch ICBMs under attack should be reduced significantly if US forces are alerted since the United States has so many more warheads available. In short, when alerted, the United States could more readily afford to risk losing its silo-based ICBMs to a surprise attack.

The SSBN force might be vulnerable to gradual attrition over time, particularly if a large-scale theater campaign were underway at the same time. At worst, however, its capability should 'degrade gracefully', and policymakers might not even be aware that a few SSBNs had been attritted. Other than that, SSBNs should be able to operate as long as their supplies last and their crews hold up. In a really protracted crisis, boats could be brought in one at a time for provisions and crew changes with very little loss in overall force capability.

The bomber force could also be maintained at very high levels of alert if adequate preparations were made in advance. If the bombers were dispersed and maintained on strip alert, adequate logistics support would be required. If part of the force were maintained on airborne alert, sustained operations would require adequate maintenance support to turn the bombers quickly when they landed.[18] Otherwise, there could be an extended period of vulnerability for a significant fraction of the force when they came off airborne alert. Proper preparation can prevent that, however.

The survivability of strip alert aircraft, particularly those at main operating bases, remains dependent on escape after tactical warning of an attack. Aircraft are likely to be at a higher state of readiness (e.g. crews on board, aircraft lined up for takeoff) during an alert and, therefore, should have a better chance of escaping before attacking missiles could arrive. Aircraft at dispersal bases might not have to react at all. That would really depend on the size of the attack and the likelihood that the enemy could have identified the dispersal bases.

Fixed C^3 sites would remain vulnerable during an alert. Major radar installations, command posts, and communications nodes could be destroyed in an attack. That would limit the flexibility of the command structure for major replanning of attack options and eliminate much of the warning network for providing assessment of subsequent attacks. However, the mobile alternates should suffice to perform the most rudimentary functions of the C^3 network: warning of an initial attack, keeping the NCA 'plugged in', and transmitting orders to strategic forces. Like the other mobile elements of the strategic force, the C^3 system has endurance problems, but these are all solvable, particularly if there has been no actual nuclear attack, with adequate support and preparation.

Effectiveness of US nuclear forces

Figure 5.1 shows the total number of weapons available to the United States on day-to-day alert and on full alert. The day-to-day alert force totals about 4000 warheads plus about an additional 1000 warheads on SSBNs in transit to their patrol zones. The fully generated force would include about 9500 warheads, the largest increase being in bomber weapons.

Figure 5.2 shows the notional effectiveness of those forces in targeting installations in the Soviet Union. The chart shows only targets 'covered' (i.e. those at which a weapon arrives and

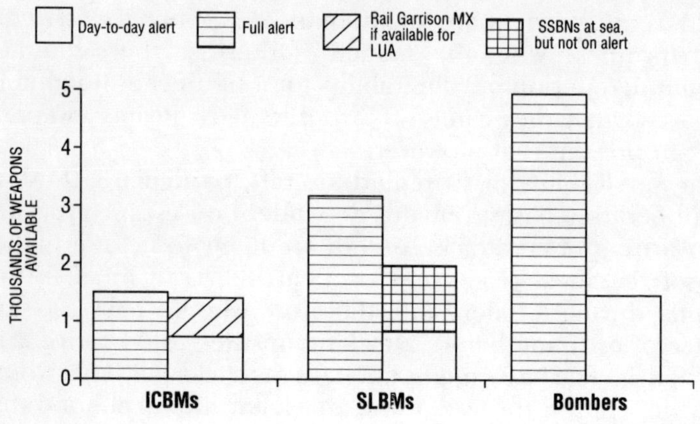

Figure 5.1 Impact of alerts on weapons availability[19]

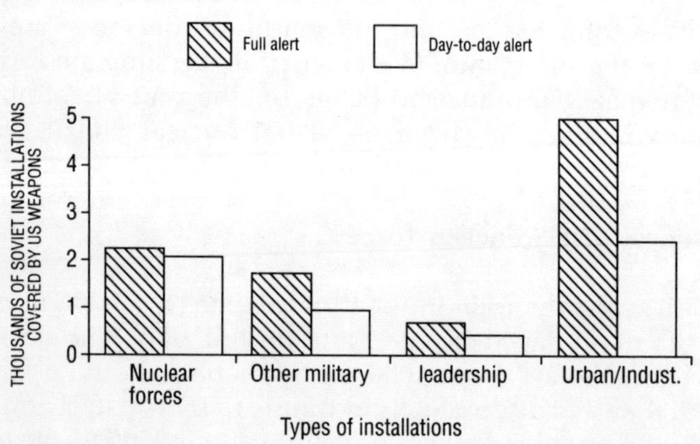

Figure 5.2 Potential effectiveness of US strategic forces – exemplary weapons allocation[20]

detonates) not destroyed, although the distinction is not particularly important for most installations, especially when current and future weapons are employed. The chart also overstates the damage to the Soviet Union somewhat since it assumes that all the US weapons are employed against the Soviet Union or its Warsaw Pact allies. None are held in reserve or used against other countries. Still, even allowing for diversion of some forces for other missions, this START-constrained force would exceed the target coverage publicly stated for the SIOP of ten years ago and would be even more effective in destroying targets.

The real message from Figure 5.2 is that US forces could do massive damage to the Soviet Union from either a day-to-day or a fully alerted posture. That result is hardly surprising, but this almost self-evident truth needs to be rederived occasionally. The fully-alerted forces could achieve somewhat broader target coverage, particularly against urban–industrial installations and conventional military bases, and would achieve higher degrees of expected damage against some installations. The results in Figure 5.2 assume that vulnerable ICBMs are successfully launched under attack. Launch under attack is less important when U.S. forces are fully generated, since so many more warheads would be available. However, even if the US forces had to respond to an attack from day-to-day alert posture, failure to launch ICBMs successfully on warning of the attack would not dramatically reduce the effectiveness of the US response. The United States does not, of course, publicly announce how particular weapon systems are targeted. It is reasonable to assume, however, that a large fraction of the US silo-based ICBM force is targeted against Soviet silos. ICBMs have traditionally been the best prompt, hard target-killing weapons in the force and, therefore, the most appropriate to use against Soviet silos. That is particularly true if they are to be launched under attack, since a launch in error would not result in dropping warheads in downtown Moscow! Also, the importance of the mission is somewhat dubious anyway, so a failure would not be a catastrophic loss. Thus, if US ICBMs did not launch under attack in a day-to-day alert the largest impact on the bars in Figure 5.2 would be in the nuclear threat category. The other bars would drop, but not much. The resulting damage to the Soviet Union would still be enormous, far exceeding the kinds of minimum damage goals traditionally associated with assured destruction (e.g. delivery of at least 400 equivalent megatons, or one 'McNamara').

Another point to note is that the alerted US forces do not pose a qualitatively different threat to the Soviet Union than the day-to-day alert forces do. In particular, *alerting US forces provides few, if any, added incentives for a US first strike.* If the Soviet Union is on day-to-day alert, its bomber forces are currently maintained at such low levels of alert that they would theoretically be vulnerable to *any* kind of attack. Very few weapons would be required. When alerted, they would presumably be at a higher state of readiness and dispersed. If they prepared adequately, their alert force should be relatively invulnerable to any US attack, regardless of whether the United States was generated or not. If their preparations were inadequate, even the day-to-day US alert force could do the job.

Similarly, the Soviets – knowing their own vulnerabilities much better than we ever could – might be concerned about attacks on their C^3 network. If such attacks were to have any chance of success, the United States would almost certainly have to execute them while the Soviets were on day-to-day alert. Otherwise, there would be so many options for redundant critical nodes that the United States could never be confident of success even with fully generated forces. On the other hand, if the United States could somehow identify critical vulnerabilities in the Soviets day-to-day C^3 operations – a most unlikely event – it could probably exploit them with a small attack using its day-to-day alert forces to maximize surprise. Thus, the ability of the United States to attack Soviet command and control depends on Soviet vulnerabilities, not US alert levels.

5.4 WHAT RISKS ARE ASSOCIATED WITH ALERTS?

One might reasonably ask, 'If alerts are so great, why don't we stay on alert all the time?' There are several reasons.

Accidents can happen

One of the reasons that the United States decided to eliminate routine airborne alerts for bombers is that alerts can be dangerous. Aircraft crash periodically during routine training exercises. Such crashes would be much more serious if the aircraft had nuclear weapons aboard. Past experience with such nuclear accidents has caused the United States to be very reticent to put nuclear-armed aircraft in the air without very good reason. Maintaining a large airborne alert force would just magnify the risks.

Airborne alert is a somewhat extreme example. Not all alert procedures are this dangerous. Still, any large military exercise inevitably involves some accidents. Accidents are unfortunate in any case, but those involving nuclear weapons could be catastrophic.

Alerts can be expensive and difficult to maintain

Operating forces on alert costs money. Moreover, the wear and tear on personnel and machines can be debilitating. Even maintaining day-to-day alerts for current US strategic forces is very taxing on crews and is, at the very least, tough on morale.

Maintaining alerts requires more people, more logistics support including spare parts, and higher reliability equipment (which comes at a price). In times of tight budgets when force structure is at risk, spending money to sustain high alert rates is not going to be popular with the services. Even in good times, 'sustainability' has a difficult time competing for resources, particularly in an arena where many have trouble suspending disbelief sufficiently.

Sustaining alerts for extended periods during protracted crises also requires detailed operational planning, extensive preparations in advance, and serious training. The demands for resources are proportionately greater and less palatable. Developing this capability requires a serious effort, but is generally straightforward. The problem areas are well-known, and are generally well-understood thanks to the host of studies on strategic force endurance that have been conducted periodically when the subject was in vogue.

The subject is important because a *lack of an ability to sustain alerts during a crisis is a potential source of crisis instability* that could increase the pressure on decision-makers to take precipitous action. A serious treatment of crisis management must take this problem into account.

Authority devolves downward

Alerting forces, particularly if that involves dispersal, inevitably leads to a measure of devolution of authority to lower-level commanders. That means some loss of negative control – the ability to *prevent* lower-level commanders from acting – by central authorities. This has been a perennial concern in the nuclear age, and various technical and operational safeguards have been built into the system to minimize the risks. Still, the danger cannot be dismissed out of hand, especially since the *perception* of risk of loss of control is unavoidable.

Incidents could occur

In addition to accidents, *incidents* – direct confrontations between antagonists' forces, unexplained disappearances of forces, etc. – inevitably occur during crises. The Cuban Missile Crisis was replete with incidents – the U-2 that was shot down over Cuba, the other U-2 that overflew the Soviet Union, the various encounters between US ASW forces and Soviet submarines, etc.

The simple fact of life is that *incidents are inevitable in any serious crisis.* We have to accept that and be prepared to deal with them. The fundamental problem for managing strategic forces in a crisis is to try to minimize the chances that they will be directly involved in incidents or that incidents that do occur increase the pressure on decision-makers to use strategic forces. Fortunately, in past crises most incidents have involved non-strategic forces and the chances are that that will remain true in the future. Still, alerts have to be designed so that they do not exacerbate incidents.

The perception and political impact of alerts is uncertain

Nuclear alerts send signals, whether we like it or not, to potential enemies, allies, neutrals, and our own population. As noted earlier, the United States used nuclear alerts to send political signals to the Soviets in both the Cuban Missile Crisis and the 1973 Middle East War.

Unfortunately, sending a clear signal is not so easy and even if it were, there is no telling how others will perceive it.[21] The

United States alerts its forces by declaring DEFCONs, which number 1 through 5 – 5 being normal peacetime (except for SAC, which normally maintains DEFCON 4 alert) and 1 being virtual war.[22] The DEFCON system, however, is necessarily imprecise – a blunt instrument for translating policy concepts into operational practice. Trying to do so can lead to incidents precisely like the one described by Sagan in which the Joint Chiefs of Staff, in trying to implement Secretary of Defense Thomas Gates' direction for a 'quiet increase in command readiness', ordered a DEFCON 3 alert, which was a much more aggressive posture than Gates intended and was denounced by Soviet Premier Khrushchev as 'provocative'.[23] The DEFCON system itself is imprecise because it provides considerable latitude to lower-echelon commanders to take particular actions or not as they see fit. Thus, it would be extraordinarily difficult for an outside observer to deduce merely from watching US military actions what the DEFCON level was. Only in the movies can the Soviet Union instantly conclude, without intercepting a DEFCON message, that the United States has just gone to DEFCON 2!

Even if the Soviets were to deduce that the United States had gone to DEFCON 2, what should they make of it? US policymakers could not possibly understand all the implications of a DEFCON alert themselves.[24] How could they possibly expect the Soviets to get a clear picture of US intentions from it?

Others are likely to get unintended messages from an alert as well. One tangible – and presumably quite unintended – effect of the US DEFCON 3 alert during the 1973 Middle East War was that it provided the NATO allies of the US with direct evidence that the United States had unilateral options for employing its nuclear weapons stationed in Europe. Since the DEFCON message went through US rather than NATO communications channels, there was no consultation with other NATO allies. The other NATO countries had probably always suspected that such options for US unilateral action existed, but could choose not to explore such a potentially divisive subject as long as there was no public evidence to force the issue. The fact of the alert made a political confrontation unavoidable.

The point is that alerts can have unintended and unpredictable political consequences. One point for US policymakers to ponder is whether they would *prefer* nuclear alerts to be *interpreted as* (aggressive) *demonstrations of resolve or as prudent* (nonaggressive) *measures taken for self protection.* The latter would be much more consistent with promoting stable crisis management.

5.5 WHAT ARE SERIOUS POTENTIAL PROBLEM AREAS FOR THE UNITED STATES IN FUTURE CRISES?

Some of the most serious potential flashpoints in future US–Soviet confrontations are likely to involve forces and geographic areas somewhat peripheral to the main focus of strategic thinking. If there are serious risks of a crisis getting out of hand, or a conventional war escalating to this nuclear level, this is where they are most likely to occur.

Soviet submarines off the US coasts

The possibility of Soviet submarines off the US coasts has been a longstanding headache to US defense planners. Figure 5.3 illustrates the problem: missiles from Soviet submarines could cover all of the United States. (The arcs shown in Figure 5.3 represent 2000 nmi range missiles. Shorter-range missiles could still be quite effective.) SLBMs launched from Soviet SSBNs near the US coasts could reach most US targets in a matter of minutes, perhaps before the United States could react. Particularly vulnerable would be SAC bomber and tanker main operating bases, Washington DC, home bases for other C^3 aircraft, and a few other key C^3 installations. In total, that would be only a few tens of installations to attack, well within the capabilities of the 3–4 SSBNs that the Soviets have at times routinely kept on station off the US coast. A successful attack could destroy a disproportionate fraction of the US strategic force and might disrupt, or even prevent, the dissemination of Emergency Action Messages (EAMs) to direct US nuclear forces.

The United States has spent great amounts of time, money and effort over the years trying to cope with a short time-of-

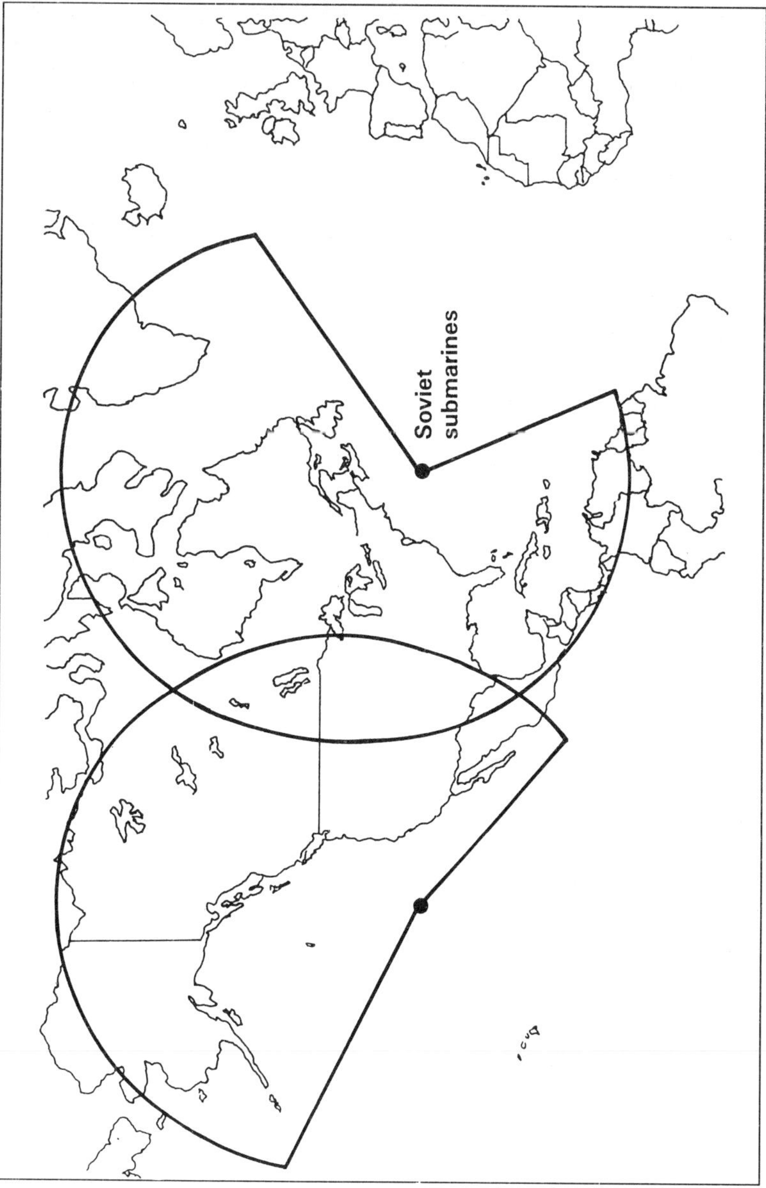

Figure 5.3 Soviet submarines off the US coasts are a perennial concern

flight SLBM attack. The United States relies on tactical warning systems and high levels of readiness for alert bombers and C^3 aircraft to react quickly enough to counter such a threat. Still, responding that rapidly would be dicey at best.

Soviet SSNs operating near US coasts are a serious concern as well. SSNs have always been a potential threat to US SSBNs so their presence near US SSBN home ports would be a concern. Cruise missiles are much slower than ballistic missiles, but would be very difficult to detect, particularly with existing US warning systems. Thus, the United States might get no warning at all of such an attack.

Therefore, the United States must be concerned about both Soviet SSBNs and SSNs operating near its shores. The Soviets might choose to withdraw their SSBNs to bastions and keep the SSNs back to protect them. If so, the threat might disappear. On the other hand, if the Soviets were to deploy their submarines off the US coasts in the future, they would be much harder to deal with because the newer Soviet submarines are much quieter, and therefore less vulnerable to US ASW than current Soviet submarines. In a crisis, *the United States would be much more vulnerable to an SSBN or SSN attack if its forces and C^3 network were on day-to-day alert than if they were fully alerted.*

Possible future air confrontation in the north

An emerging problem is a future air confrontation in the north. The problem is illustrated in Figure 5.4. As the United States has moved toward a bomber force that emphasizes standoff cruise missile carriers, the Soviets have countered by developing appropriate aircraft to mount a far forward air defense to engage the bombers before they can launch their cruise missiles.[25]

In addition to flying long-range interceptors accompanied by tankers and airborne warning aircraft from northern bases in the Soviet Union, the Soviets would have strong incentives to try to capture forward bases beyond Soviet territory. Operating fighters out of such bases would make sustaining a forward defense much easier. A forward air defense of this sort would pose a formidable threat to US bombers.

The United States has several potential counters available, most of which could lead to direct confrontations between US

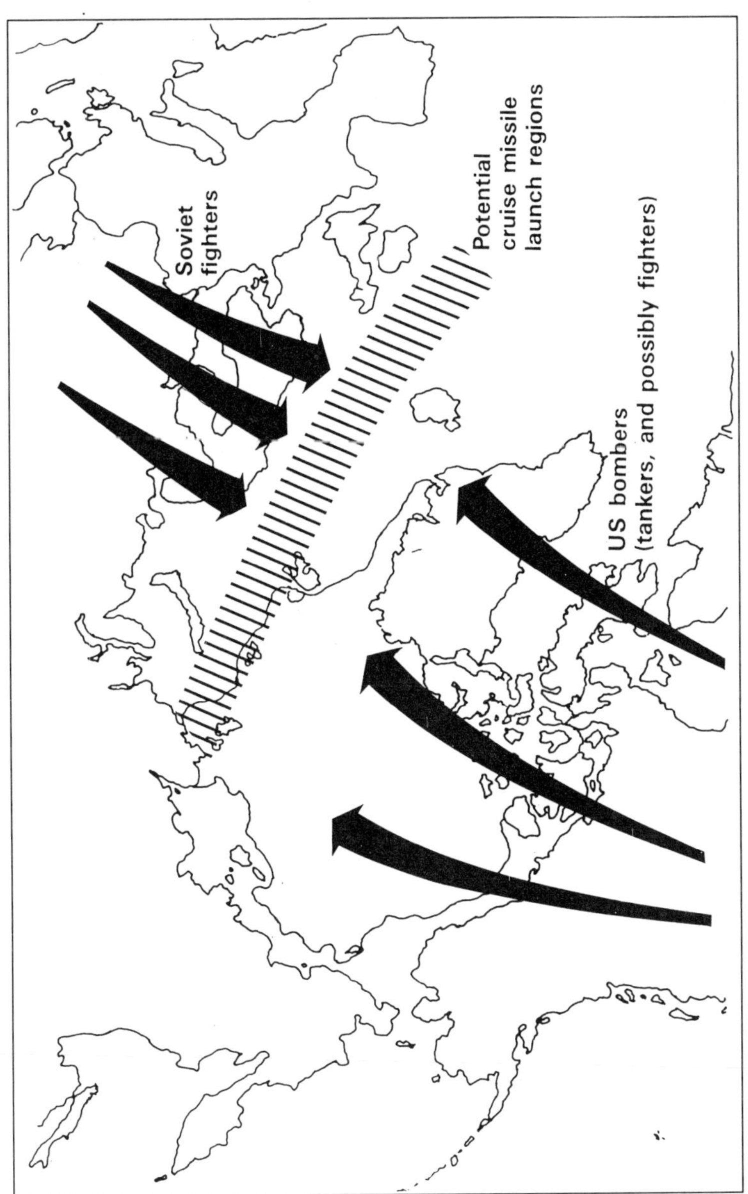

Figure 5.4 Possible future air confrontation in the north

and Soviet forces prior to any decision to launch nuclear attacks. First, the United States could deny the Soviets use of forward air bases. That would probably require either engaging the Soviets on the ground to prevent their taking the bases in the first place or attacking the bases, probably with aircraft or cruise missiles, to make them unusable for the Soviets. In either case, direct military engagements between Soviet and US military forces would be very likely.

Next, the United States could move its own long-range fighters to northern bases to protect the bombers and other aircraft. Such a force would also, of course, be useful for engaging *Soviet* bombers; it would increase tension during a crisis and increase the risk of incidents. However, the United States could not afford not to counter a Soviet forward air defense. The military risk would be too high, particularly if the United States opted to rely on a standoff cruise missile force in lieu of penetrating stealth bombers.

A completely different kind of air confrontation might occur if there were a theater war in progress in Europe and the Soviets mounted an amphibious operation against NATO's northern flank. One of the most potent counters to such a Soviet assault would be for the United States to employ heavy bombers armed with a variety of conventional weapons against the Soviet fleet. Since a conventional war was in progress, the bombers would certainly be fair game for Soviet air defenses as would Soviet fighters for NATO fighter escorts that the bombers might employ. One Soviet commentator, however, has raised the concern that the United States might use this sort of bomber operation as a cover to launch a bomber precursor strike against strategic targets in the Soviet Union.[26] How the Soviets would react to such a perceived threat is unclear, but the United States would have to be somewhat concerned that they might overreact. On the other hand, the military advantage to the United States of using heavy bombers in some conventional operations in the north is likely to be too overwhelming to forgo, simply to ease perceived Soviet paranoia.

The air situation in the north is going to become increasingly ambiguous and dangerous as time progresses. The military incentives for both sides to try to operate there are too strong to ignore for both strategic and theater campaigns, so collisions may prove unavoidable. Both sides will have to understand that, and manage crises accordingly.

Naval confrontation in the north

Similar kinds of problems could lead to naval confrontations in the north. One problem is the Soviet surface fleet. It could threaten NATO in a European campaign. It could also – accidentally or intentionally – position itself along SAC bomber approach routes to the Soviet Union and try to shoot down any bombers or other aircraft that flew within range of its missiles and provide early warning to land-based air defenses of bombers that it could detect but not shoot down. The problem is illustrated in Figure 5.5.

A likely US counter would be to dispatch SSNs to the north to engage the surface ships. Those SSNs, however, could also threaten Soviet SSBNs, presumably a matter of great concern to the Soviets. Also, they might, if armed with cruise missiles, threaten Soviet land targets as well.

Again, the military advantages to both sides of operating their naval forces this way might outweigh any hypothetical escalation rates. However, such operations would be even less transparent than air operations in the north, so the attendant risks would be substantial.

Ambiguous nature of intelligence collection systems

In past crises, there were problems with spy planes. Neither side would rely much on aircraft to collect intelligence in future crises, so those problems are not likely to recur. However, others might appear. In particular, there is a natural tension between intelligence-collection systems as means to enhance CBMs and as targeting tools to help locate dispersed aircraft or mobile ICBMs, for example. Depending on how each side viewed the other's intelligence-gathering systems, either or both could begin interfering with the other's systems – jamming; direct attack of satellites, ground stations, launch facilities, etc. Such actions could not only intensify the crisis, but also complicate the introduction of CBMs to help defuse it.

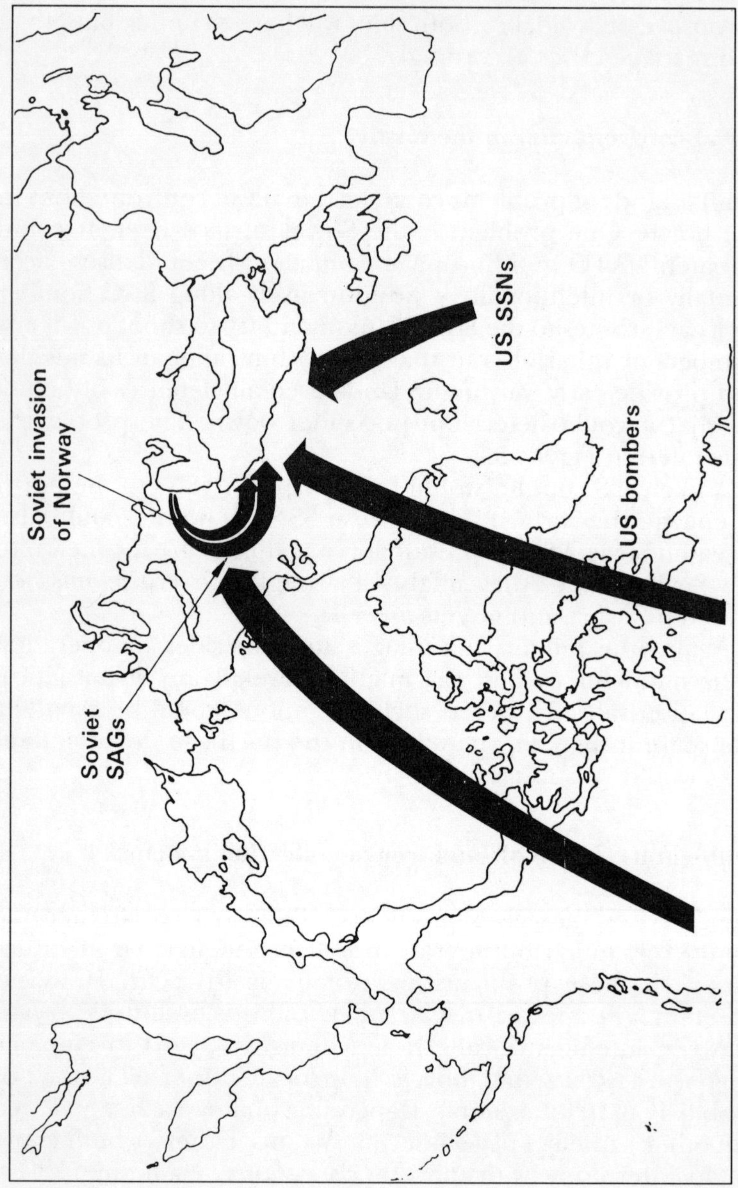

Figure 5.5 The naval confrontation in the north

5.6 POSSIBILITIES FOR DE-ESCALATORY CBMs

The basic premise of considering de-escalatory CBMs as crisis-management tools is that altering nuclear alert procedures or standing down from alerts in a measured, orderly way might contribute to the peaceful resolution of a crisis. Such CBMs might, in principle:

- reassure potential adversaries by concretely demonstrating the intentions of all sides to resolve a crisis peacefully
- reduce the military threat to potential adversaries

Richard Darilek has covered the objectives of CBMs elsewhere in this volume. There are several basic tests for any CBMs:

- Do they increase or decrease crisis stability?
- Do they impose unacceptable military or political costs on any of the players?
- Are they likely to reduce the risks of accidental war?

In addition, there are practical questions – Can particular CBMs actually be implemented? Can they be verified? Are they really likely to be effective?

At the strategic level, the fundamental issue is the impact of CBMs on crisis stability – the degree to which neither side has an incentive to strike first, even in a crisis when all of the choices appear unpalatable. There are two primary sources of crisis instability:

- the current or impending vulnerability of one's own forces or supporting systems (i.e. a 'use them or lose them' situation)
- exploitable vulnerabilities of enemy forces or supporting systems

CBMs are strategically desirable to the degree that they enhance crisis stability. CBMs that might actually decrease crisis stability could only be adopted at some risk. Complicating the strategic equation is the possible impact of CBMs on theater conflicts that might be either ongoing or imminent.

Possible CBMs

Possible CBMs have been widely discussed.[27] A number are

listed in Table 4. Most involve returning generated forces to a normal alert status. Some go farther and actually impose specific restrictions on force operations. All fall into two general categories: those which increase transparency of operations and those which restrict operations. The former seek to reduce the risk of misperceptions by the other side and positively reinforce statements of benign intentions. The latter are intended to reduce the threat to both sides and minimize the risks of direct confrontations or other provocative incidents.

Table 5.4 Possible de-escalatory confidence-building measures

CBMs that increase transparency	CBMs that restrict operations
Non-interference with tactical warning systems Non-interference with intelligence collection systems Monitored return to main operating bases of: – bombers – tankers – mobile ICBMs – C^3 aircraft – other mobile C^3 systems Notifications of: – bomber airborne operations – stand-downs	Keep-out zones – ban forward-deployed submarines – ban forward-deployed military aircraft Keep-in zones – SSBNs in bastions Restrictions on airborne alert, particularly for bombers Restricted operating areas for conventional forces

Evaluating CBMs

In evaluating CBMs, there is a crucial distinction to be made about what one expects them to accomplish. If the crisis has been resolved politically and all that is required is an orderly stand-down regimen to demonstrate good faith, then developing adequate procedures and confidence-building measures is easy. If the crisis has not been resolved and the United States is expected to stand down from alert to demonstrate benign intentions, designing adequate CBMs is infinitely more difficult, perhaps impossible.

Standing down in response to a political solution to a crisis should be straightforward to implement and easy to monitor.

The United States could stand down in stages as shown in Table 5.5, gradually returning to a day-to-day alert even from the highest levels of force generation. With the current and planned communications systems available, there should be no problems issuing the orders to any of the forces and being confident that they would receive them. Nor is there any reason that recovering and reconstituting the forces efficiently should pose any problems *if adequate preparations are made in advance.* For example, there is no reason why bombers cannot be recovered, even from airborne alert, a few at a time, refueled, given minor maintenance if necessary, provided with new crews, and returned to normal alert status with minimal risk. Old scenarios (e.g. fearing to return bombers to their bases after an alert because a period of dramatically increased vulnerability) should never occur if proper plans are developed, adequate maintenance capability is provided, and sufficient attention is given to SSBNs, and C^3 aircraft.

Monitoring this kind of stand-down should be routine, since all that is basically required is to keep track of the numbers of things at home bases. National technical means are probably adequate for most of these tasks, assuming they are still functioning. On-site monitors at home bases could also be employed to provide added confidence that forces really were returning to normal alert.

An important point to note is that the dynamics of risk and the cognitive processes of political leaders are likely to be very different during the de-escalatory part of a crisis following a political resolution than during an ongoing crisis, perhaps accompanied by a conventional war, with the issue still in doubt. In a de-escalating crisis, both sides are probably looking for reassurance that their antagonists are acting in good faith in implementing agreed-to stand-down measures. If both sides stand down prudently, there should be no 'windows of opportunity' when one side could really benefit from launching a first strike. At the very worst, even if an attacker were able to destroy, say, a large portion of the bomber force on the ground, the surviving forces would be more than ample to destroy his society. There would simply be no percentage in developing an elaborate ruse to lure part of an opponent's forces into a vulnerable position only to be destroyed by the rest of his forces. In this case, an opponent has a choice – a political

Table 5.5 A strategic stand-down procedure for the United States

Stage	*Actions*	*Supporting airborne*	*Monitoring options*
1	Remove SSBNs in transit from full alert	rest crews	none possible
	Withdraw forward-deployed SSBNs to broad ocean areas	rest crews	none likely
	Return bombers and tankers from airborne alert (if they were there) a few at a time to dispersal bases	turn bombers quickly; change crews; maintain strip alert or cancel bombers	none likely
2	Return SSBNs to port a few at a time	reprovision; change crews; maintain alert in port	national technical means (NTM) or on-site inspectors
	Return bombers and tankers to main operating bases a few at a time	turn quickly; change crews; maintain high strip alert; do necessary maintenance	NTM or on-site inspectors
3	Resume normal alert for bombers, tankers, and SSBNs	do necessary maintenance; cycle crews	on-site inspectors, NTM for some aspects
	Resume normal alert for SICBM and silo-based ICBM	cycle crews	none likely

Table 5.5 A strategic stand-down procedure for the United States *(cont'd)*

4	Return Rail Garrison Peacekeeper to garrisons a few at a time	maintain garrison alert; cycle crews	NTM or on-site inspectors
5	Return Rail Garrison Peacekeepers to normal alert	do necessary maintenance; cycle crews	on-site inspectors for some aspects
	Return airborne C^3 aircraft not normally airborne to dispersal bases	conceal aircraft, maintain communications on ground; do maintenance; rest crews	none appropriate
6	Gradually return mobile C^3 assets to home bases	normal maintenance, cycle crews	none appropriate, except for aircraft at known MOBs
	Revoke any delegations of nuclear authority*	———	none appropriate
	Return NCA successors to normal duty*	———	none appropriate
	NORMAL DAY-TO-DAY ALERT		

* To revoke all conditional delegations or leave all NCA successors vulnerable, might never be appropriate, even in peacetime.

settlement which he has already accepted. He is not faced with the classical crisis-instability problem: being forced to choose among a set of unattractive alternatives and perhaps choosing an even partially effective nuclear strike as the least odious option available.

Dealing with an unresolved political crisis is quite another matter, and the sort of de-escalatory CBMs considered here are likely to be of little use. As Vick and Thomson have pointed out, they are not very powerful tools.[28] Indeed, they could actually exacerbate a crisis. But a symbolic and militarily 'insignificant' CBM (e.g. a unilateral declaration, etc.) might be useful in influencing perceptions. Militarily there may not be much to be done, but 'squishy' CBMs may buy time and provide opportunities for negotiations.

First, consider the implications of alerted US strategic forces on the choices that a US decision-maker is likely to face during a crisis. Alerting his forces has eliminated most of the real nightmare scenarios:

- An attempted decapitation attack would almost certainly fail, a fact that Soviet leaders should also be able to perceive, hopefully deterring them from even considering such an option.
- The bomber force, if dispersed and/or on airborne alert, would be much less vulnerable to a short-time-of-flight SLBM attack. Even the bombers remaining on main operating bases would be at a higher state of readiness and more likely to be able to escape quickly if necessary.
- Mobile ICBMs, particularly Rail Garrison Peacekeepers if deployed out of garrison, would be much less dependent on tactical warning.
- The likelihood that forces would react effectively to tactical warning of an attack would be much greater than in peacetime because the crisis would probably have solved the usual credibility problems associated with warning in peacetime.
- Launching silo-based ICBMs under attack would be much more likely to work. However, overall US force effectiveness would depend much less on launching ICBMs under attack, so a US decision-maker would have more flexibility to risk riding-out an attack if he lacked confidence in his warning systems.

In general, US decision-makers should be under much less pressure to act precipitously with strategic forces alerted. The consequences of *not* acting are much reduced in virtually all conceivable scenarios. Attacks on Washington, SAC headquarters, NORAD headquarters, SAC main operating bases, etc. would still have major impact, but would not be devastating, as they might be if US forces were not on alert. Thus, there would be no need to react precipitously to ambiguous warning, perhaps of a small attack, as there might be if US forces and C^3 assets had not been generated. *Thus, the consequences of 'incidents' should be dramatically reduced by having forces on alert during a crisis.* If the same incidents occurred during a crisis with forces on day-to-day alert and thus more vulnerable, the cognitive impact on decision-makers could be much more serious and the tangible risks much more real.

It is also unlikely that alerting US strategic forces would exacerbate a crisis much, except for making Soviet leaders a bit grumpier. (Presumably, they would not be in the best of humor anyway.) Many past concerns are simply outdated. There is virtually no chance that technical or operational failures with modern strategic systems could lead to an accidental war unless decision-makers are totally psychotic. (And if they *are* totally psychotic, the crisis is beyond the help of CBMs!) For example, the danger of false tactical warning of a missile attack leading to an accidental war has always been a matter of concern. However, with US forces and C^3 systems generated, the only sort of irrevocable decision that a US NCA might have to make would be to launch vulnerable ICBMs on warning of attack. Today and in the future only an inconceivably pathological tactical warning system failure could cause a false alarm that resembled a serious attack on silos. The apparent attack would have to be large. The trajectories of the attacking missiles would have to be on credible azimuths to attack silo fields. The launch points would have to be credible. A decision-maker would probably insist on dual phenomenology warning – that is, detection of an attack by both radar and infrared sensors, for example – before launching ICBMs under attack. It is hard to imagine a warning system failure of this magnitude, and even if it were to occur, US decision-makers *still* would be under less pressure to act during a crisis if forces were alerted than if they were not. The much larger force available to the United States because of the alert would provide policymakers with a cushion. Even if the attack proved to be real and the United States chose not to launch on warning, the additional warheads available in the alerted force would more than compensate for the lost ICBMs, as noted earlier. Concerns about trivial warning systems failures, such as those from systems like Cobra Dane – an intelligence collection system that is added to the warning network during alerts – are simply frivolous.[29]

Similarly, the alerted forces themselves are unlikely to increase the risks of war. The main requirement is sufficient logistic support and adequate operational procedures to sustain alerts for extended periods of time if necessary.

As suggested earlier, alerting US forces does little to increase the risk that the Soviets face. To the degree that they really worry about clever US precursor attacks from bombers or submarines, they would be just as much at risk from US day-to-day alert forces since only relatively small numbers of weapons would be required. Even more fundamentally, the *Soviets* would be more vulnerable on day-to-day alert since they normally maintain very low alert rates for their bomber forces. Similarly, their C^3 network would be more vulnerable on day-to-day alert, although that network probably looks much more vulnerable to them than it would to US attack planners. In short, the fact that US forces are on alert should not present the Soviets with new sets of problems that would destabilize the crisis.

The main point is the following: *the alert is not the problem; the crisis is the problem.* Alerting nuclear forces generally helps more than hurts. CBMs that only address stand-down measures treat the symptom, not the disease.

Even worse, most CBMs do not address some of the real potential sources of confrontations in a US–Soviet crisis that were described earlier. Table 5.6 summarizes some of these problem areas and the relevance of selected CBMs. The problems the United States has to solve are:

- keeping Soviet submarines away from the US coasts
- preventing Soviet surface naval forces from either supplementing Soviet air defenses against bombers or from supporting amphibious operations on NATO's northern flank
- preventing Soviet aircraft from operating out of forward bases beyond the borders of the Soviet Union

Table 5.6 Prospects for avoiding confrontations in associated areas

Potential problem areas	*Military implications*	*Prospects for CBMs*
Soviet submarines off US coast	• Less severe threat if US forces alerted • Both SSNs and SSBNs are threats • Soviet sub quieting complicates ASW	• Keep-out zones – probably not enforceable • Unilateral actions would help – Soviets might choose not to forward deploy submarines
Naval confrontations in the north	• Soviet surface navy strategic and tactical threat – threat to bombers • Submarine confrontations likely – strong incentives for US to move SSNs forward	• Keep-out/Keep-in zones – hard to enforce • Unilateral actions – rules of engagement may help – bastion strategies
Air confrontations in the north	• Strong incentives for both sides to move aircraft forward • Confrontations likely and dangerous	• Ban on forward aircraft deployment – probably verifiable – would greatly reduce risks at low cost • Unilateral actions – avoid airborne alerts

There appear to be two possibilities for at least reducing the dangers of confrontations in these areas. One is unilateral action. Examples include:

- US avoidance of airborne alert for bombers (which is probably a good idea anyway) or maintenance of alert lines well behind any possible areas of confrontation
- withdrawal of Soviet SSBNs, SSNs, and surface forces into bastions, which might be their strategy of choice

Another is *declared rules of engagement.* The United States could state very clearly to the Soviets that:

- it considers any foreign submarines close to its coasts to be a severe threat to security and that it will sink any submarines that it can find
- that it will not allow the Soviets to move combat aircraft to northern bases outside the Soviet Union
- that it will not deliberately send SSNs into northern waters either to attack Soviet SSBNs or to attack land targets, but that it would employ SSNs against Soviet surface fleets that moved against Norway or positioned themselves to threaten SAC bombers
- that it would not use heavy bombers to launch a first strike against the Soviet homeland, but that it would use heavy bombers with conventional weapons against the Soviet fleet if it moved against NATO's northern flank

Some of these declared rules of engagement would be quite similar in practice to CBMs such as 'keep-out' or 'keep-in' zones. There are subtle distinctions, however, that could prove important in an actual crisis. Compliance is a key issue with CBMs. Failure to comply with an agreed-upon CBM is itself an issue, and charges to that effect, particularly if the evidence is ambiguous, could exacerbate a crisis still further. Others have no special obligation to honor such US statements, but would presumably take them into account in evaluating their own options. Moreover, the ability of the United States to enforce such restrictions is less of an issue than it would be with formal CBMs. For example, a formal CBM such as an SSBN keep-out zone near the US coasts implies some level of confidence that the United States could actually enforce such a ban. By contrast, the United States could state that it would attack any foreign submarine detected near US coasts even if it had very little capability to locate submarines. This kind of latitude in interpretation could be useful in managing a crisis.

The Soviets might not be particularly pleased by these unilateral pronouncements by the United States. However, declared rules of engagement could provide some of the advantages of CBMs by reducing ambiguity in US operations and making clear US interests and intentions. The Soviets might not even object to some of the restrictions. For example, they might not care about invading Norway during a specific confrontation with the United States, so might be willing to forgo some military actions that the United States might even respond with their own declared rules of engagement, conceivably even leading to a dialogue with the United States on rules of the game that might serve the same function as CBMs. There are limits to what such an approach can accomplish, but it might provide a little leverage to reduce risks in a crisis.

5.7 CONCLUSIONS

Successful application of CBMs to stand down US strategic forces during a crisis presupposes a political resolution of the crisis. Then, an orderly, phased return of US strategic forces to day-to-day alert monitored by either on-site inspectors, notional technical means, or both should be straightforward to orchestrate. The key is returning forces slowly, in stages, and in the proper order so that periods of vulnerability can be minimized while the other side is reassured of US good intentions.

If the crisis has not been resolved politically, standing down from alert is probably not wise and CBMs can only contribute at the margin to reducing tensions. Alerting US strategic forces generally tends to stabilize rather than destabilize a crisis because:

- US strategic forces and C^3 are much less vulnerable when alerted
- US forces are not much more threatening in a first-strike sense when alerted
- technological and operational improvements have significantly reduced the risk of accidental war.

Alerts involve serious risks of specific kinds of confrontations in particular regions, that could escalate: air and naval confrontations in northern regions; and risks of Soviet submarines off the US coasts. These confrontations, which usually involve supporting forces, might or might not arise, depending on the details of the particular crisis. However, the military risk of overlooking, say, Soviet forward deployment of fighter aircraft or SSBNs would probably be too great for the United States to accept, and CBMs are probably too weak to rely on. Some unilateral actions, like avoiding airborne alerts, could reduce risks somewhat. Also, declaratory rules of engagement for particular problem areas may at least help the other side understand US concerns and actions, thereby reducing the dangers of misperception and miscalculation.

Alerts involve inherent risks, but crises are dangerous by definition. Incidents are inevitable. Policymakers have to expect them and be prepared to respond sensibly. In general, *incidents are less dangerous during a crisis if forces are alerted than if they are not* because forces are less vulnerable and there is less incentive for decision-makers to take precipitate action. Again, *the alert is not the problem; the crisis is the problem.* CBMs that treat the symptoms rather than the disease can do more harm than good.

The risks of both crises and alerts should not be minimized. Militarily, striking first is *always* preferable to striking second, analytical studies to the contrary not withstanding. Thus, policymakers will always be under some pressure to go first in a crisis regardless of what 'rational' calculations show. As a result, the safest course for the Soviet Union and the United States is to avoid confrontations that could escalate. To borrow a phrase, 'The only way to win is not to play!'

In that vein, strategic alerts should not be used to signal political resolve. As instruments of policy, they are too blunt for sending finely-tuned messages. Instead, they should be employed, if at all, to signal prudence and concern. That is, they should look defensive, not offensive.

The United States must design procedures to operate its strategic forces in a safe, stable way during crises and to minimize the risks as they stand down. That should be straightforward to accomplish and has more to do with sound military practice than CBMs *per se.* However, improving the endurance of strategic systems, developing practical operational procedures, and adequate training will require resources, and that means competing in a very difficult arena. If the United States does not invest these resources, then the danger inherent in at least very high levels of alert might increase substantially.

NOTES

1. See, for example, Herman Kahn's discussion of the First World War and possible future analogies in Herman Kahn, *On Thermonuclear War,* 1969 Second Edition (New York: Free Press), pp. 357–75.
2. The best discussion of alerting procedures for US nuclear forces available in the open literature is Bruce G. Blair, 'Alerting in Crisis and Conventional War', in Ashton B. Carter, et al. (eds), *Managing Nuclear Operations* (Washington, DC: Brookings Institution 1987), pp. 75–120.
3. In addition to technical questions about whether they *could* actually be recalled, some of the factors that might influence the crews' decisions include:
   - their perception of the general political climate
   - how far along they are in their mission,
   - their degree of confidence in SAC's ability to recover quickly and to execute a coordinated attack later should the need arise,
   - the state of the safety devices on their weapons,
   - their confidence in the validity of any recall order
   - the sort of indoctrination and training they have received, and the degree of their shared values, regarding how best to err: on the side of avoiding an unnecessary nuclear war or of making sure they deliver their weapons.
4. See, for example, Sagan's description of the 'unintended' DEFCON 3 alert in Scott D. Sagan, 'Nuclear Alerts and Crisis Management', *International Security,* Vol. 9, no. 4, Spring 1985, pp. 102–6. Another example is the much-publicized false alarm of a missile attack that occurred in November 1979 when an exercise tape was accidentally loaded into a NORAD computer. The readiness of the bomber force was briefly raised before the error was discovered. Ibid., p. 135 and Ashton B. Carter, 'Sources of Error and Uncertainty', in Carter, et al., p. 629.
5. Some Genie-related incidents occurred during the Cuban Missile Crisis. Scott D. Sagan, 'Accidents at the Brink: the Operational Dimensions of Crisis Stability', unpublished paper, February 1989, pp. 26–9.
6. CINCSAC General Thomas S. Power is said to have sent a message to the Pentagon *in the clear* confirming the readiness of SAC forces with the express purpose of signalling the Soviets that US strategic forces were prepared for war. Sagan 1985, p. 108.

7. Henry Kissinger, *Years of Upheaval* (Boston: Little, Brown, and Company, 1982), pp. 587–9.
8. Beyond the 'signal' sent by the US nuclear alert, there was some inherent danger and possible coercive substance involved, regardless of what policymakers may have intended. As Blechman and Hart have observed, by introducing an implicit nuclear threat in a conflict involving an ally – Israel, in this case – with which the United States had strong historical and political ties, the Unites States was initiating an escalation process that it might not have been able to control. Barry M. Blechman and Douglas M. Hart, 'The Political Utility of Nuclear Weapons: The 1973 Middle East Crisis', *International Security*, Vol. 7, no. 1, Spring 1982, pp. 132–56. Thus, the actions by the United States could conceivably have led to a direct nuclear confrontation with the Soviet Union *regardless of the fact that 'rational' calculus would clearly argue that the stakes in the crisis for the United States and the Soviet Union were not worth the risks of a nuclear confrontation.* The recognition by policymakers on both sides of the risks of uncontrollable escalation in confrontations, particularly those in which one or both superpower has strong historical interests, may be a major factor in explaining the prudence with which the United States and the Soviet Union have generally approached each other in the nuclear age.
9. For a description of the operational concept of Rail Garrison Peacekeeper, see Barry E. Fridling and John R. Harvey, 'On the Wrong Track? An Assessment of MX Rail Garrison Basing', *International Security*, Vol. 13, no. 3, Winter 1988/1989, pp. 113–41.
10. For a succinct description of the SICBM system concept, see Donald A. Hicks, 'ICBM Modernization: Consider the Alternatives', *International Security*, Vol. 12, no. 2, Fall, 1987, pp. 177–8.
11. William M. Arkin and Richard W. Fieldhouse, *Nuclear Battlefields: Global Links in the Arms Race* (Cambridge, Mass.: Ballinger, 1985), p. 45 and Congressional Budget Office (CBO), 'Modernizing U.S. Strategic Offensive Forces: Costs, Effects and Alternatives', November 1987, p. 72.
12. CBO, p. 70.
13. Donald B. Cotter, 'Peacetime Operations: Safety and Security', in Carter et al. 1987, op. cit., p. 50.
14. The seminal work in the open literature on US strategic C^3, its vulnerabilities, and their ramifications is Bruce G. Blair, *Strategic Command and Control: Redefining the Nuclear Threat* (Washington, DC: Brookings Institution, 1985). Another classic is Paul Bracken, *The Command and Control of Nuclear Forces* (New Haven: Yale University Press, 1983). For an excellent discussion of tactical warning systems, see John C. Toomay, 'Warning and Assessment Sensors', in Carter et al., pp. 282–321.
15. Some of these potential vulnerabilities include: the vulnerability of the NCA to a surprise attack, the vulnerability of fixed command centers such as Strategic Air Command Headquarters and North American Air Defense Command Headquarters, the vulnerability of key command and control aircraft to attack on the ground, the vulnerability of satellite ground stations to direct attack, the vulnerability of satellite commun-

ications links to disruption, jamming, and nuclear effects, similar vulnerabilities in other communications systems, vulnerabilities of warning systems, particularly ground-based radars, to attack or disruption.

16. Blair 1985 takes the danger seriously. Carter dismisses the possibility of decapitation somewhat cavalierly but concedes the complications that disrupting the US command system could cause the United States in retaliating after a Soviet first strike. Ashton B. Carter, 'Assessing Command System Vulnerability', in Carter et al., pp. 607–10. Whatever the reality, *perception* of a problem could be almost as serious as the problem itself.
17. Blair 1985, pp. 241–80 and Congressional Budget Office, 'Strategic Command, Control, and Communications: Alternative Approaches for Modernization', October 1981.
18. The bombers must be returned to prearranged bases in small numbers over a sufficient period of time to allow the returning bombers to be refueled, to have maintenance done if necessary, probably to have new crews assigned, and to be maintained at an appropriate level of readiness to be launched quickly if necessary. Such a recovery regimen would require considerable planning, preparation, and discipline, but could certainly be done if the task were given sufficient priority.
19. The following alert rates are assumed for the various components of the US strategic forces. CBO 1987:

	Alert status	
System	Day-to-day	Fully generated
ICBMs		
– silo-based	0.95	0.98
– RG Pk	0.95	0.98
– SICBM	0.90	0.95
SLBMs	0.67 (at sea)	0.95
	0.33 (fully	
Bombers	alerted)	0.98
	0.30	

20. For the purposes of this particular set of calculations, the number of arriving US weapons was calculated by applying the following arrival probabilities:

Weapon	Arrival probability
Air-launched cruise missiles (ALCM)[8]	
– B-52 or B-1 launched	0.77*
Gravity bombs	
– B-1	0.60
– B-2	0.80
Gravity bombs	
– B-1	0.72
– B-2	0.90
SLBMs	0.80
ICBMs	0.95

* The Advanced Cruise Missile (ACM) could presumably do better

The potential target coverage was derived by scaling the results of an earlier SIOP, Desmond Ball, 'The Development of the SIOP, 1960–1983', in Desmond Ball and Jeffrey Richelson (ed.), *Strategic Nuclear Targeting* (Ithaca, NY: Cornell University Press, 1986), p. 81 to take into account the different number of arriving weapons in the notional force employed in this analysis.

21. Ramberg discusses some of the problems of interpreting political signals during crises. Bennett Ramberg, unpublished paper, May 1989, pp. 60–85.
22. The DEFCON system is discussed by Blair 1987 and the various levels defined elsewhere as well. Sagan 1985, p. 101 and Kissinger 1982, pp. 587–8.
23. Sagan 1985, pp. 102–6.
24. Sagan is correct when he expresses doubts about the feasibility of expecting civilian authorities to master the intricacies of DEFCON procedures. Ibid., p. 138.
25. See the discussion Soviet incentives for and moves toward a far forward air defense in James T. Quinlivan, *Soviet Strategic Air Defense: A Long Past and an Uncertain Future*, RAND P-7579, September 1989, pp. 21–4.
26. Cited in Quinlivan, p. 21.
27. See Joseph Nation, *The Utility of De-Escalatory Confidence-Building Measures* P-7571, The RAND Corporation, Santa Monica, June 1989 and Alan J. Vick and James A. Thomson, *The Military Significance of Restrictions on Strategic Nuclear Force Operations.* N-2113-FF, The RAND Corporation, Santa Monica, April 1984.
28. Vick and Thomson, pp. 28–30.
29. Sagan 1989, pp. 31–2, 64.

6 De-escalation and Soviet Nuclear Operations

David Frelinger

6.1 INTRODUCTION

Many writings have appeared over the years on nuclear forces and nuclear strategy. This chapter focuses on the prospect that certain de-escalatory measures will allow and even encourage Soviets leaders to 'stand down' (i.e. return to peacetime operations) their nuclear forces after a crisis, despite conflicting motives for keeping forces on alert. Standing-down forces is one of many de-escalatory measures the Soviet and the United States might consider as a way to build confidence in nuclear crisis termination.

This chapter will not delve into the dark corners of Soviet command and control, nor will it walk the reader through the labyrinth of Soviet military writings. Instead, it will show how technology underlying Soviet strategic nuclear forces combines with Soviet doctrinal preferences to offer both hope and concern over the ability of the Soviet Union to properly de-escalate their forces following a crisis.

The specific issues to be addressed include:

- Are alerts likely to make things better or worse in a crisis from a Soviet military perspective?
- To what degree do alerted nuclear forces themselves contribute to the danger of the crisis?
- Do activities by non-strategic nuclear forces contribute to instability during a crisis and make de-escalation of military forces more difficult?
- Are there de-escalatory measures, especially stand-down measures, that enhance crisis stability and reduce the risks of unintended conflict?

6.2 ANALYTICAL ENVIRONMENT

A number of problems, most notably a realistic description of Soviet nuclear operations, makes discussion of de-escalatory matters problematic. Among these problems are: classification of information; a probable divergence between doctrine and practice, including actual practice during a crisis; and a very limited supply of historical evidence.

Classification of information

While the United States provides only limited information on the operation of its nuclear forces, information on nuclear alert procedures in the Soviet Union is an even greater mystery. Like their US counterparts, Soviet military leaders hold operational details closely, lest an adversary find a weakness in the system that might be exploitable in a war. As one result, most Soviet discussions of strategic nuclear operations are couched in terms of historical analogies to the Second World War, more commonly called by the Soviets the Great Patriotic War. These historical analogies do not present much of a picture of how present-day systems work, and instead attempt to subtly tell a story that could communicate something of importance about present-day nuclear operations to the proper audience within the Soviet military. Soviet military writers *do discuss* nuclear operations, but for the most part, their writings are in the form of analogies to conventional military operations. Western analysts must decipher the code used by the Soviet writers in order to understand how the lessons of the past apply to contemporary Soviet strategic nuclear operations.

Classification hampers discussion of Soviet strategic nuclear operations in two ways. While the Soviets guard the details of their operations quite closely, the United States similarly seeks to protect what it gleans of Soviet strategic nuclear operations. Detailed references on Soviet nuclear operations similar to those produced by Bruce Blair and Paul Bracken on US strategic operations are not available.[1] Soviet military writings – when they do not deal with historical analogy – typically focus either on broad concepts or on details of military operations research that make extracting policy relevant material difficult. The excellent work of Stephen M. Meyer is the most cogent description of Soviet nuclear operations to appear in the open literature.[2]

Doctrine vs practice

A great deal of work has been done in the West to mine Soviet military writings for hints about how the Soviets *think* about nuclear operations in order to support making reasonable predictions about how the Soviets *would conduct* strategic nuclear operations in a crisis. The sad truth is that the divergence between doctrine and real-world military activities makes such analysis and prognostication difficult. One of the principle causes of this divergence is the unpredictable human element in decision-making.

Predicting how Soviet commanders and their forces will actually operate based on their doctrine is quite risky since the human element can intervene at many points in the process. Individual commanders might dispense with doctrine and instead substitute their own judgments about what would be best for the Soviet Union. For instance, commanders might not believe intelligence that would lead them to conduct a preemptive attack under 'official' doctrine.

The Soviet civilian leadership maintains ultimate control over nuclear forces. Therefore, the attitudes of political leaders towards nuclear conflict are quite important. Unfortunately for Western analysts focusing on Soviet military writings, the attitudes of these members of the political leadership are probably not adequately reflected in writings on Soviet military doctrine. Consequently, the divergence between Soviet military writings and the actual conduct of nuclear operations may be far greater than that already postulated.

Extrapolation from historical data

There are two major problems when using the historical record: the record is very sparse, and even if the record were more complete, the rapid change in technology has made useful insights very shortlived. In the United States, the study of nuclear operations and behavior in crises has long been the province of serious scholars who patiently wait for the declassification of crisis data or who have access to both the principal actors and the minutes of critical crisis deliberations. In contrast, the Soviet Union has allowed far less discussion and investigation of how it has behaved in crises. Without access to the internal workings of the decision-making process, intentions cannot be gleaned from actions. Analysts might know whether a missile force had or had not been readied, or that some ship had been moved to or from a port, but not *why* such events had occurred.

Even if the Soviets do finally open their records to study, then a number of problems best described by Buchan in Chapter 5 emerge. Among these are extremely limited data, anecdotal evidence, and dated evidence.

The greatest threat to reasonable analysis is the age of the evidence and the dramatic changes in weapons technology that have occurred over the years to make extrapolation from earlier behavior very questionable. Take, for instance, changes in rocket design in the ICBM force. Formerly dependent on the use of non-storable corrosive liquids (which made them slow to respond and difficult to hold at the ready), Soviet ICBMs now use solid fuels so they may be held at the ready for long periods of time, and respond more rapidly than systems that use non-storable fuels. A forecast of contemporary Soviet nuclear operations based on this antiquated data would falsely show that alerts are time-consuming and difficult to maintain, which they clearly are not today.

6.3 SOVIET DOCTRINE FOR NUCLEAR WAR: A US PERSPECTIVE

Soviet military writings contain a number of themes that provide insight into how the Soviets view strategic nuclear operations. Among these fundamental themes of Soviet strategic nuclear operations are:

- nuclear war grows out of conventional coalition warfare, and therefore 'surprise attacks' are unlikely
- nuclear targeting emphasizes the destruction of nuclear forces, associated command and control installations and

personnel, projection forces, political administrative centers, and economic facilities

- preemption is preferred to Launch on Tactical Warning (LOTW)/Launch Under Attack (LUA), which is preferred to riding-out a US attack[3]
- unconventional warfare, deception, and direct action activities will play an important part in the period before a general exchange.

Soviet writers assume that general nuclear war would grow out of large-scale coalition warfare. Therefore, Soviet planning usually assumes that while the timing of a nuclear exchange will not be known, a bolt-from-the-blue attack is very unlikely. Instead, the Soviets concentrate on the danger of missing warning indicators and failing to act accordingly. Soviet authors argue that the best time to strike an attacker is before he has the opportunity to launch his attack against the Soviet Union. This preemptive theme disturbs US defense analysts, especially when it is viewed in conjunction with forces well-suited for preemption.

Soviet targeting presumably reflects a Soviet interest in damage prevention and concentrates primarily on attacking an adversary's offensive forces.[4] Soviet strategic nuclear forces seem to satisfy the damage-limiting doctrine by depending on highly-accurate, heavily-fractionated ICBMs such as the SS-18. By emphasizing the ICBM force, the Soviets ensure that the majority of their strategic nuclear warheads will be able to reach the United States in 30 minutes or less. This quick attack could disrupt a US attack before it got underway.

While the Soviets have a doctrine emphasizing preemptive attack, Soviet military writings recognize the difficulty of actually doing so during a crisis. Consequently, the Soviet command and control system is designed to operate should the Soviets fail to successfully preempt an attack. The apparent robustness of the Soviet command and control structure, along with hints from their military writings, suggests that the Soviets are fairly confident about the ability of their command and control structure to survive attack.[5] A belief in the ability of the command and control structure to survive is a prerequisite for the Soviets to contemplate riding-out an attack, since a US strike on the Soviets would logically include command and control elements of Soviet nuclear forces.

Because the Soviets view strategic nuclear conflict as an element of a larger coalition war, their military doctrine emphasizes the interaction of nuclear and conventional forces. The strategic nuclear phase of the conflict is envisioned as occurring after the United States and its allies have decided to use nuclear weapons. The Soviet strike would take place in the context of either launching their forces prior to the execution of the American attack (preemption), after warning of attack by sensors (LOTW), following the initial nuclear detonations (LUA), or after riding out an attack (rideout).[6] For the Soviets, controlling when to launch the forces can be a significant determinant as to how well they do in achieving their wartime objectives, and define to some extent how the Soviets will respond to perceived threats during crisis de-escalation.

6.4 ACTIONS IN AN ALERT

Why go on alert?

Alerts increase the ability to go to war. The increased ability to go to war stems from improved reaction time, greater survivability, and increased numbers of weapons available. The Soviet Union has not associated alerts with sending overt political messages, such as the US did in its 1973 nuclear alert associated with the Yom Kippur War.[7]

What are the military objectives?

Nuclear forces are put on alert in order to:

- reduce their vulnerability
- increase the number of weapons available to execute an attack
- increase the readiness of forces
- insure that commands can reach the majority of forces
- insure the continuity of command.

Alerting Soviet nuclear forces would probably involve increasing their readiness by recalling personnel and making sure the equipment was capable of responding rapidly to attack orders. The particulars would vary between the ICBM, SLBM, and bomber portions of Soviet strategic nuclear forces.

A second element of Soviet preparations would then be to disperse critical support and command personnel from main operating bases. Dispersal of the command and support personnel would have the twofold effect of increasing the possibility that the Soviets could conduct extended nuclear operations against an adversary, reducing the chances of an adversary killing those responsible for operational control of the nuclear forces either in a first strike, or after a Soviet preemptive attack.

Since the political leadership is ultimately responsible for the release of nuclear weapons, the political leadership would also have to be dispersed and protected against the effects of a nuclear attack. Preparations for protection of the leadership include the use of dispersal sites, fixed very-hard command centers, dispersal sites, and a variety of mobile command posts that all could be used to protect the leadership and allow it to control forces.[8]

Operations in an alert

Strategic forces

According to the US Department of Defense, the Soviets traditionally keep only a fairly small fraction of the SSBN force at sea (10 to 30 per cent) as a secure retaliatory force, and virtually none of the bomber force available for immediate launch.[9] Consequently, the Soviets could greatly increase their ready weapons by alerting these two elements. SSBNs could be sent to either bastions (areas defended by Soviet naval and air forces) or under the polar ice cap. Once deployed away from port to these relatively safe locations, they are less vulnerable to attack by either strategic nuclear weapons or conventional Anti-Submarine Warfare (ASW) operations. Once the SSBN force has been alerted and dispersed, the Soviets would have many more weapons available than on a normal day-to-day alert. The SSBN force would also be better able to withstand a large scale nuclear attack or a sustained ASW campaign conducted during the course of a conventional conflict preceding a nuclear exchange.

The ICBM force cannot be enhanced a great deal since more than 80 per cent of Soviet ICBM forces are ready for launch in peacetime.[10] The Soviets could also increase the number of ICBMs available by returning to alert their ICBMs forced down for repairs. The Soviets might enhance the survivability of their mobile ICBM force by dispersing the SS-24 and SS-25 mobile ICBMs. It would be difficult for an enemy to target mobile ICBMs once they are dispersed.

The current Soviet bomber force is held at very low alert levels on a day-to-day basis and could not be expected to survive a surprise attack. Because of this, the Soviets would have to alert this force to make it usable in a nuclear exchange. Even if alerted, the current bomber force would only make a small contribution to attacking targets in the United States.

A larger bomber force would give the Soviets incentives to utilize it.[11] The Soviets might consider measures that would enhance the survivability of the bomber force. These measures include:

- dispersing some bombers from their main operating bases to other interior airfields.
- developing a larger tanker force to support bomber operations and to decrease dependence on forward bases
- placing some bombers on airborne alert.

Of these measures, the simplest and least provocative would be to increase the number of dispersal bases for the bombers, and thus to make them difficult to target. The resultant force could be dispersed at a very large number of airfields, all of which would have to be targeted by US ballistic missiles – preferably short flight-time SLBMs – in order to have a high probability of catching any aircraft on the ground.

Developing a tanker fleet to support the bomber force would be more costly for the Soviets than simply developing elaborate dispersal plans, but a tanker fleet would create an opportunity to support strategic offensive operations. It would also enhance the capabilities for a broad range of strategic defensive and conventional operations.[12]

The most extreme effort the Soviets might make is placing aircraft on airborne alert during a crisis.[13] However, airborne alerts are very expensive to keep up, can be misinterpreted, and can lead to unexpected interactions with enemy forces. Airborne alerts will strain both the support system for aircraft as well as aircrews if a large fraction of the bomber force is maintained on alert. Airborne alerts consume great deals of fuel, decrease opportunities for preventative maintenance, and wear out flight crews by forcing them to operate up to their limits of endurance.

Airborne alerts may contribute greatly to instability if a crisis drags on beyond a few weeks. For example, unless the support system is configured to keep the aircraft aloft for an extended period of time, its exhaustion would force a partial stand-down of the force as the only alternative to using it for an immediate attack. An airborne alert might be used to hide preparations for an attack, simply by making the US accustomed to the presence of the bombers fairly far forward, as well as regular operations in a third country, such as Cuba. Airborne alerts could lead to Soviet bombers and any accompanying escorts to be intercepted by US fighters as they protected US aircraft operating near the Soviet Union in support of conventional military operations.[14]

Non-strategic forces

An alert of nuclear force would likely be preceded by preparation for major conventional operations. Alerted conventional forces would presumably prepare both to conduct independent operations and to support strategic nuclear forces. Theater nuclear forces would play a significant role in supporting operations against bases housing forces that threaten the Soviet Union. Strategic defensive forces would try to erect an effective air defense against US bombers and cruise missiles. The Moscow ABM system would be brought up to its maximum state of readiness. Naval forces would prepare for both defending submarine bastions against US ASW attack and for conducting offensive ASW operations and general surface warfare, directed especially against US aircraft carriers and surface ships armed with land-attack nuclear weapons.

A general alert of Soviet forces would greatly increase the number of Soviet military forces operating around the periphery of the Soviet Union, as well as forward of the Soviet Union, to prevent US forces from approaching the Soviet homeland. The result of this alert would be to increase greatly the chance of Soviet forces meeting with US naval and air forces. The potential for incidents probably increases in proportion to the number of interactions.

A general alert might also lead the Soviets to engage in a variety of measures intended to deceive US intelligence. They might begin active operations in the United States to either track US forces or to attack US strategic forces and command and control directly. The potential consequences of such activities are tremendous. For example, if during a period of tension, someone with a shoulder-fired SAM were discovered near a US bomber base, or the base from which NEACP (the President's airborne command post) operates, the United States might have to conclude that preparations for a Soviet first strike were occurring.

6.5 ASSESSMENT OF STAND-DOWN MEASURES ON FORCE OPERATIONS

Potential options for stand-down

There are many possible scripts for standing down US and Soviet nuclear forces. These options range from: a 'crash' stand-down in which all the forces quite suddenly go from full alert, to day-to-day alert to a 'gradual' stand-down over weeks with either pre-arranged or *ad hoc* agreements on time, place, and manner of strategic force deployments. A gradual stand-down might occur as a result of negotiations aimed at de-escalating the crisis.

The range of possible combinations is large, and worthy of a serious study. However, all of the possible stand-down measures are intended to perform two basic, yet contradictory functions: increase the confidence of both parties that the other side is not seeking a military advantage while at the same time insuring that neither party's strategic forces become too temptingly vulnerable to attack. One of the main benefits of going on alert is that the available forces become larger and are consequently better able to absorb an attack and retaliate. At the same time, however, the survivability of some forces may decrease because the alert increases the number of deliverable weapons arrayed against it.

A crash stand-down

A 'crash stand-down' is what can occur when all strategic nuclear forces are brought immediately down from alert status. 'Crash' refers to the fact that after a rapid stand-down, strategic nuclear forces can be in a lower state of readiness than they were before the alert. This decrease in capability is caused by the need to perform deferred maintenance on aircraft and missiles, to reprovision SSBNs, and, perhaps most important, to give crews needed rest.

A 'crash' stand-down is what typically appears in popular accounts of nuclear crisis termination, in which the political crisis suddenly ends and strategic forces are miraculously returned to normal day-to-day alert *without any catastrophic loss of capabilities.* The maintenance requirements of particular systems, such as missile guidance systems, or transporters for mobile missile systems such as the Soviet SS-25 transporter and the American Hard Mobile Launcher (HML), or aircraft avionics dictate how deep and long the sag in capabilities might be. Without knowing the details of the systems involved, it is possible only to note that this is a potential problem with standing down the forces rapidly.

A gradual stand-down

Stand-down measures must effectively manage the transition period from alert to day-to-day operating levels by insuring that balance might be struck between the conflicting set of objectives mentioned above. Any effective means of stand-down, regardless of the details of the operation must:

- minimize the vulnerability of at least one significant portion of each party's strategic forces (or minimize the combined vulnerability of a significant number of forces)
- build confidence by standing down forces most threatening to the adversary
- maintain control of the forces by standing down C^3 last.

When standing down their forces, the Soviets have to choose which portion of their strategic forces they would rely on for deterrence during the transition period. The Soviets would always have the option of simply bringing deployed mobile assets home and announcing a policy of launching under attack. Such a policy would put the Soviets in a fairly strong position with regard to determining US actions, but would result in a less stable world – one where the Soviets would have to resort to launching an attack based on potentially unreliable early indications of an attack against them. Consequently, a *desirable* stand-down posture should allow the Soviets to meet their basic set of targeting requirements without having to LOTW/LUA.

SSBNs, the most secure element of Soviet strategic forces, could not be brought home without revealing their position and exposing them to attack. Clearly it would be foolhardy for the Soviets to bring the majority of their SSBNs home immediately after a crisis, unless some other portion of strategic forces could perform the SSBNs' job of striking soft targets even after riding out a US attack.

Fortunately, the Soviet Union could keep their mobile ICBMs dispersed for survival and use that force as a hedge against the SSBN force being destroyed in port. Mobile ICBMs have the advantage of being no more or less dangerous to the United States when they are deployed away from their casernes. SSBNs, on the other hand, have the capability to surreptitiously approach the United States and to threaten US bombers and command and control elements with short time-of-flight missiles.

Bomber forces are likely to be the most attractive force to stand-down. Bombers are more difficult to hold on alert and to stand down than other elements of the Soviet strategic nuclear forces because of their relatively high maintenance requirements. These maintenance demands mean that the Soviets would probably have to return the bomber force to a lower state of readiness *regardless of the status of the crisis* just to maintain their effectiveness.

The Soviets would also have to at least *begin* to stand down activities not directly related to Soviet strategic nuclear forces (e.g. conventional force operations, some intelligence gathering, etc.) since continuation of these could send the wrong signals to the United States. Among the activities that the Soviets would have to forgo are intrusive intelligence and covert action activities; and interference with means of control over US strategic nuclear forces.

Intrusive intelligence-gathering activities by the Soviets might include the activation of base-watchers to determine the level of alert at US military facilities, actively trailing US mobile ICBM forces (such as the Rail Garrison MX), and perhaps conducting operations directed at the US C^3I networks. Such activities might be benign, or they might actually involve direct action against US assets to disrupt the alerting process. If any of these activities were detected in the US, especially during a stand-down period, the US would have to assume that the Soviets were at best unable to control their forces, and at worst were planning to exploit the stand-down period for military advantage. In either case, the US would have to react in order to protect itself from the Soviets, thereby reinvigorating the crisis.[15]

Soviet doctrine as described in their military literature stresses the importance of radio-electronic warfare, particularly as a tool for disrupting the actions of an adversary during the early stages of a conflict. Recent arms control measures have banned such activities as interfering with strategic command and control links to forces, but while such activities might be banned, they may still be lurking in some operational plan to be executed during a crisis. C^2 links might also suffer from jamming activities directed against tactical command and control systems.

What the Soviets might lose by standing down

Standing-down Soviet strategic forces means that the Soviet Union would have to forgo many of the benefits gained from alerting its forces, and they might enter a transitional state that made Soviet forces even more vulnerable to attack than when they were at their day-to-day posture. Are Soviet strategic nuclear forces as robust as their command and control system? Could Soviet forces survive a US preemption under the worst case and still meet basic Soviet targeting requirements? Questions like these underlie much of the discussion of crisis stability from the Soviet perspective.

It is clear that the Soviets can stand down their forces if they have an incentive to do so. The Soviets need not make their forces unacceptably vulnerable to preemption unless they make gross errors in force management, but the Soviet leadership would have to recognize that there are benefits and losses associated with standing down their forces. The Soviets will lose a number of capabilities by standing down their forces. These include:

- an inability to conduct a short warning attack on US C^3IW and bomber bases
- a loss of a large residual force if the US is allowed to strike first.

A large residual force allows the Soviets to hedge against catastrophic failure of Soviet forces, compensate for a greater-than-expected US threat, and conduct extended nuclear exchanges.

A conspicuous stand-down of forces, such as the recall of SSBNs to home waters and the return of alerted boats to port where they could be seen by US national technical means, would decrease the total number of survivable weapons by making all submarines in port vulnerable to attack.[16] A stand-down of the sort described would not, however, eliminate the threat against the United States. If the Soviets keep even a few quiet SSBNs at sea, they could perhaps approach the US without being detected. The dramatic effect, though, would be to force the Soviets into giving up a large reserve force of weapons, since the SSBNs in port could be targeted by US forces, and would not likely survive a US attack.

A large nuclear reserve is important to Soviet military planners because it allows the Soviet Union to have weapons dedicated against peripheral targets around the Soviet Union, and against other nuclear powers such as France, Great Britain, and (perhaps most important from the Soviet's standpoint) the People's Republic of China. The reserve force is also important to the Soviets because it allows them to conduct extended nuclear operations against the United States. Whatever the merits of planning for extended nuclear operations, the Soviets apparently do consider them a possibility and have structured their forces accordingly. Consequently, the Soviets would probably emphasize the survivability of their secure nuclear reserve forces in any stand-down operation.[17]

A simple analysis of Soviet weapons and targets suggests a great deal about how the Soviets would have to operate their forces. Doctrine and common sense suggest that the Soviets would prefer preemption to launch under attack, and launch under attack to riding-out an attack.[18] If one accepts that the Soviets have a set of targeting requirements implicit in their military writings, then the Soviets would have to insure the destruction of American nuclear forces, as well as other military targets, command and control systems, and war-supporting industries.

In the basic analysis that follows, the US attack against the Soviets is assumed to proceed to completion (e.g. all US weapons including bomber-delivered are allowed to reach their targets).[19] The Soviet weapons are categorized to reflect the survivability of those forces in the face of a US attack. The following assumptions were used:

- fixed-silo ICBMs, bombers, and submarines in port are survivable only if launched prior to the arrival of US weapons
- mobile ICBMs and SSBNs at sea are assumed to be completely survivable
- all non-operational weapons (including those down for maintenance) are non-survivable.

If one compares the number of Soviet warheads on alert prior to a US attack and those sure to survive an attack with the estimates of warhead requirements (see Figure 6.1), it is clear that the Soviets would have to LOTW/LUA to meet their requirements. The size of the US hard-target requirement is very large relative to the number of fully survivable hard-target-capable warheads, and the Soviets cannot meet their requirements following a US attack. However, the Soviets can be confident of attacking all the soft targets in the US even after absorbing a US attack – *providing* Soviet forces had been alerted first. Over 60 per cent of the Soviet's soft-target capable weapons come from generated SSBNs. Unalerted, these forces could cover perhaps only half of the soft-target requirement.

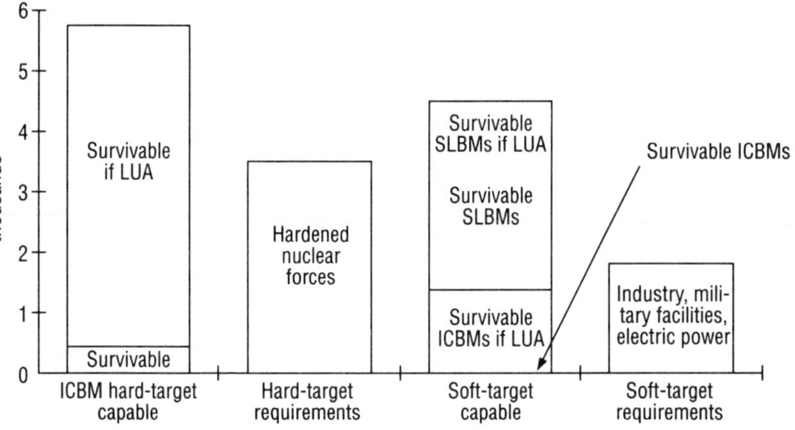

Figure 6.1 Current Soviet warhead availability and requirements

The Soviets must currently LOTW/LUA to meet the requirements for destruction of US hard-targets if the US is allowed to initiate the exchange. However, by the late 1990s, unilateral actions by the US and Soviet Union and the effects of arms-control treaties will change these results substantially. Unilateral actions include Soviet development and deployment of land-mobile ICBMs, and the further development of the US Trident D-5 SLBM, which is capable of attacking the full spectrum of targets, including hardened targets such as ICBM silos. Arms control enters the equation by sharply shrinking the total numbers of weapon available, and creating incentives to alter the mix of forces fielded.

Figure 6.2 illustrates Soviet targeting capabilities and requirements under the same scenario, but including these anticipated changes. The notable change from today is that both forces are assumed to be constrained to a START agreement, and that a large fraction of the US and Soviet forces is mobile. The effect of the United States and the Soviet Union pulling a large fraction of the ICBMs from their silos is twofold: the Soviets have decreased the need to LOTW/LUA their force based on meeting targeting requirements, and the American hard-target set has decreased in size by moving a large fraction of the ICBM force out of silos.[20] The soft-target set is amply covered by survivable ICBM and SLBM warheads not needed to

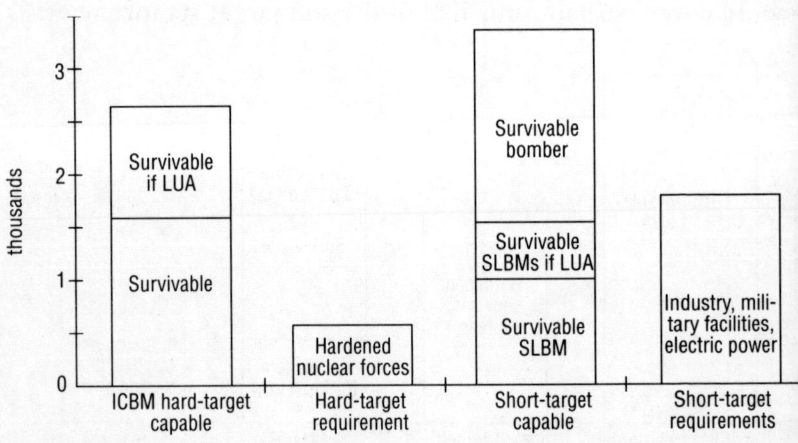

Figure 6.2 Late 1990s Soviet warhead availability and requirements

meet the hard-target requirements. The addition of a very large bomber force provides a hedge for failure of either the SSBN or ICBM force, provided the bomber force is capable of being launched prior to the arrival of US weapons.

It is interesting to note that by the late 1990s a large fraction of the US hard-target force will be based on Trident D-5 missiles which the Soviets cannot target, and the Soviet hard-target capable force will in turn be spread between mobile ICBMs and fixed heavy ICBMs, about half of which cannot be targeted by the US once they have been alerted and dispersed for survival.[21] The net effect of the changes will be that the majority of the nuclear forces for each side will have become effectively invulnerable.[22]

Soviet gains from standing down

While the Soviets lose some military capabilities, there are also military gains. We have seen that alerts greatly enhance the ability of the Soviets to both withstand attack and to deliver a larger blow against any adversary. Two perfectly reasonable questions are: 'Why not remain on alert?' and 'Why don't the Soviets always maintain a much larger fraction of their strategic forces on alert than they do on normal day-to-day alert?'

The Soviets gain from standing down their strategic forces by:

- reducing wear and tear on personnel and material
- reducing information to the US about generated Soviet force posture
  - (i) keeping deployment locations of mobile systems unknown
  - (ii) decreasing opportunities for the U.S. to search for unique signatures of mobile systems
- enhancing control of Soviet forces

Alerting strategic forces is costly; it stresses both personnel and machines as hours of duty are extended and routine maintenance is skipped in the attempt to keep both the human and mechanical elements of the forces at their maximum state of readiness. For example, consider SSBNs. The Soviet system of manning SSBNs involves the use of a single crew per submarine, unlike the dual-crew system in use in the United States. If all the boats were sent to sea at the beginning of alert, this would force crews that had just finished to deploy again to sea, perhaps with minimum provisions. SLBMs aboard the submarine might have had to forgo routine maintenance, resulting perhaps in a less than normal system reliability. Over the short run, these costs might be acceptable but as the alert dragged on, a prudent Soviet planner would want to alleviate them. By decreasing the alert rate somewhat, more maintenance could be conducted and a large fraction of the submarines could be expected to have both reliable weapons and crews.

A second, and perhaps more compelling reason for the Soviets to stand down their forces as soon as possible, is that they would be very concerned that the United States might learn particularly sensitive details regarding force operations during a crisis. While the Soviets might expect the United States to observe Soviet military operations keenly during peacetime, during a crisis period the US would presumably target the Soviet Union for extraordinary attention, looking for indications that the Soviets were planning to attack. Under this intense scrutiny, a Soviet planner should be concerned that the US might learn about weaknesses in the Soviet operational plans simply by observing activities in the field.

For instance, Soviet mobile ICBMs can be considered relatively invulnerable against attack once deployed because their location is not known well enough to permit delivery of nuclear weapons against their location. If, on the other hand, the United States had an opportunity to closely observe an actual mobile ICBM deployment (perhaps complete with efforts to deceive the US), the US might find some unique signature of the system, or flaw with how they were conducting operations. If the US found some quick and consistent way of identifying the location of the mobile ICBMs, they might easily destroy them.

In the business of conducting these operations, the less an adversary sees, the more confident one is that he won't find a flaw. Indeed, even after the crisis has abated, the Soviets would probably have to alter their practices significantly just to be sure the Americans didn't know the current operational plans for the mobile systems.

Soviet concerns about maintaining control of nuclear weapons also provide an incentive for standing down forces. The Soviets have historically had a centralized military establishment. The nuclear weapons command and control structure is probably even more centrally controlled than the conventional forces C^3 structure. Even if the Soviets implement a system using permissive action links (PALs) to prevent unauthorized use of nuclear weapons, they might still face losing control of those weapons. Tactical nuclear weapons that might have been dispersed in conjunction with the general alert are particularly worrisome.

Gains from a US stand-down

The Soviets would also gain if US forces returned to a lower state of alert. A Soviet military might want to see a variety of US forces stand down. The forces of greatest immediate concern to the Soviets are US strategic nuclear forces. Soviets would like to see that the US was returning forces capable of delivering short time-of-flight weapons – namely SSBNs, and possibly ending any US airborne alert of bombers out of concern over a leading-edge cruise missile attack.

Because US SLBMs threaten C^3IW systems, the Soviets would probably like to see the number of US SSBNs returned to normal quite rapidly. The Soviet desire for removing the threat would conflict with the requirements of US SSBNs assigned to NATO as well as British and French submarines stationed near the Soviet Union. All these forces, especially those not armed with the long-range Trident missiles would have relatively short flight-times for missiles launched at the Soviet Union. The tension between achieving military objectives and building confidence is complicated by the multi-national character of the SSBN threat; this and verification problems would make such things as SSBN 'keep-out zones' of any sort particularly difficult to establish. Consequently, any agreement on SSBN might appear asymmetrical with the Soviet submarines being asked to remain in the bastions, with US, French, and British submarines given freedom to operate in most waters.

One consequence of the asymmetry in the stand-down of SSBN forces might be Soviet insistence on an offsetting stand-down of the US bomber forces. By keeping US bombers restricted to activities over North America, even airborne alerts might be tolerable to the Soviets. Indeed, the US could probably tolerate a phased stand-down of the bomber force by initially dropping back to dispersed strip alert, and eventually returning to main operating bases. A gradual stand-down of US bomber forces does not dramatically increase the vulnerability of Soviet strategic nuclear forces, although a somewhat smaller percentage of US bombers might successfully escape a Soviet preemptive attack. By insuring the US had a somewhat smaller surviving bomber force, the Soviets might partially offset the decrease in survivability and effectiveness of their SSBN force.

The Soviets have expressed concern over US naval forces operating near the North Cape of Norway, and in the Sea of Okhotsk – both bastions for Soviet SSBNs. Soviet leaders would welcome US stand-down efforts here. The primary threat from US naval forces to the Soviet SSBN fleet comes from attack submarines which, when supported by other naval forces, could threaten the survival of SSBNs in the bastions. The actual magnitude of the US threat is debatable as Soviet submarine quieting continues; however, the Soviets would still be concerned about having US forces operating immediately in and around the SSBN bastions. Consequently, the Soviets might also insist on a withdrawal of US ASW forces from near their bastions.

A final area of concern for the Soviets is forces armed with nuclear weapons that would operate near the Soviet periphery. These forces include US carrier battle groups, and all surface ships and submarines armed with nuclear-armed Tomahawk cruise missiles. In the 1950s when carrier aviation had a more prominent role in nuclear weapons delivery than it does today, the Soviets began their longstanding concern over US aircraft carriers approaching the Soviet Union. Since then, the US has de-emphasized the role of surface ships in the delivery of strategic nuclear weapons, but the Soviets still spend a great deal of effort to destroy these forces. The problem here is that the carrier is the centerpiece of the US surface forces and would have to be deployed near the Soviet Union prior to the outbreak of a conflict for it to have a decisive effect in any short war. Consequently, the US would be reluctant to withdraw those forces prematurely.

The second class of measures the Soviet military might desire would be those that make the US forces vulnerable to preemption and enhance the ability of the Soviets to obtain their wartime objectives. Dispersal of US mobile ICBMs would frustrate the Soviets by making preemptive targeting difficult. Returning the ICBMs to their casernes would make them targetable, particularly if attacked in conjunction with C^3I to prevent a US launch before the Soviet attack has been completed.[23]

6.6 CONCLUSIONS

The Soviet strategic nuclear forces have no structural impediment to their standing-down after a crisis. As one RAND researcher pointed out early in this exercise, it is only logical that a strategic nuclear force can be 'de-alerted' after a crisis without endangering the integrity of the force. Modern nuclear forces can be properly managed as to allow them to return to their pre-alert levels of readiness without necessarily making the forces any worse-off than when they were on normal day-to-day alert.

Soviet strategic nuclear forces suffer from no structural flaw to prevent them from being gracefully returned to normal day-to-day alert following a crisis. The underlying technology allows the Soviets to manage their forces in a manner consistent with going on alert without having to either 'use or lose' those forces. Soviet military doctrine, while emphasizing preemption, has always taken into account the possibility that the Soviets might not be able to preempt. A situation in which the Soviets have returned to essentially normal operations without commensurate US actions is an undesirable, but not a necessarily unacceptable possibility for the Soviets. Consider for example the Soviet SSBN force. Usually the Soviets keep less than 30 per cent of their SSBN force at sea and safe from preemptive attack. When alerted they might put between 50 and 75 per cent of the SSBN force to sea. A submarine lost during an alert represents a much smaller fraction of the Soviet's capabilities than one lost under non-alert conditions. Losses in the context of a crisis situation or stand-down effort may seem more ominous and may excite decision-makers into considering all sorts of dark possibilities, yet objectively the losses are less significant than they are during normal operations. The disparity between the objective danger of incidents, and the perceived danger to the forces means that a very real possibility of unnecessary escalation of a crisis exists. As long as Soviet and American forces interact with each other, incidents must not only be planned for, they must be expected as a normal part of operations when forces, both conventional and strategic nuclear, are at a very high state of alert.

In the late 1990s, the Soviets will be able to reliably cover a large fraction of the US target set with mobile ICBMs maintained on alert buttressed by a bomber force, without raising fears of a short-warning attack in the United States. SSBNs, capable as they are, generate fears of short-warning attacks in the United States and could be counted on to carry a stabilizing role during the stand-down process. Asymmetries in geography and political systems allow the Soviets to depend on mobile ICBMs and bombers during a stand-down, and at the same time, rapidly return the SSBN force to day-to-day operations. While not eliminating completely the threat of a short-warning SSBN attack on the US mainland, it would be a significant confidence-building measure. Because returned SSBNs will represent a large portion of the Soviet strategic nuclear reserve, this measure would allow decision-makers in the US to be more confident that the Soviets were not contemplating an attack on the United States.

No plans for standing-down nuclear forces will work unless preparations are made to handle the transition period. Along with operational plans for returning the strategic nuclear forces to normal alert status, a system designed to deal with incidents during the transition period must also be created. Indeed, incidents either during or after a crisis could lead to the outbreak of war between the US and the Soviet Union. Some analysts argue that the mindset of decision-makers during and after a crisis predisposes them to perceive an incident between US and Soviet forces as the precursor to a major exchange. However, the objective conditions of the opposing strategic forces do not necessarily lead to this conclusion. When alerted, both the US and Soviet strategic nuclear forces are better prepared to withstand attrition due to military incidents than they are during day-to-day operations, and the strategic nuclear C^3I system is alerted and better able to withstand attack. Nonetheless, given the number of forces involved in a worldwide alert of forces, the chances are very high that some sort of military incident might occur. Indeed, the accident might even involve the nuclear forces themselves, or even the use of nuclear weapons. In any case, the magnitude of the disaster stemming from unintentional escalation demands that both the military and political leadership be sensitized to these events in order to avoid exaggerating the importance of such incidents when nuclear forces and C^3IW systems are alerted and least vulnerable to attack.

The notion of incidents occurring as a normal part of operation does not extend into the homelands of the US and the Soviet Union. The distinction here is not that of geography *per se*, but is a distinction in terms of the sort of assets put at risk by those operations. Operations in either nation's homeland would threaten the command and control network of their respective strategic nuclear forces. While they are alerted for protection, C^3IW systems are not interchangeable to the same degree as the strategic offensive forces. This means that both the US and Soviet Union are probably very sensitive to intentional or unintentional threats to elements of their C^3IW systems.

Managing a transition after an alert will be a difficult task. The difficulty will not lie with the management of the forces, since both US and Soviet forces can be moved between a fully-alerted posture and normal operations without making either party an attractive target for attack. As with many situations in today's world, the human element, as embodied in the political relations between the United States and the Soviet Union, will be the ultimate determinants of the stand-down and confidence-building process.

NOTES

1. Bruce G. Blair, 'Alerting in Crisis and Conventional War', in Ashton B. Carter, John Steinbruner, Charles Zraket (eds), *Managing Nuclear Operations* (Washington, DC: Brookings Institution 1987), pp. 75–120, and Paul Bracken, *The Command and Control of Nuclear Forces*, (New Haven: Yale University Press, 1983).
2. See Stephen M. Meyer, 'Soviet Nuclear Operations' in *Managing Nuclear Operations*, Ashton Carter et al. (eds), op. cit., pp. 470–531.
3. Launch on Tactical Warning (LOTW) is the policy of launching the strategic nuclear forces based on tactical indications received from warning sensors such as satellites and radars. Launch under attack (LUA) is the policy of launching the strategic nuclear forces based both on information from warning systems and confirmed nuclear detonations. The worst case for the Soviets would be launching their forces after riding-out a US attack, and launching their forces after the arrival of all the US weapons.
4. See 'Soviet Nuclear Targeting Strategy' in *Strategic Nuclear Targeting*, Desmond Ball and Jeffrey Richelson, eds, (Ithaca and London: Cornell University Press), pp. 84–108.
5. The Soviet strategic nuclear C^3I system is comprised of soft, hard, and mobile command centers for military and civilian leadership. The command and control structure includes a variety of fixed and mobile assets which provide the Soviet leadership with the ability to communicate with and control their strategic nuclear forces. The command and control structure contains airborne command posts, deep underground shelters and many hardened facilities, leadership relocation sites, mobile communication links that would be activated in crisis time, redundant communication links to strategic forces via satellite. HF, LF, VLF, and land-lines. See Meyer, and US Department of Defense, *Soviet Military Power: An Assessment of the Threat 1989* for a discussion of the Soviet C^3I system. For a discussion of the vulnerabilities of US C^3I vulnerabilities, see Blair.
6. These four cases can actually be treated as three cases (at this level of detail): preemption, where the undegraded Soviet force is launched against the US without any serious time-pressures on the command and control network; LOTW/LUA, where a mostly undegraded force is launched against the United States with a severe time-constraint on dissemination of the execution order and rapid response of the forces; and the rideout case, where the Soviets must respond after a full US attack.
7. Indeed, the Soviets apparently handle their nuclear forces more conservatively than the United States. If this pattern holds, it is unlikely that the Soviets will use alerts to convey political messages.
8. *Soviet Military Power: An Assessment of the Threat 1989*, pp. 43–4.
9. Meyer, p. 494.
10. Ibid.
11. Should the Soviet Union and the United States arrive at a START

agreement favorable to bomber forces, the Soviets might expand their bomber force. The Soviets could exploit START's favorable counting rules for penetrating bombers, and along with the almost non-existent continental air defenses in the United States, arrive at a much more powerful force (measured in deliverable warheads) than their current mix of weapons. See Paul Stockton's chapter for more details on the START agreement.

12. Whether or not the Soviets build a large bomber force, a tanker fleet for operations outside Europe seems likely. An early indication of an expanded Soviet bomber force might be a growth of the tanker force.
13. Airborne alerts were abandoned as a routine measure due to cost considerations, fear of accidents following a number of crashes of nuclear-armed bombers, and a growing confidence in the ability of early-warning systems to provide sufficient warning time for the bombers to escape from bases.
14. There would be a number of interactions between US and Soviet forces in a nuclear crisis, although the most disturbing would be those between strategic bombers and naval forces. US naval surface forces have to be very wary of Soviet bombers armed with anti-ship missiles, and consequently cannot be expected to allow any aircraft, let alone a bomber, to approach their formation without being challenged in some way, as demonstrated recently in the Persian Gulf. In a crisis, aircraft commanders should avoid unnecessary contact with naval forces.
15. Intrusive US efforts against the Soviets would also likely produce a strong response.
16. The submarines in port could still be on missile alert since their missiles could reach the United States. However, while the submarines could be used in the initial strike against the US their warheads could not be withheld for later use because of their vulnerability to attack. Furthermore, they would not offer flight-time advantages compared to ICBM forces.
17. The Soviets have a variety of measures of effectiveness for nuclear forces appearing in their literature. The best-known (Anureyev's Lambda) is a snapshot of an exchange showing the relative performance of the opposing nuclear forces.
18. Indeed, any nuclear power would prefer the aforementioned hierarchy since it follows a path of from minimum to maximum demands on the responsiveness of the C^3 network and on the forces.
19. The exact composition of current Soviet forces is based on Thomas Cochran, William Arkin, Robert Norris, and Jefferey Sands, *Nuclear Weapons Databook: Soviet Nuclear Weapons*, Volume IV, (New York: Harper and Row, 1989). START-compliant forces are based on information from the Soviet Academy of Science's Institute for World Economic and International Relations.
20. The fate of the mobile ICBM force and that of the Soviet ICBM forces is up in the air at the time of writing. It appears that the mobile ICBM force may not be built by the US for budgetary reasons, and that it be exchanged in negotiations for a decrease in the number of MIRVed mobile ICBMs deployed by the Soviets.

21. It has been suggested that dispersing the mobile ICBM force is provocative, but it is true only so much as it reflects the apparent level of concern over the survivability of the ICBM force during a crisis (e.g. the risk of war is seen as increased). SSBNs are generally considered stabilizing elements because of their survivability.
22. The Soviet SSBN force is not assumed to be hard-target capable, though if the Soviets do not have MIRVed land mobile hard-target killers, they might choose to develop a missile similar to Trident D-5.
23. The Soviets would have to assume that the US might LUA or LOTW, but the Soviet military would prefer to fire at a concentrated, rather than at a dispersed American target base.

Part III

Future Prospects and Conclusions

7 De-escalatory Confidence-building Measures after START

Paul N. Stockton

7.1 INTRODUCTION

The very notion of examining de-escalatory CBMs in the context of the START negotiations appears odd. Given the immense progress in US–Soviet relations, of which the proposed START agreement is emblematic, the risk of the two nations stumbling to the brink of war seems increasingly remote. Why bother analyzing CBMs designed to help resolve such an improbable event?

The obvious answer is that relations between the US and the Soviet Union – or whatever array of nations succeed it – could take an unforeseeable turn for the worse. Once ratified, the START agreement is supposed to remain in force for seven years, more than enough time for political tensions to return with a vengeance. This suggests a more prudent question: if our two nations do stumble to the brink of war, will the START agreement affect the prospect for de-escalatory CBMs? And if the US and Soviet Union pursue deeper force-reductions in a follow-on 'START II' agreement, could that agreement be designed to facilitate more effective de-escalatory measures?

Yet, there is still another, more skeptical, inquiry that should be made. In an era of friendly relations and enthusiasm for arms-control reductions, have we overlooked ways that START might threaten efforts to defuse a crisis? Indeed, might START provisions that initially appear most helpful for de-escalation prove especially dangerous during a crisis?

This chapter sets the stage for addressing such questions by outlining the START agreement and offering a brief overview of how START might affect the prospects for CBMs. Then, after examining some specific CBM proposals in light of START, an analysis will be made of the de-escalatory problems and opportunities that a START II treaty might create.

7.2 KEY ELEMENTS OF THE START AGREEMENT

That START could have dramatic, far-reaching implications for confidence-building initiatives is not immediately apparent. After all, CBMs focus on the operation of military forces; in contrast, START concentrates on 'structural' arms-control issues, particularly the numbers and types of forces to be deployed by the United States and the Soviet Union. Richard Darilek notes in Chapter 1 that this distinction tends to split CBM initiatives from structural arms-control agreements such as START. Nevertheless, whether intended or not, the force limits and verification provisions of START will alter the prospects for a broad range of possible confidence-building initiatives.

START's overall limit on warheads will cause surprisingly little of this impact. Dramatic cuts in total warhead levels seemed likely when the START agreement first took shape. President Reagan and President Gorbachev agreed at their 1986 meeting in Reykjavik that START would impose a 50 per cent cut in strategic forces, leaving both sides with 6000 total 'accountable' warheads. But accountable is the key word. US and Soviet negotiators have agreed that not all warheads will be counted on a one-for-one basis. For example, penetrating bombers such as the B-2 will be counted as carrying a single warhead, even though they can actually carry 15 or more bombs and short-range attack missiles. Sea-launched cruise missiles will not be counted against that limit at all (although both sides have agreed that they will not deploy more than 880 SLCMs while the treaty remains in force).[1]

These counting rules will minimize the overall force reductions actually required by the agreement. If the United States deploys all the forces under START planned by Department of Defense and armed services, the US would have to cut its current warhead total of about 13 000 by as little as 10 to 20 per cent.[2] Soviet reductions below the current total of approximately 11 000 warheads will also be well below the 50 per cent cut originally envisioned by Bush and Gorbachev.[3] Of course, economic and domestic political pressures may limit the number of new weapons actually deployed under START, thereby curtailing efforts to take full advantage of the counting rules. But the fact remains that START will require only modest overall force reductions, minimizing any significance that such reductions might have for confidence-building initiatives. The CBM implications of truly deep cuts, which may occur in a START II agreement, will be discussed later in the chapter.

Nevertheless, START I will impose stringent sublimits on some particular types of weapons. Most striking are the constraints on ballistic missiles. Fifty per cent cuts would be required in the Soviet force of 308 SS-18 ICBMs and in Soviet ballistic missile throw-weight (with that reduced throw-weight level becoming the new ceiling for both sides). The agreement would also impose a ballistic missile warhead sublimit of 4900, under which the Soviet Union would have to reduce such warheads by about 50 per cent. (US reductions would be 37 per cent.)

Within these ballistic missile sublimits both sides will have considerable latitude to modernize their forces. The US did attempt to limit modernization in one key area: in April 1990, President Bush proposed a ban on mobile MIRVed ICBMs such as the Soviet SS-24 and the US mobile-based MX. But Gorbachev rejected that proposal, and the two sides agreed during the June 1990 summit that each could deploy up to 1100 warheads on mobile ICBMs under START. A close look needs to be taken at how these sublimits and mobile ICBM deployments will affect the prospects for confidence-building initiatives.

An analysis is also needed of the way that measures to verify compliance with these treaty restrictions could create new opportunities, and problems, for CBMs. The verification provisions of START were not designed as CBMs *per se.* Nevertheless, they could serve some important confidence-building purposes. The most obvious is to promote military 'transparency' by providing increased knowledge of the other side's military forces. Baseline inspections to determine existing force levels, measures to track the number and location of deployed missiles and bombers, the monitoring of missile production facilities – all these measures could help create confidence-building transparency.

Verification provisions may also have an impact on de-escalatory CBMs. Given the stringency of the sublimits imposed by START, the wide array of forces they limit, and the complexity of the counting rules applied to them, extensive and intrusive measures will be established to help verify compliance with the agreement. On-site inspections will play a particularly important role. Under the INF treaty of 1988, each side has stationed as many as 200 inspectors on the other's territory in order to conduct baseline inspections and verify that INF forces have been taken out of operation and destroyed. Yet, according to US Army Brigadier-General Roland Lajoie, Director of the On-Site Inspection Agency, the job of INF verification 'is infinitely easier than on-site inspection for a START agreement'. START deals with many more types of weapons, and attempts to limit them rather than ban them entirely (as was done by the INF treaty). As a result, a much larger number of on-site inspectors will be required, and they will need access to a much broader array of missile bases and other sensitive military facilities.[4] What new kinds of CBMs might these inspectors make possible, especially during the de-escalation phase of a severe crisis? And what escalatory problems might arise from efforts to monitor compliance with START as such a crisis evolved?

7.3 DE-ESCALATORY CBMs UNDER START

Ideally, de-escalatory CBMs could help the US and the Soviet Union wind down a confrontation by offering tangible evidence of their intent to do so, without increasing crisis-instabilities or exposing either side to unacceptable military risks. Glenn Buchan and David Frelinger have evaluated a number of possible CBMs from the standpoint of crisis-stability and related criteria. The following section examines how the START sublimits, and verification provisions for ICBMs, bombers and SLBMs will affect the prospects for such de-escalatory measures.

ICBM-related confidence-building measures

The START agreement will create new opportunities, and also new difficulties, for CBMs involving ICBMs – especially mobile ICBMs. To assist efforts at verifying compliance with mobile ICBM sublimits, START will impose basing restrictions and other constraints that might make CBMs more practical. This is particularly true of proposals to send de-escalatory signals during a crisis by shifting the deployment modes of mobile ICBMs. For example, if missiles were ordinarily stationed in a few small base areas during peacetime, but were widely dispersed during a crisis to make them less vulnerable to attack, they might eventually be brought back to their base areas as a de-escalatory CBM.[5] START could facilitate such measures by restricting where (and under what circumstances) mobile ICBMs could be deployed, and by establishing procedures to help monitor compliance with those restrictions.

The precise nature of these restrictions may not be agreed to by the United States and the Soviet Union until shortly before the treaty is signed. However, the United States has suggested some deployment schemes that provide a general framework for analyzing the implications for CBMs. For rail-mobile ICBMs such as the US Rail Garrison MX, the US has proposed that a small number of bases would be established where the missile-carrying trains would be stationed in peacetime. Those trains would be dispersed over a much larger area if a crisis broke out,[6] conceivably, they might be returned to their garrisons to help wind-down that dispute, with their return monitored by national technical means. For road-mobile ICBMs, such as the US Midgetman, a number of deployment options have been proposed for START. One proposal would create a system of three concentric deployment areas. The inner area would be the so-called restricted deployment area, where all the main basing and support facilities would be located. Outside this area would be a much larger deployment zone for peacetime operations and training exercises by a predetermined portion of the ICBM force. Beyond that zone would be a still larger region where, in a crisis or with advanced notification, ICBMs could be deployed.[7] Again, the ICBMs could conceivably be returned to the inner area as a de-escalatory CBM.

Crisis-stability implications

What impact would this CBM have on crisis-stability as the US and Soviet Union attempted to step back from a confrontation? Dispersing ICBMs into the outer area would not increase the threat posed by those missiles, which could attack enemy forces just as effectively from the inner zone. Dispersal would, however, reduce the vulnerability of ICBM forces and thereby reduce incentives for an enemy strike. This raises a potential problem for stability: if ICBMs were vastly more survivable after dispersal than before, the Soviets might perceive an advantage in striking when dispersal begins, making the onset of dispersal a potentially destabilizing event. Such considerations would probably play a limited role in Soviet calculations even if war seemed imminent, given the relatively small proportion of US counterforce-capable warheads deployed on ICBMs. Nevertheless, it would be prudent to reduce any such dramatic disparities between pre- and post-dispersal force survivability. In road-mobile systems, for example, a good percentage of the force deployed could constantly be deployed in the middle concentric area where targeting them would be difficult. Rail-garrison basing of the MX (in which missile-carrying rail cars would be kept in relatively small areas in peacetime) may be less amenable to such stabilizing measures.[8]

Once ICBMs were fully dispersed in a crisis, some portion of them could be returned to the inner deployment areas as a CBM. Doing so would signal that the perceived likelihood of war had declined, since the returned forces would be more vulnerable to attack. But is this effort to send such a signal counterproductive? The ability of ICBMs to launch an attack is not diminished by bringing them back; they are still as potentially threatening as before. At the same time, a mutual return of ICBMs would increase the vulnerability of both sides to attack. An adversary might even propose such a return in order to improve its position to launch a first strike. What one side embraced as a stand-down measure to build confidence could be exploited by the other as a set-up for attack.

This suggests that mobile ICBMs should be returned to their inner deployment areas only after the crisis was defused, rather than using that return to facilitate an end to the crisis. At most, a phased return of ICBMs might be considered as a balance between the desire to send tangible de-escalatory signals, and the need to guard against dangerous increases in vulnerability.

Down-loading, verification and CBMs

The counting rules of START will also create some new problems involving ICBMs and confidence-building initiatives. The rules for counting ballistic missile warheads under START are different from those under SALT. With SALT, each ICBM or SLBM was assumed to carry the maximum number of warheads with which those particular types of missiles had been flight-tested. Under START, the United States and the Soviet Union will simply state how many warheads each of their ballistic missiles is carrying, *regardless* of how many their missiles have carried in flight tests.

This change in counting rules was motivated in part to improve crisis-stability. START would allow each side to down-load their ICBMs to carry fewer MIRVs, thereby permitting a large number of launchers and easing the problems associated with high warhead-to-launcher ratios. What made this counting change possible was a change in verification attitudes and procedures. SALT assumed that each missile carried the maximum number of warheads with which it had been tested, in large part because there was no way to verify whether such a missile was carrying fewer warheads. However, under the assumption that the Soviets would agree to fairly intrusive sorts of on-site inspections, START negotiators concluded that the United States could determine the number of warheads carried by a missile to an adequate degree.

The precise nature of such on-site inspections has yet to be settled. One possible means proposed by the United States in March 1988, would be for inspectors to select a deployed ICBM at random and hold nuclear radiation sensors over the missile after the nose cone has been removed, thereby determining the warhead load by counting the number of emitters. In any case, such verification measures are almost certain to involve intrusive access to deployed missiles, in addition to portal monitoring at missile assembly sites.[9]

On Capitol Hill, skeptics of the treaty are already highlighting the risk that the Soviets will attempt to 'break out' of such warhead limits by deploying additional warheads on down-loaded ICBMs.[10] They argue that once an ICBM has been flight-tested to carry a maximum number of warheads, it would be a relatively simple engineering task for the Soviets to add warheads to reach that maximum number over and above the stated missile load.

How significant this problem is in military terms is open to question. Given the large number of Soviet warheads that will remain under START I, the additional warheads offered by a Soviet breakout might not seem as militarily decisive as treaty opponents suggest. But in political terms, the fact that the issues have already been raised suggests that breakout concerns could become significant during a severe crisis (when the value of additional ICBM warheads would seem most attractive to the Soviets and of greatest concern to the United States).

One means of reducing fears over warhead-breakout would be to permit additional on-site inspections of US and Soviet ICBMs during a crisis – that is, to allow a larger portion of ICBM forces to be checked for warhead-loadings than would ordinarily be permitted. More comprehensive evidence that the Soviet Union was still complying with its warhead limits would reduce concerns that US ICBMs had been made more vulnerable to a first strike. Inspections could also reduce political tensions by demonstrating that both sides were honestly fulfilling their START commitments. And by easing such concerns and mutual suspicions, on-site inspections might serve as an important de-escalatory CBM.

However, while greater inspection rights might seem useful for de-escalation, the US may be reluctant to grant Soviet inspectors such additional access during a crisis. Even under the inspection provisions already envisioned for START, Amy Woolf of the Congressional Research Service argues that the Soviet Union will be able to use START inspections to gain important intelligence information about US forces. According to Woolf:

> It is inevitable that Soviet inspectors will have access to sensitive information, about systems limited by START and those that are not affected by the treaty, that the United States would rather not reveal.[11]

This desire to avoid revealing sensitive information about the location and other characteristics of US forces would be all the stronger during a severe crisis, when the adversary could use such information to help plan a strike. Soviet leaders would be similarly reluctant to allow US inspectors – that is, spies – access to Soviet forces as long as war seemed at all possible. Thus, while greater inspection rights might be useful as a de-escalatory CBM, security concerns will argue against any such initiatives.

In fact, during a severe crisis, the issue would not be whether to allow additional inspection, but whether to allow pre-established, treaty-required inspections to continue. The desire to limit access to sensitive intelligence information has already led to one apparent case of interference with existing inspection rights under the INF treaty. In March 1990, US inspectors at the Votkinsk missile facility were attempting to use an X-ray 'cargo scan' to verify that a missile exiting the facility was not a banned SS-20, but rather an SS-25 (which is also produced at Votkinsk but is a strategic weapon unconstrained by the INF treaty). Soviet guards reportedly drew their pistols and prevented US inspectors from conducting the scan.[12]

Note that this misunderstanding over inspection occurred in peacetime, when political tensions were extremely low. During a crisis, when both sides would be far more worried about giving the enemy access to sensitive intelligence information, such misunderstandings would be far more likely. And even if political leaders deemed the continuation of inspections a necessary risk, military commanders at individual bases might take unauthorized action to limit such access.

Of course, it would be precisely during a severe crisis that mutual suspicions would be at a height; each side would have the strongest interest in verifying continued compliance with the treaty, and would be most worried if its access to enemy forces were suddenly denied. Yet it would be at that same time that each side would have the greatest incentive to protect its forces from espionage or worse and would find it most attractive to limit access to those forces. Such a denial of access would not be undertaken lightly. But precisely because of the political import the opponent might see in such a move, restricting on-site inspections could heighten the perceived likelihood of war.

Recall that START permits the down-loading of ICBMs in order to strengthen crisis stability. But during a crisis, the measures necessary to verify compliance with those designated warhead loads may collapse, in a manner that could prove destabilizing indeed.

SSBN-related CBMs

Earlier chapters have suggested a number of possible de-escalatory CBMs involving ballistic missile submarines, where changes in deployment modes or other stand-down measures might help consummate negotiated agreements to end a crisis, increase political trust, and help return superpower relations to a more normal status. For example, the gradual return of SSBNs to port that had been put out on patrol during a crisis might provide tangible evidence of a willingness to return to such normal status. Other CBMs might help defuse a potentially explosive confrontation by reinforcing crisis stability, through measures to enhance SSBN survivability (such as SSBN sanctuaries) or to limit the first-strike threat posed by these submarines (such as keep-out zones). How would the provisions of START influence the potential value and practicality of these confidence-building initiatives?

The most important implications for CBMs will stem from the declining number of ballistic missile submarines under START. A number of analysts have argued that the agreement's ballistic missile sublimits will lead to a drastic cut in the number of SSBNs deployed by the United States, unless that smaller number of warheads can somehow be spread over a larger number of submarines (or the required cuts are made primarily in the ICBM force). While still a Senator, Vice-President Dan Quayle noted that the Trident SSBN carries an 'embarrassingly large number of missiles' – 24 – and that each of those Trident missiles carries an 'embarrassingly large number of warheads' – eight. Assuming that the United States relies on Tridents under START and retires the older Poseidon SLBMs, the United States could end up with a force of 15 to 19 SLBMs by the mid-1990s, with perhaps as few as ten SSBNs at sea at any one time (down from the current 20).[13]

This analysis assigns too much blame to the START treaty for the decline in SSBN numbers. Ted Warner and David Ochmanek point out that regardless of START, the US Navy had already planned to have a total force of only 20 SSBNs (all Tridents) by 1999.[14] Nevertheless, the fact remains that US SSBN numbers are likely to decline sharply while the START treaty remains in force. This is all the more true because options for increasing those numbers, such as developing and deploying a smaller SSBN, or buying additional Tridents and disabling some of their launching tubes, would be enormously expensive and therefore politically difficult.[15]

Not all possible CBMs will be affected by this decline in SSBN numbers. For example, proposals to establish SSBN 'keep-out' zones are designed to reduce the threat that ballistic missile submarines could launch a short-warning attack on command centers and other targets. However, because that threat can be posed by a very small number of SSBNs, any decline in SSBN numbers under START is unlikely to influence either the seriousness of the threat or the merits of keep-out zones as a solution.

In contrast, if reductions in SSBN numbers somehow increased SSBN vulnerability, CBMs designed to protect ballistic missiles from attack might become more attractive. That even a sharp drop in SSBN numbers would create vulnerability problems is by no means certain. Indeed, the US Navy has chosen to accept quantitative force reductions while emphasizing qualitative improvements in the survivability of individual SSBNs. A key reason why the Navy proposed to drop to a total of 20 SSBNs under START was that, owing to the reduced noise-levels and other qualitative improvements offered by Trident SSBNs, those improvements in survivability overshadowed any concerns over quantitative decreases in the SSBN force.

However, some analysts have concluded that such a sharp decline is bound to undermine SSBN survivability. In particular, if the United States relies on fewer SSBNs, they argue that the Soviet Union would make it more practical to attempt to trail those submarines with SSNs as they left port. And while the Navy has already addressed this problem through SSBN quieting and other measures, Henry Kissinger argues that the drop in the number of US SSBNs under START will nevertheless make them more vulnerable:

> when the number of submarines is cut so drastically while the agreement leaves Soviet antisubmarine warfare forces free to grow and modernize, the vulnerability of the U.S. residual submarine force must inevitably increase.[16]

Could CBMs offer a means of boosting SSBN survivability in the face of such quantitative force reductions? Joel Witt argues that one particularly attractive option would be to create SSBN sanctuaries, or 'keep-in' zones, where the adversary's anti-submarine warfare (ASW) forces would be prohibited from entering (and where civilian vessels that could be used for covert military purposes would be barred from entering).[17] The United States and the Soviet Union might agree to establish relatively large sanctuaries such as the Sea of Okhotsk, or – as proposed by Alexi Arbatov – agree that neither side could deploy submarines or surface ASW forces within a zone extending 1000 km from the other's coast.[18] Alternatively, if trailing by enemy SSNs is determined to be the most serious ASW threat, much smaller SSN-free zones might be established contiguous to SSBN bases (with SSBNs transiting through those protected areas on their way to unprotected patrol stations in the open ocean). Witt suggests that the United States might find this approach more palatable than larger sanctuaries 'since it would enhance the ability of the American SSBNs to slip into the vast ocean basins without being followed'.[19]

Again, however, it is by no means certain that the vulnerability of US SSBNs to trailing is a serious enough problem to warrant sanctuaries. Moreover, creating sanctuaries would not eliminate the threat to SSBNs but merely shift the focus of that threat. Alan Vick and James Thomson have noted that ASW sensors might be put into the sanctuaries covertly, and that remote sensing assets (which previously collected data from tens of millions of square miles of ocean) could be concentrated on a fairly small body of water if SSBNs were stationed in such keep-in zones.[20] The problem would also exist of detecting violations of the zones by enemy SSNs, although this problem might be more manageable if only relatively small areas contiguous to SSBN bases were designated as sanctuaries.

The more fundamental question for the United States is whether the potential benefits of sanctuaries (in terms of Trident survivability) are worth the cost to other US military objectives. According to Vick, the US Navy's Maritime Strategy calls for attacks against Soviet SSBNs even before a conventional conflict escalated to nuclear exchanges. Former Secretary of the Navy John Lehman claimed that American SSNs would attack Soviet SSBNs 'in the first five minutes of the war'.[21] Indeed, it is the desire to reduce this US threat to Soviet SSBNs that helps make sanctuary proposals so attractive to the Soviet Union.[22]

From the perspective of de-escalation during a crisis, calling off such attacks (or forgoing them entirely by creating SSBN sanctuaries) might offer a useful political signal. It is also possible that crisis-stability might be strengthened if Soviet leaders knew that their SSBNs were safe from attack, thereby minimizing pressures to 'use them or lose them'. Again, however, granting Soviet SSBNs that guarantee of survival could sacrifice other US objectives. Admiral James Watkins, the former Chief of Naval Operations, has stated that during a conventional war 'antisubmarine warfare forces would continue to destroy Soviet submarines, including ballistic missile submarines, thus reducing the attractiveness of nuclear escalation by changing the nuclear balance in our favor'.[23] Creating sanctuaries would inhibit such operations. Unless a fundamental shift in US policy eliminates the goal of killing SSBNs, or the evolving ASW threat makes sanctuaries more necessary for the survival of Trident submarines, the prospects for adopting this confidence-building measure remain poor.

CBMs involving bombers

The START agreement is structured in a way that could increase the potential need for bomber-related CBMs. According to Robert Einhorn of the State Department's Policy Planning Staff, the sublimits and counting rules of START are designed to 'encourage the evolution of force structures that rely more heavily on less destabilizing systems'.[24] Einhorn and other Bush Administration officials argue that bombers and air-launched cruise missiles (ALCMs) are less destabilizing than ballistic missiles; the faster speeds and shorter warning-times offered by ballistic missiles make them more suitable for conducting surprise attacks. Accordingly, while START puts sharp sublimits on ballistic missile warheads, heavy ICBMs and ICBM throw-weight, air-breathing forces (i.e. ALCMs and bombers) face no equivalent constraints. In fact, the permissive counting rules accorded to penetrating bombers and ALCMs are supposed to encourage their deployment at the expense of ballistic missiles. As Einhorn puts it: 'cutting more deeply into ballistic forces than air breathing forces will serve the overriding goal of enhancing stability'.

CBMs involving bombers could become far more important under these circumstances. Buchan argues that if the Soviet Union deploys aircraft well north of its borders during a crisis, while US bombers are also kept on airborne alert in northern areas, a serious risk of confrontation could emerge. The need to minimize such risks would grow if both sides relied more heavily on bombers. Accordingly, restrictions on forward deployments and airborne alerts and explicit rules of engagement for air forces could become all the more attractive under START.

However, while the agreement has been structured to encourage a heavier reliance on bombers, other factors – especially the cost of building and maintaining bombers – are working against this sort of force evolution. General Colin Powell, Chairman of the Joint Chiefs of Staff, has testified to Congress that the B-2 bomber needs to be deployed in order to take advantage of the counting rules of START.[25] But the congressional drive to cut defense spending has jeopardized that program. The Soviet Union is also cutting back on production and deployment of its own modernized strategic bomber, the Blackjack.[26] Thus, while bomber-oriented CBMs may still be useful under START, that agreement has yet to encourage the sort of reliance on bombers that could make such CBMs essential.

7.4 DE-ESCALATORY CBMs AND START II

Although the current START agreement will make only modest reductions in overall force levels, US and Soviet negotiators have begun discussing the possibility of making much deeper reductions in a follow-on, START II treaty.[27] Neither side has yet declared how deep these cuts should be. However, Soviet officials have emphasized their eagerness for reductions far greater than those made in START I. Soviet Deputy Foreign Minister Victor Karpov has stated that 'as soon as START I is signed, we should start negotiations on START II' aimed at cutting thousands of warheads from remaining forces.[28] US analysts outside the government have suggested that a 50 per cent cut below START I levels (leaving a total of roughly 3000 accountable warheads) could be a likely focus of negotiations.[29]

START II is also likely to target specific kinds of weapons for especially deep cuts. Karpov suggested that the follow-on agreement might eliminate entire classes of existing weapons. President Bush has been still more specific. He has proposed that START II eliminate all MIRVed ICBMs. And while President Gorbachev rejected that proposal, he did so not because the plan was too radical, but because it did not go far enough – particularly in terms of cutting other forces (such as bombers and SLBMs) which the United States relies on more heavily than the Soviet Union.[30]

There will be many other hurdles to negotiating a follow-on treaty that reduces forces so deeply, including the question of how third-country forces will be dealt with. Nevertheless, deep cuts are moving on to the negotiating agenda. Assuming that overall warhead levels were reduced to approximately 3000 under a START II treaty, what new sorts of opportunities and difficulties would emerge for CBMs?

Force vulnerability and CBMs

The prospect of radical force reductions will raise a host of concerns over the adequacy of US (and Soviet) strategic forces under a START II agreement. In particular, deep cuts could magnify concerns over force vulnerability during a crisis. If the US and the Soviet Union agree to rely on far fewer weapons for deterrence, the ability of those remaining weapons to survive a first strike will be of special concern. Declines in force survivability that would be deemed marginal at current warhead levels may, after deep cuts, seem far more destabilizing during a crisis.[31]

The effect of deep cuts on force vulnerability and prospective de-escalatory CBMs could indeed be great. For example, one possible de-escalatory measure would be to return mobile ICBMs to their initial pre-crisis basing area. Although such a return might increase the vulnerability of the ICBMs to attack, depending on the specific characteristics of the deployment mode, this risk would be limited under START I by the fact that so many warheads would remain on other systems. With far fewer weapons to rely on under START II, de-escalatory CBMs that even marginally threatened force-survivability might become less acceptable.

The most obvious way to offset these vulnerability concerns would be to replace existing weapons with more survivable forces, and to structure the START II agreement accordingly. But the desire to save money through deep cuts will tend to undermine political support for such weapon improvements. Could CBMs provide a cheaper way of bolstering force survivability, thereby making deep cuts (and the CBMs themselves) more acceptable? To put it in still more ambitious terms: might CBM proposals be integrated with deep cuts to form a single coherent START II agenda, bridging the historic gap between structural arms control and CBMs?

A preliminary answer may be found by examining the possibility of SSBN sanctuaries. The US has been far less supportive of this proposal than the Soviet Union, in large part because only the Soviets believe that sanctuaries would be valuable for strengthening SSBN survivability. Deep force-reductions will not necessarily drive the US toward the Soviet position; the US Navy may continue to believe that sanctuaries are completely unnecessary for Trident survivability. Nevertheless, if the Soviet Union concludes that the decline in SSBN numbers under START II makes sanctuaries all the more necessary, the US might agree to those sanctuaries in exchange for other Soviet concessions.

But the value of CBMs for survivability is open to question. Such operational arms-control measures usually do nothing to physically eliminate potentially threatening enemy forces (a task more the province of structural arms control). As long as US ASW forces remained unlimited by START II, the possibility would always exist that the US would use them to violate Soviet SSBN sanctuaries. And while actually doing so might provide a useful warning indicator to the Soviet Union, that would be of cold comfort once the destruction of Soviet SSBNs began.

Moreover, even if CBMs could help make deep cuts more negotiable with the Soviet Union, those cuts should not be viewed as an end in themselves. Force reductions (and any CBMs packaged with them) must be judged in terms of overall security goals. Agreeing to create sanctuaries would conflict with objectives deemed crucial by the US Navy – in particular, according to Admiral Watkins, the need to strengthen deterrence by threatening Soviet SSBNs with destruction. It might be argued that the US should de-emphasize such objectives under START II in favor of granting Soviet forces a greater degree of assured survivability. But nothing about deep cuts will automatically compel such policy shifts, and as long as CBMs run afoul of competing security goals, prospects for adopting them will remain limited.

CBMs and the risk of treaty violations

Deep force-reductions may increase concerns over the possibility of warhead-breakout or other treaty violations. Under START I, the military significance of such violations will be limited by the fact that so many warheads are already deployed. At the far lower force levels established by START II, the perceived risk of a warhead breakout could intensify, particularly during a crisis. Measures to verify compliance with treaty restrictions might play an important confidence-building role under these circumstances.

However, as discussed in the context of START I, on-site inspections could cut two ways in terms of confidence-building. On the one hand, each side would be extremely interested in verifying that the other side was adhering to warhead limits during a crisis. On the other hand, each side would be reluctant to grant the other additional inspection access to its strategic weapons, and might even be tempted to deny the verification rights already agreed to – at the very time when such a denial would be most troubling to the adversary. Deep cuts would do nothing to ease this potential problem. On the contrary: with both sides relying on far fewer forces, and the potential importance of a warhead-breakout all the more significant, the risks of on-site inspection to confidence-building and crisis-stability could grow.

7.5 CONCLUSIONS

The START agreement will create far more problems than opportunities for de-escalatory CBMs. Returning mobile ICBMs to their pre-crisis basing areas, creating SSBN sanctuaries – these and other prospective CBMs all involve liabilities that START does nothing to ameliorate. And on-site inspections, far from offering a solution to warhead breakout concerns arising under START, could create new threats to efforts at de-escalation.

The prospects for CBMs under START II are still worse. Although deep cuts will tend to magnify concerns over force vulnerability, CBMs cannot be counted on to resolve such problems, and indeed may become even less attractive as vulnerability concerns grow.

NOTES

1. Matthew Bunn, 'SAC Force Proposal: 1200 Warheads Under START?', *Arms Control Today*, February 1990, p. 31.
2. Amy Woolf, *The Strategic Arms Reduction Treaty: Major Elements of the Agreed Framework*, Congressional Research Service, Washington, DC, 4 June 1990, p. 1.
3. Alexi Arbatov, 'START: Good, Bad, or Neutral', *Survival*, July/August, 1989, p. 292.
4. Lajoie has not yet estimated the total number of inspectors that the US will require. However, he has noted that INF deals with nine missiles, all ground-based, and required the United States to monitor only one 'portal' at a Soviet missile production facility (Votkinsk). START involves 21 missile systems that are air-, ground- and sea-based, and have multiple portals. The result: the scope and cost of inspection for the START Treaty will be 'vastly greater' than that of INF. David Riley, 'Mutual Glasnost', *Government Executive*, July 1988, p. 44.
5. See, for example, Joseph Nation, *Force Standdown and Crisis Termination*, P-7292-RGS, The RAND Corporation, Santa Monica, CA, December, 1986, pp. 24–5.
6. Barry Fridling and John Harvey, 'On the Wrong Track?', *International Security*, Winter 1989, pp. 123–32.
7. Steven A. Hildreth, *Arms Control: Negotiations to Reduce Strategic Offensive Nuclear Weapons*, Congressional Research Service, Washington, DC, 23 June 1989, p. 7.
8. Fridling and Harvey, pp. 123–32.
9. James R. Blackwell, 'Contributions and Limitations of On-Site Inspection in INF and START', in Lewis Dunn, *Arms Control Verification and the New Realities of On-Site Inspection* (Lexington, MA: Lexington Books, 1990), p. 116.
10. Former Senator and now Vice-President Dan Quayle was prominent among these skeptics as recently as 1988. Dan Quayle, 'The Pitfalls of STARTing Now', *RUSI Journal*, Summer 1988, pp. 50–51.
11. Amy Woolf, *On-site Inspections in Arms Control: Verifying Compliance with INF and START*, Congressional Research Service, Washington, DC, 30 October 1989, p. 44.
12. Rowland Evans and Robert Novak, 'Missile Crisis', *Washington Post*, 16 March 1990, p. 23.
13. Quayle, p. 50, and Hans Binnendijk, 'START: A Preliminary Assessment', *Washington Quarterly*, Autumn 1988, p. 13.

14. Edward Warner and David A. Ochmanek, *New Moves* (New York: Council on Foreign Relations, 1989), pp. 46–8.
15. Tridents cost approximately $2 billion a copy; schemes to deploy more of them within START, much less to develop and deploy an entirely new small SSBN, would face enormous political hurdles in Congress. See Michael Gordon, 'Stocking the Atomic Arsenal: How Much Deterrence to Buy', *New York Times,* 23 May 1990, p. 1.
16. Henry Kissinger, 'START: A Dangerous Rush for Agreement', *Washington Post,* 24 April 1988, p. D-7.
17. Joel Witt, '"Sanctuaries" and Security', *Arms Control Today,* October 1980, pp. 1–7.
18. Alan J. Vick, 'Building Confidence During Peace and War', *Defense Analysis,* Vol. 5, no. 2, p. 105.
19. Witt, p. 7.
20. For a good critique of possible sanctuary areas, see Alan J. Vick and James A. Thomson, *The Military Significance of Restrictions on Strategic Nuclear Force Operations,* N-2113-FF, The RAND Corporation, Santa Monica, CA, April 1984, pp. 21–4.
21. Vick, pp. 106–7.
22. Michael M. May and John R. Harvey, 'Nuclear Operations and Arms Control', in Ashton Carter, John D. Steinbrunner and Charles Zraket, eds, *Managing Nuclear Operations* (Washington, DC: The Brookings Institution, 1987), pp. 722–3.
23. Ibid.
24. Robert Einhorn, 'The Emerging START Agreement', *Survival,* September 1988, p. 390.
25. R. Jeffrey Smith, 'US Proposal Favors Strategic Bombers', *Washington Post,* 8 February 1990, p. 30.
26. Michael Gordon, 'U.S. Says Soviets Will Field Fewer of Its Latest Bombers', *New York Times,* 5 June, 1990, p. 5.
27. The Bush Administration announced on 11 February 1990 that it would begin discussions with the Soviet Union on Soviet proposals for strategic arms reductions beyond START I. Michael Gordon, 'US Invites Ideas from the Soviets on Strategic Cuts', *New York Times,* 12 February 1990, p. 1. See also R. Jeffrey Smith, 'US, Soviets at Odds on Arms Pact Details', *Washington Post,* 13 February 1990, p. 17.
28. R. Jeffrey Smith, 'Soviets Press US for Deeper Reductions in Strategic Weapons', *Washington Post,* 25 February 1990, p. 14.
29. Warner and Ochmanek, pp. 60–62.
30. Michael Gordon, 'US Urges a Ban on Some Missiles But Soviets Say It's Too Limited', *New York Times,* 8 April 1990, p. 1.
31. This may occur even though the *relative* number of surviving warheads would not change. However, the *psychological* consequences of increased force vulnerability might be very destabilizing at suggested START II force levels.

8 Non-Superpower Nuclear Crisis De-escalation

William C. Martel[1]

8.1 INTRODUCTION

How we think about nuclear crises is inevitably a product of the cold war and the times when crises and confrontations involved the two nuclear superpowers and their clients. From the strategy and concepts of deterrence to the broader American doctrine of containment after the Second World War, the almost singleminded focus of thinking about nuclear crises centered on the dangers in a US–Soviet conflict. It was only natural that they would gain the most attention because they had by far the largest nuclear arsenals and could have inflicted the greatest havoc if a crisis had escalated into a conflict.

The fact is that crises during the cold war involved the superpowers and dominated most of the analytic work on nuclear crises. Now, however, we are entering an age in which states other than the nuclear superpowers – the United States, Soviet Union, United Kingdom, France, and China – will possess nuclear weapons, the means to deliver them, and therefore the wherewithal to become involved in nuclear crises.[2] It is inevitable that a growing number of states will possess nuclear weapons by the end of the twentieth century.

Why should we care about non-superpower nuclear crises (NSNC)? The simple reason is that the prospect of the United States and Soviet Union or their allies being drawn into a regional nuclear crisis could presage the outbreak of a larger and more dangerous superpower crisis. An excellent example is the 1973 Yom Kippur War when the United States detected that Israel was mating nuclear warheads to its aircraft.[3] Such an action could have drawn the superpowers into a far more dangerous crisis than that which occurred.

As we witnessed in the Middle East Crisis in 1990, fears that the superpowers will be involved in such crises are fading rapidly. The irretrievable fact, however, is that nuclear crises pose significant risks for many states. We can only imagine what the current crisis in the Persian Gulf would be like if Iraq were a nuclear power. The US and the West would face the prospect that vital economic centers in the Persian Gulf, most notably petroleum fields and refineries in Saudi Arabia and Kuwait, could be destroyed at any time. One certain consequence of the destruction of the oil supply would be massive disruption of the economies in the West and the East.

Nor is it in any state's interest to have nuclear weapons used in regions close to their homeland or against their friends or allies. All states, not just the superpowers, are compelled by the prospect of a regional nuclear war to take these issues seriously. More than that, however, there are a number of questions that we should ask about potential nuclear crises. Will there be NSNC? What are their characteristics and who are the likely antagonists? Are these crises likely to be unstable? Can these crises be controlled by outside powers or the antagonists themselves? Should other states try to terminate these crises and can they be terminated? This is the appropriate time for scholars and policymakers to contemplate both the issues that will arise in these incidents and the actions that will be necessary if we are to control these crises without incurring terrible losses to ourselves and others.

This chapter explores the dynamics of crises involving states other than the superpowers that possess nuclear weapons or other weapons of mass destruction. It analyzes the kinds of NSNC that may occur in the next couple of decades and outlines some principles for defining conceptually the nature of such crisis. Second, it discusses the kinds of antagonists and crises that we are likely to confront in the future. Third, it examines whether de-escalatory measures for nuclear forces and other CBMs can help to terminate non-superpower crises.[4] Finally, it reflects on some of the issues that shape the thinking on nuclear weapons and deterrence in the emerging political order.

What do we mean by NSNC?

We can define NSNC in several ways. They can be seen narrowly as events that are significant to outside powers because nuclear weapons or other weapons of mass destruction are used or are seen as imminent. NSNC could begin when states that possess nuclear weapons are involved in a crisis, and these states take actions designed to make nuclear or conventional forces ready for use, thereby signalling to other states that nuclear weapons could be used. The broader and more satisfying definition is that NSNC analytically cover the entire range of events on the spectrum of heightened tensions, political crises, and conflicts between states that possess nuclear weapons. This implies that de-escalatory measure (DM) and other CBMs should not apply only when a nuclear conflict is imminent but through all stages of a crisis.

The intent is to make the term 'NSNC' cover a wide range of circumstances because it makes it easier to understand the nature of these crises and the role of DMs in crises involving regional powers. A narrower focus would limit our inquiry to a small subset of the crises that occurred in the past or that could occur in the future. This intellectual framework for NSNC provides a foundation for considering methods and approaches to terminating or de-escalating crises between nuclear-armed states.

8.2 ORIGINS AND STRUCTURE OF NSNC

The intellectual proposition that is embedded throughout this chapter is that American, allied, and presumably Soviet thinking about nuclear crises necessarily reflect their own cultural biases, experiences and previous actions. They were, after all, the antagonists in two nuclear crises: the 'real' crisis in 1962 over the presence of Soviet missiles in Cuba, and the 'lesser' crisis in 1973 during the Yom Kippur War when American nuclear forces were alerted in response to the potential deployment of Israeli nuclear weapons and the movement of Soviet airborne forces to the Middle East. To the extent that other nuclear-armed states (the United Kingdom and France) were involved in these crises, they played a decidedly minor role as allies of the United States rather than contestants.

There are three assumptions that should guide our thinking about nuclear crises that could occur between the end of the twentieth century and the beginning of the next. The first is that towards the end of the cold war, the superpowers (the US, the Soviet Union and China) and major powers like the United Kingdom and France are substantially less likely to find themselves in crises with other similarly powerful nuclear-armed states. With the collapse of communism, the revolutionary changes in Eastern Europe and the Soviet Union, and the decline in East–West tensions, it is increasingly difficult to imagine a war involving nuclear weapons between the nuclear giants.

Second, during the next two or three decades, regional nuclear crises involving the emerging nuclear powers (Israel, Pakistan, India, Brazil, South Africa, Iraq, and Iran, at a minimum) are more than a remote possibility. For example, in early April 1990, border tensions over the state of Kashmir put India and Pakistan on the brink of war.[5] Recent events in the Iraq–Kuwait crisis suggest that the prospect of war between the superpowers and regional powers has increased.

Third, in future nuclear crises, the ability of superpowers and second-tier nuclear powers (the United Kingdom, France and China) to exercise political control will be quite limited. One reason is that we have no evidence that these nascent nuclear powers will adhere to the 'rules' of the nuclear era or that they will be as cautious or risk-averse as the superpowers. The United States and Soviet Union always acted on the assumption that the potential devastation of a nuclear conflict imposed powerful limits on behavior. Today, however, there are sound reasons for questioning whether the rational and pragmatic paradigm of deterrence will apply in future crises. Moreover, the end of bipolarity probably will mean less control by the superpowers over former clients, which now are more willing to take risks and follow their own agendas.

It is difficult to determine whether nascent nuclear powers will adhere to the nuclear rules of the game. Consider for illustrative purposes the case of Iran and Iraq. The dilemma is how to demonstrate to our satisfaction that potential nuclear powers such as Iran and Iraq will be rational actors in a nuclear crisis when they were involved in a nearly decade-long war in which nearly one million died. How reticent will they be to use nuclear weapons when the 500 000 casualties that Iran suffered in the war with Iraq is comparable to the losses it would suffer in an Iraqi attack with several nuclear weapons against military, economic, and urban targets – or that Iraq would suffer in an Iranian nuclear attack? Who could have imagined that Iraq would challenge the United States and the rest of the world, given the vast military and economic resources that can be brought to bear on it and thus outstrip it in any process of escalation?

These events hardly constitute absolute evidence of systemic irrationality, but it nonetheless highlights that no automatic connection exists between the standards that existed during the nuclear crises of the cold war and those that could occur in the future. Recent Iraqi and Israeli posturing over Iraq's threat to retaliate against Israel with chemically-armed ballistic missiles is not reassuring.[6] Nor is the sequence of events in the Iraq–Kuwait crisis.

Reasons for NSNC

It is not difficult to explain why NSNC could occur in the future. There are two trends that have changed the ability of states to possess and use nuclear weapons. The first is the proliferation of nuclear weapons. More nations now possess nuclear weapons than was the case two decades ago and an even larger number are likely to possess them in the next several decades. In addition to the United States, the Soviet Union, China, France, the United Kingdom, and India, there are the putative nuclear powers: Israeli, South Africa, and Pakistan; and those that may become nuclear powers in the not-too-distant future: Argentina, Brazil, Iraq, Iran, and possibly South Korea and Japan.

The second is the proliferation in the means for delivering nuclear weapons.[7] A number of states, including China, have been selling ballistic missiles with ranges of a thousand or more kilometers. As *The Economist* warned, 'At least 22 third-world countries are at present trying to buy or build [ballistic] missiles.'[8] In addition to ballistic missiles, many of these states have or soon will have advanced aircraft which are capable and highly effective instruments for delivering nuclear weapons. Israel, for example, has relied on aircraft as the primary means for delivering nuclear weapons. Many states are in a similar position.

The broad point is that the technologies which are necessary for inclusion in the nuclear club have become more widely available, and this has almost certainly expanded the number of potential antagonists in nuclear crises.

Simply having nuclear weapons and delivery vehicles does not necessarily mean that crises are more likely to occur or that they will be fairly regular events in the next century. Nor does it offer any contrary evidence that nuclear crises are a predictable consequence of states learning the destructive power of nuclear weapons and their potential for devastating a society. One hopes that the proliferation of technologies somehow may educate the Third World about the horrors of war and thus we will face crises but not nuclear wars.

Regrettably, it is difficult to argue convincingly that the number of states that possess nuclear weapons provides a reliable indicator of the probability that these crises will occur. Because the number of states that will own nuclear weapons is growing, the implication is that nuclear crises are far more likely to occur. However satisfying this linear reasoning is, it simply does not provide useful insights into the political, economic, or military forces that will fuel these crises, the events that may unfold in a crisis, or the policies that outside powers may pursue to prevent or terminate them.

It is evident, however, that some of the states that are or may soon become nuclear powers have been troubled by a variety of tensions. Some have been involved in wars with their neighbors in recent years. For example, even though South Africa is among the states that seem less likely to be involved in NSNC, it is embroiled in a bitter domestic contest over apartheid, has been involved in disputes with neighboring states, and could see a radical change in the power structure during the next decade.[9] On the subcontinent, India and Pakistan have longstanding animosities that have resulted in wars. In 1990 these states were involved in military alerts on their common border that involved several hundred thousand troops and that had clear implications for a potential nuclear crisis. We could even speculate about a splintering of the Soviet Union into warring republics, each with a substantial number of nuclear forces.[10]

The more extreme and worrisome cases are in the Middle East and Persian Gulf. Israel has a long history of tensions with its Arab neighbors and has been involved in several wars with them. Both Iran and Iraq have longstanding animosities toward both one another and other states in the region, most recently evidenced by the Iran–Iraq War and the recent Iraqi invasion of Kuwait. On the other hand, there are states in South America like Argentina and Brazil that seen less likely to become involved in NSNC because their disputes have been less violent.

Is it safe to infer that NSNC will follow from the 'causes' which dominated earlier crises, or that a state's historical record is one sign of its candidacy for involvement in NSNC? A variety of reasons exist for the involvement of nuclear-armed states in NSNC.

The first and most probable are *political* conflicts over territory or the tensions that are rooted in historic animosities. One example is the Iran–Iraq War, waged for territorial reasons after an invasion by Iraq in 1980 and fueled by longstanding tensions and the determination of idiosyncratic leaderships to avoid losing. There are religious or ideological forces that motivate these crises, as we saw in the tensions between the Sunni and Shi'ite sects of Islam in the Iran–Iraq War.

Even if there are ideological and political frictions, *economic* forces will be a factor in crises that develop between nuclear-armed states. The decision of Iraq to invade Kuwait for oil revenue presumably was in part taken for economic reasons.

It is important to emphasize that the causes of NSNC are not likely to parallel those that fueled superpower nuclear crises. Unlike the ideological differences that fueled the cold war and various crises between the superpowers, the violent antagonisms that many potential actors in NSNC feel toward one another are rooted in extreme *religious* differences. Many states or peoples have deeply-rooted antagonisms that go back in some cases for thousands of years and thus are far more enduring than the decades-deep antagonism between the United States and the Soviet Union. At the same time, the United States and Soviet Union do not share the common borders that can contribute to tensions and crises. The same cannot be said of many of the regional powers in the Middle or Far East which will possess nuclear weapons in the next decade or two.

8.3 TAXONOMY OF EVENTS

In order to have any analytic value, observations about events in these crises must not be tied to specific regions, states, or particular scenarios. If we are to evaluate measures and actions that can be taken by the superpowers or antagonists to terminate or de-escalate NSNC, the best step is to derive general principles about the evolution of NSNC that transcend the actions of individual states. The advantage to working through the mechanics of these crises is that it helps to identify significant factors in the termination of NSNC, and deduce whether and how NSNC can be terminated before they escalate.

Actions with nuclear forces

There are a number of actions that can be taken with nuclear forces during NSNC. We should note, however, that at any point these crises could de-escalate or stalemate if both states limit themselves to actions that did not go beyond alerting their nuclear forces.

Alert nuclear forces. The lowest operational level in NSNC is when a state alerts its nuclear forces.[11] This can be done covertly even though it is nearly certain that outside powers will detect these actions, or overtly in order to use public gestures as a way to send a signal of intent. The practical effect is to lessen the vulnerability of the forces, and to alert others to the seriousness of the crisis.

One imagines that the response of the other state(s) would be to alert their own nuclear forces, both as a counter to the original alert and to lessen and thereby equalize the vulnerability of their nuclear forces. In contrast to the superpowers, however, these states may not have the intelligence facilities that are necessary to detect the size, location, or readiness of the opponent's deployed forces.[12] This suggests that much of the activity by antagonists in NSNC may be conducted in the blind. Unlike the superpowers, these states will have quite limited means for gauging the extent of the adversary's preparations. One effect may be to increase the probability of surprise attacks and more generally to make these crises less stable.[13]

Threats to employ nuclear weapons. In NSNC states could threaten to use their nuclear forces. The threat could be made in public in an ambiguous form – that it will use whatever force is necessary to resolve the crisis – or, less likely, as a bold statement of the intent to use nuclear weapons. An alternative is that the threat to use force could be made in private communications to one or several states in a region and may not explicitly mention nuclear weapons.

Threats to use nuclear weapons could be related to conditions in an ongoing conventional war. Moreover, nuclear threats against urban areas could escalate both the conventional war and the crisis.

Nuclear first-use or preemption. Faced by alerted nuclear forces or the threat, even if it is not stated explicitly, that another state may use nuclear weapons, states might use nuclear weapons first against a variety of targets in anticipation that the opponent is about to do the same. In contrast to the superpowers, however, these states may not have credible preemptive options. We will examine in the next section a number of factors which will determine how nuclear weapons could be used in NSNC.

Retaliation or follow-on use. Once a crisis has escalated to the point where nuclear weapons have been used, the victim(s) of the attack(s) can respond in kind with nuclear weapons. This is not to exclude the possibility that retaliation will take the form of other means, such as war with conventional forces, terrorism, or economic sanctions, but only to note that a state which is attacked with nuclear weapons will at least consider retaliation in kind with nuclear weapons. The options and timing of retaliation can vary, as we examine in the next section.

Factors affecting nuclear use

Small Nuclear Arsenals. States involved in NSNC are likely to have relatively small nuclear arsenals with perhaps 100 and at *most* several hundred weapons. Thus, any nuclear attacks perforce will be quite limited. Nonetheless, nuclear powers will be able to inflict moderate to severe damage. Although these attacks will not be large by the standards common in US or Soviet parlance, they will be immensely significant to countries like Iran, Saudi Arabia, Pakistan, Israel, or India. An attack with ten nuclear weapons against urban targets, for instance, would have devastating consequences for any of the smaller societies as it would destroy, for all practical purposes, the core of that society.

The number of attacking and surviving warheads probably will not vary in relative terms depending on who strikes first or second, for two reasons. The first is that these states are unlikely to have the ability to destroy their opponent's forces. This is significantly different from a superpower exchange in which each nation has the ability to destroy proportionately more weapons than it launches if it attacks first, even though the ability to retaliate with surviving forces is not eliminated. Until the developing countries reach the point where they possess accurate ballistic missiles with multiple warheads, their ability to destroy nuclear forces will be highly constrained because the exchange ratios would favor the victim of the attack. When we reach that point in the next several decades, these crises will be far less stable.

The second is that nuclear weapons are likely to be used on a *quid pro quo* basis. States will not have large numbers of weapons or the ability to employ large packages of nuclear weapons, and hence will use nuclear weapons quite sparingly. This lessens the value of using nuclear weapons first and enhances crisis stability. It also suggests that these states will use nuclear weapons on a small scale in response to the adversary's actions.

Limited delivery means. The nascent nuclear powers will have quite limited means for delivering nuclear weapons. While some states will possess relatively inaccurate ballistic missiles, the majority will rely on aircraft as the primary means for delivering nuclear weapons. They will rely on aircraft because they offer greater precision and reliability than primitive, first-generation ballistic missiles. States that possess missiles could use them against a wide range of targets, but countries armed with ballistic missiles are no more likely to preempt than those without them because these missiles will not be accurate enough to destroy nuclear forces. While the superpowers almost certainly would use ballistic missiles or aircraft in an initial attack, smaller states are more likely to use missiles to attack urban areas. This, too, will change when these nations develop more advanced and accurate ballistic missiles.

States do not necessarily have to follow this targeting scheme. For instance, political and economic centers do not have to be targeted at the outset of a conflict but could occur toward the end of the conflict. Likewise, attacks against targets of military value could occur later in a NSNC.

States may behave in quite unexpected ways. For example, instead of engaging in ineffective counter-military attacks, an irrational and vengeful state might attack one or two political or economic centers at the outset, leave nuclear forces or other forces of mass destruction intact for the moment (perhaps believing that it cannot destroy the enemy's nuclear forces), and hope to convince the victims to terminate the crisis. One example is an attack by Iraq with chemically-armed ballistic missiles against Israel. As in the West, a less powerful state might be intimidated and thereby compelled to terminate the NSNC if it were confronted by the imminent destruction of its cities. It is conceivable that states will want to avoid urban centers or keep retaliation proportionate to the attack in order to avoid further escalation. It is equally conceivable, however, that these states will act in unpredictable ways. The United States and outside powers, therefore, should not expect that other states will follow the 'western logic' of nuclear deterrence.

Potential targets. There are three potential types of targets in NSNC. In preemptive or first-use attacks, *military* targets include nuclear forces (e.g. missile sites or airfields) and command and control locations. If the crisis is precipitated by a conventional war, a range of targets that is associated with conventional forces (e.g. troop formations, supply depots, and so forth) could be attacked. There also are *political* targets; leadership sites (possibly in urban areas), urban areas, and targets of political or religious significance, such as the Great Mosque in Mecca. The third are *economic* targets, which include industrial facilities, oil refineries, and ports, to name but a few.

Geography. NSNC will be regional events that are likely to involve a relatively small number of states who are able to attack targets in the intermediate range (1500 miles or less). The regions from which NSNC could originate are the Middle East, Far East and Latin America. With the exception of China, and perhaps India in the more distant future, none of these states could mount attacks of intercontinental range. But the fact that NSNC are likely to be regional affairs during the next several decades does not necessarily imply that the superpowers and other large powers will be excluded from involvement. The Soviet Union, for instance, lies within range of potential nuclear-armed states in the Middle East and Far East that harbor ideological and political hostility toward the Soviet Union. And the United States has deployed forces in Saudi Arabia in the Iraq–Kuwait crisis. The United States and Soviet Union clearly could be drawn into NSNC.

In the taxonomy of events that could occur in NSNC, several circumstances are likely to dominate any use of nuclear weapons. The first is that there will be little warning of an attack. These states do not have sophisticated warning systems and will not be able to detect an attack until nuclear detonations occur. The consequence is that NSNC could be quite unstable. In particular, if states fear that a surprise attack could disrupt their command and control of nuclear forces and endanger their ability to conduct a retaliatory attack, incentives to use nuclear weapons first could increase.

Second, a factor that mitigates the tendency toward instability is that these states will not possess credible means to destroy nuclear forces on a preemptive basis. They have no reason to fear that they will lose nuclear forces in a counter-military attack, concerns regarding the command and control of weapons notwithstanding.

Third, any exchange of nuclear weapons in NSNC will be quite small, typically on the order of fewer than ten weapons. Most states will not possess large nuclear arsenals and the weapons that they do have will be low-yield. A 'typical' exchange might be a regional attack conducted with a small number of weapons delivered by inaccurate ballistic missiles or aircraft.

Fourth, the targets in NSNC will be primarily political and economic in nature. These states will not have the means to conduct counterforce attacks against nuclear forces, but will be able to strike cities and economic facilities. Such attacks could be extremely effective and able to inflict relatively high levels of damage if directed against industrial facilities or urban populations.

8.4 TERMINATION OF NSNC

There are fundamentally two types of NSNC – those that involve the use of nuclear weapons and those that do not. Whether nuclear weapons are used will have a profound effect on the ways in which NSNC may be terminated. In this section we consider some of the choices that outside powers are likely to confront. The next section examines DMs and their value to both antagonists and outside powers.

No nuclear use – gradual wind-down

In view of the enormous economic and human costs that a nuclear war poses, states simply may allow a crisis to wind-down before nuclear weapons are used. If states pursue risk-averse strategies, they will avoid actions that escalate the crisis. Throughout a crisis there will be pressures on the antagonists to take unilateral or bilateral actions that are designed to defuse the crisis. Here we examine two broad approaches and their associated risks that outside powers will face.

Do-nothing strategy. If nuclear weapons have not been used, outside powers will face less pressure to take any explicit actions or measures to force the antagonists to terminate a crisis. Incentives to wait as long as possible at the sidelines in the hope that intervention is not necessary will be consistent with the cautious behavior of the superpowers and regional nuclear powers. At the same time, if outside powers intervene they run the risk that the antagonists could respond with force, including the use of nuclear weapons.

An important component of thinking in the West may be the belief that these matters are best left to the antagonists, for two reasons. The first is the belief that other states have no right to intervene unless nuclear weapons are used. This thinking may be a reflection of isolationist tendencies in the United States. It may also be a product of colonialism and the inclination to avoid intervention in the affairs of other states unless the circumstances are compelling. The second is the hope that these crises will de-escalate on their own. While there may be some reluctance to intervene, this probably will fade once nuclear weapons have been used. States may feel that it is proper to intervene only *after* nuclear weapons are used.

There are many reasons why outside powers, especially those that are within the range of the nuclear forces of the antagonists, will think that the risks of intervention are too great. But the fact that outside powers are likely to hesitate before they intervene does not provide evidence of a predisposition to stand idly by while a crisis escalates to a nuclear conflict. In these circumstances, the best route for outside powers is to engage the antagonists in negotiations.

Negotiated termination. One mechanism for terminating a crisis is for outside powers to help the antagonists negotiate an end to the crisis. A nuclear crisis can be brought to an end through negotiations in one of two ways. The first case entails appeals by the antagonists to outside powers for their help in starting negotiations both before or after the use of nuclear weapons. In the second case, outside powers can be proactive, serving as intermediaries in the negotiations and using their power or influence to induce the states to negotiate. Their interest could reflect concerns that if the crisis remains unchecked, it will escalate to the point where outside powers are attacked.

There is a range of negotiation measures available to outside powers. This includes outside powers and international organizations who could help the warring parties with negotiations. Perhaps the most important is to offer their 'good offices' in beginning negotiations between the antagonists. While this could occur at any stage in a crisis, it is more plausible before the use of nuclear weapons. Another would be proposals to stand down the antagonists' nuclear forces and to implement other CBMs in order to buy time and thus avoid war. CBMs would have their greatest value when negotiations with outside powers have started. For example, superpower support for de-escalatory measures would add credibility and momentum to the process. Also, outside powers might offer to use their national technical means to de-escalate the crisis by verifying that the alert level of nuclear forces has been reduced or that the forces have been 'stood down'.

In many ways, the prospect of outside powers choosing to intervene reactively through negotiation is the most satisfying, given the Soviet Union's domestic plight, its reluctance to engage in external military actions, and historical US isolationist tendencies. It is an option that minimizes the risk to outside powers because it does not put them in the middle of a crisis, does not force them to choose sides or appear to do so, and does not compel them to use force if a crisis is resolved by the negotiations. However, outside powers may be more likely to take an active role in the de-escalation process, including the use of force, if negotiations fail and the crisis is seen as threatening superpower interests.

Nuclear use

The grim alternatives to the above scenarios are those that escalate to the use of nuclear weapons. While the antagonists could continue to use nuclear weapons, it is more likely that the conflict would be terminated by the antagonists themselves or with the help of outside powers. Any hesitation to do so almost certainly will fade once the outside powers confront the devastating effects that nuclear attacks will have on their vital interests. However, if these states are not rational actors, wanton destruction may not end the crisis. Still, the antagonists are more likely to recoil from the prospect of further nuclear attacks and to look favorably on the efforts of outside powers to end the crisis if they cannot do so themselves.

Once a crisis has reached the point where nuclear weapons are used, powerful pressures will build on outside powers to intervene. While NSNC can be terminated by both the explicit actions of the antagonists and the actions of outside powers prior to nuclear use, outside powers may be certain to intervene once nuclear weapons have been used. In fact, the antagonists may hope the use of nuclear weapons will force outside powers to intervene because of outside powers' fears of the effects of a nuclear war on their interests or their eventual involvement.

Enforcing an end to a crisis. If a crisis reaches the point where nuclear weapons are used, outside powers will have to consider measures to end it themselves. If the antagonists have not responded to attempts to end the crisis through negotiations, outside powers may have to *compel* the antagonists to end the crisis. The clear implication of 'enforced termination' is that outside powers threaten or actually use force to end the crisis. At one extreme, outside powers collectively could threaten to use both nuclear or conventional force against the nation that uses nuclear forces first or even against all states which use nuclear weapons.

Outside powers and regional states are likely to understand that the risks of intervention in NSNC cannot be taken lightly. They must understand that the decision to use force against the antagonists could make them potential victims of a nuclear attack. Would outside powers attempt to prevent a limited regional nuclear war from escalating to a full-scale attack with tens or perhaps several hundreds of weapons? Quite simply, non-intervention increases the chances that nuclear weapons will be used, creating chaos among the allies that contribute to regional stability. That prospect makes it easy for us to cite compelling political, military, or economic reasons for states to believe that intervention is consistent with their interests. Very few outside powers will believe it is sensible, given the dangers inherent in a situation in which states are trading nuclear blows, to watch idly as the antagonists inflict great harm on themselves and others.

Four categories of states or political entities could feel compelled to help avert further nuclear use. The first are regional powers that do not possess nuclear weapons. They will have the strongest motivation to end a crisis but the least military leverage. In many cases the best they will be able to do is to act as intermediaries. The second are the regional powers which are themselves nuclear-armed. These states will be able to influence events because nuclear powers can implicitly threaten the military involvement of outside nuclear powers. The third are the superpowers as well as the already-mentioned nuclear-armed states that can use their nuclear and conventional power to put pressure on the antagonists. Their leverage is a direct function of their ability to use nuclear weapons and the belief that they will intervene to prevent the destruction of economic and political interests. Finally, supra-national institutions, most notably the United Nations, have some limited ability to put pressure on the antagonists to terminate the crisis.

Termination measures before or after nuclear use

If outside powers decide that the use of force is the only way to terminate NSNC, it may reduce their options to actions that disarm the antagonists. What options would be available? An effective option would be to destroy the antagonists' nuclear forces before the regional crisis threatens to spiral out of control. There are punitive measures as well. A broad range of military and civilian targets could be attacked with conventional weapons in order to destroy the ability to use nuclear weapons or to use military forces. During the Gulf Crisis of 1990, the multi-national force in the Middle East attacked a number of facilities in Iraq both to forestall attacks with chemically-armed ballistic missiles and to weaken the Iraqi military.[14]

Powerful states may be able to exercise considerable influence if they convince the antagonists that the costs of allowing the crisis to continue are greater than the antagonists are willing to accept. That strength is increased if these states act in concert, as part of an alliance (e.g. NATO or the Warsaw Pact), or in cooperation across alliance boundaries. In today's world, it is not too difficult to imagine the United States and the Soviet Union acting in cooperation to end a crisis if the crisis escalates to the point where they or their interests were threatened with nuclear weapons. Even the *non-nuclear* crisis involving Iraq produced a remarkable degree of US–Soviet cooperation.[15]

The great powers will possess far more credibility than the less powerful states when it comes to the threat to use force to end a crisis, particularly if they act in concert with other states. This does not mean, however, that lesser powers have only a marginal role in terminating a crisis. Smaller states are not precluded from taking decisive actions to increase their capability, as the Israeli attack in 1981 against Iraq's nuclear reactor at Osirak testifies. The possession of nuclear weapons strengthens this credibility.

8.5 TERMINATION AND DE-ESCALATORY MEASURES

De-escalatory CBMs may play important roles in the termination of NSNC. DMs involve more than simply standing-down nuclear forces; they can directly influence the ability to terminate or at a minimum de-escalate crises before they spiral out of control. Thus, it is useful to examine the relationship between the value of de-escalatory measures and events in NSNC discussed above.

Hypothetical de-escalatory measures

There are several examples of de-escalatory measures that could be used to terminate NSNC. The first is for the antagonists to refrain from alerting their nuclear forces when tensions increase or to reduce the readiness of forces in a crisis.[16] While the reconnaissance capabilities of these states will be quite modest, the standing-down of nuclear weapons and their launchers may be passed along to the antagonists by outside states that detect these actions.

The second is for states to forgo actions that indicate an increased perception of war. For example, refraining from evacuating leadership cadres or urban populations signals that conflict is not anticipated and that the increased vulnerability of their societies is an acceptable risk.

A third measure is to terminate the hostilities that created the pressure to use nuclear weapons. The most likely source of pressure to use nuclear weapons in NSNC is a conventional war that both sides are seeking to win. Losses on the battlefield are a powerful incentive for states to use nuclear weapons, and thus ending a conventional war will reduce these pressures.

Factors affecting the value of DMs

DMs can have two broad functions. First, they should add order to the undoubtedly disorderly actions of nations which threaten nuclear use to signal how serious the crisis has become. Second, they can provide firebreaks to contain a crisis before nuclear weapons are used. De-escalatory measures can be useful instruments both for outside powers that are searching for ways to end NSNC and as instruments by the antagonists themselves. In this review of DMs, we explore some of their consequences for and limitations in nuclear crises.

De-escalatory measures are voluntary. DMs fundamentally rest on voluntary compliance. Two important issues are whether they can be anything other than voluntary, and whether they can be made to work if they are not voluntary. By their nature, DMs are actions which, if they are to be effective, must depend on the forbearance of the states in whose name they are being employed. These measures imply that the antagonists themselves employ DMs and accept them as a useful way to help end the crisis and that there are prior agreements on the role of DMs. If outside powers are involved in the de-escalation process (e.g. as mediators), the antagonists must clearly accept or be willing to consider DMs suggested by the outside powers. If there is no such acceptance, then we are talking not of de-escalatory measures but of forced and unwelcome intervention by outside powers.

DMs reflect nuclear 'history'. If DMs and CBMs are to have some practical benefit, it will be necessary for regional nuclear powers to learn the lessons of the history of US–Soviet relations. Before these regional powers can effectively employ DMs, the major nuclear powers may wish to encourage potential nuclear powers to build their own 'history', so to speak, on nuclear issues. A fascinating question is whether these emerging nuclear powers are going to follow the intellectual style of the Americans and Soviets in the 1940s and 1950s, when large-scale, spasmodic attacks against a society dominated our thinking about nuclear deterrence or whether they will leap quietly into a stable order.

DMs depend on rational actors. If irrational actors are dominant, it will pose almost irreconcilable problems for controlling these crises. In the wake of the profound influence of the United States and Soviet Union, the developing world may have a psychological dependence on the superpowers which effectively inhibits the development of alternative responses for dealing with nuclear crises. The superpowers and other major nuclear states may, therefore, want to begin exploring the issues of termination and DMs as part of broad discussions with nascent nuclear powers on the role of nuclear weapons in the future.

Superpower interest in NSNC is uncertain. Perhaps in the future there will be superpower interest in regional initiatives that lead to the creation of approaches to managing nuclear crises and their integration into policy. De-escalatory measures are a prominent example of responses that will be useful. Until that is done, however, DMs are likely to be limited to superpower nuclear crisis termination. The larger question is whether DMs will gain the superpower institutional history that is needed before they can be practical in the 'second' nuclear age of NSNC. Outside intervention in NSNC is discussed in detail below.

Western-style DMs may not be relevant to NSNC. It was not by accident that the examples cited earlier in this chapter concerning the structure of NSNC contained references to US and Soviet experiences with nuclear weapons. These undoubtedly had a profound effect on our thinking about nuclear crises. If how we think about NSNC is a reflection of the past, and there is no reason why it should not, the states which could one day be involved in NSNC may not have faith in de-escalatory measures. They may distrust them as 'western', 'infidel' or 'imperialistic' contrivances, or as examples of attempts by the superpowers to exercise control over and meddle in the affairs of states that only now are joining the 'nuclear club'. The central question, therefore, for DMs and CBMs is whether these can be institutionalized as a regular part of state-to-state relations. Then, the problem would be manageable because we could proceed in a rather mechanical fashion to search for the points in a crisis when DMs could be useful.

The unyielding fact is that DMs are an intrinsic part of the thinking that spawned the theories of deterrence and crisis management in the 1950s and 1960s. The presumption is that the use, as distinct from the threat of using, nuclear weapons is irrational and ought to be avoided, and further that we can derive some benefit from actions which involve cooperation among states that jointly agree on the irrationality of nuclear war and that lessen the chance of war. To confirm the hypothesis that DMs are a part of the theories of deterrence and crisis management which transcend cultures and values, there are examples when states that possessed nuclear weapons exercised caution and restraint in crises or conflicts. The border clashes in Kashmir between India and Pakistan in the spring of 1990 is an excellent example.[17] Another instance was the Saudi Arabian declaration to renounce the acquisition of nuclear weapons.

While such qualities may be absent among some states, others have demonstrated that they see some merit in these 'western' inventions. There are reports that India and Pakistan now are discussing CBMs in light of their recent close brush with war.[18]

The worrisome prospect is that these measures will not apply universally to all crises, and that leaves open the possibility that some day a nuclear crisis will spiral out of control.

Reflections on outside intervention

The natural preference is for a nuclear crisis to wind-down gradually before nuclear weapons are used. Should a crisis reach the point where nuclear weapons are used, however, it is likely that outside powers will act to ensure that the crisis is terminated either through enforcement or negotiation. Any use of nuclear weapons will increase the incentive of outside powers to compel the antagonists to negotiate, even if they must use or threaten the use of their own military forces. While the antagonists will resent outside intervention, it is preferable for outside powers to incur their wrath than it is to see the uncontrolled or spasmodic use of nuclear weapons. Outside powers will rightly believe that controlling escalation and ending a conflict are in the interests of all states, especially if there are questions about the ability of antagonists to effectively control their nuclear forces. Both enforced and negotiated terminations offer a mechanism to the antagonists for stopping a war that will be destructive even if it cannot last long given the small size of nuclear arsenals in the Third World.

The threshold for intervention for outside powers ultimately is the question of whether nuclear weapons will be used. The consequences of a regional nuclear war are simply too great for outside powers to remain uninvolved. One example is the economic devastation that a nuclear attack would inflict on oil production facilities in the Middle East. Beyond the fact that the industrialized societies depend upon oil, the consequences for regional stability also would be too great to bear.

While there are no rough rules of thumb for gauging when outside powers intervene, in part because there may not be agreement among outside powers, a reasonable guess is that the detonation of one or perhaps two nuclear weapons will be sufficient to mobilize the rest of the world. At that point outside powers will attempt to get the antagonists to negotiate. Should nuclear weapons continue to be used after that, we would expect outside powers to enforce some kind of termination.

There are limits to outside intervention. First, the more aggressive and violent the termination measures, the less likely they are to be used. States are far more likely to push negotiations than they are to threaten or actually use force to end a crisis. One obvious exception is a crisis that escalates to the point where the employment of nuclear weapons threatens political, military, and economic resources, or in which the conflict threatens to spill over into other states.

Second, the more persuasive measures to end a crisis that involve the use of force clearly are the province of the more powerful states. The United Kingdom, the Soviet Union, or the United States could threaten to retaliate against a nuclear-armed Iraq, for instance, if it used nuclear weapons. However, threats from states like Iran, Egypt, or Saudi Arabia simply are not as credible because these states do not possess nuclear weapons or have the ability to use them in a decisive fashion. Negotiations are the instrument of choice for the less powerful states and the United Nations because they do not have the military power to compel states to terminate a crisis. The more important observation is that nuclear crises may be controlled best by the threat to use nuclear weapons.

The superpowers and significant nuclear powers will confront the fundamental question of whether they are willing to intervene to terminate NSNC. The corollary is whether other states will believe that the superpowers are willing to enforce DMs on non-compliant states. The superpowers have nothing to gain by allowing NSNC to reach their own, possibly violent, conclusion. They will want to avoid the dislocation that will result from destruction of economic targets, and to prevent the instability that is a likely consequence of a regional nuclear war. We can envision, however, that a nuclear war might make a region very stable if one power dominates.

If a crisis or war were to involve militarily-capable powers or the dominant regional power, remain confined to a region, and not involve the use of nuclear weapons, outside powers are unlikely to intervene militarily in the ways we have described. But that will change instantly if any outside powers or the superpowers are attacked with nuclear weapons. This is the moment when outside powers will have to decide whether and how they will intervene. It is also a time when DMs would have limited appeal unless they were enforced. The other possibility that cannot be dismissed is that if one of the antagonists in a nuclear crisis attacks an outside power with nuclear weapons, a devastating counterblow will be unleashed. It is this sort of fear that could help more than any other factor to contain a crisis.

Reflections on DMs

For the superpowers or any outside powers that do not wish to allow a nuclear crisis to escalate, DMs are a supremely rational choice, because they provide *a form for thinking about how to terminate a crisis prior to the use of nuclear weapons.* As an extension of the rational-actor paradigm of nuclear deterrence for governing the actions of states in a crisis, DMs are another mechanism to which we can point as evidence of concerted efforts to think and plan in advance about how we might act in a nuclear crisis.

There is no evidence to the contrary that DMs are more than a reflection of American and Soviet ways of thinking about nuclear crises and that these have no 'following' in the states which are likely to be involved in NSNC. The point is that outside powers may not want to become involved for a number of reasons and that this can limit the opportunities for de-escalation.

De-escalatory measures can be useful even if the domain they cover is quite limited. One reason for outlining the structure of nuclear crises is to make the point that there are three circumstances in which DMs can have value. The first is if the rational actor model applies to states that are engaged in nuclear crises. The second is if nuclear weapons have not been used in the crisis. And the third is if there is confidence in the ability of outside powers to enforce DMs. The danger is that these circumstances may not apply all of the time.

In summary, DMs can be useful to antagonists and outside powers alike if four general conditions are met. The first is that there must be some form of cooperation between the antagonists. Second, there must be common agreement on the value of termination. There would not be much sense to DMs if the antagonists were determined to destroy their enemy at all costs. Third, there must be a general consensus that the use of nuclear weapons is to be avoided (or limited) at all costs. Fourth, there has to be prior agreement on the value of DMs as a means for terminating nuclear crises. Without such agreement, states will find it difficult to undertake the cooperative and voluntary measures that DMs imply.

8.6 CONCLUSIONS

This chapter has alluded to several transcendent issues about nuclear weapons and crises that clarify how we think about nuclear weapons and the prospects for controlling or terminating NSNC. The issues have been framed primarily in the form of the questions that we should ponder in an inquiry about the relationship between nuclear weapons and future crises. This section offers some early answers to these questions.

Observations

There are several basic observations about NSNC in this chapter that should be articulated in some detail. The first is that most of our thinking on crises and de-escalation has been dominated by the experiences of the United States, the Soviet Union, and their respective allies during the cold war. It is quite likely that our experiences with nuclear weapons, ideology, and great-power politics are far too narrow for the circumstances in NSNC. To put the matter bluntly, the emphasis on 'western' experiences may be misleading and wrong for the next generation of nuclear crises.

The second is that actors in NSNC may not be rational. The contrast with the cold war could not be more stark when we consider that rationality was the dominant assumption in deterrence and in all the actions that states take to create stable and predictable points. Irrational actors are likely to be the major cause of NSNC. They will be driven by deeply-embedded religious and ideological schisms that know no counterpart in western societies. It is the presence of nuclear weapons in these societies that is most profoundly unsettling and the cause of concerns that NSNC may be quite unstable. This is the major difference between the nuclear crises in the past in which nuclear weapons were not used and those of the future in which we cannot be sanguine about the prospects for peace.

The third observation concerns the taxonomy of events in nuclear crises. States in NSNC will not have the ability to destroy the nuclear forces of their adversary in the near future. The size of their arsenals will not be affected by using nuclear weapons first or second, and hence there is no advantage to going first. But while their fear of preemption will be small, it does not mean that they will refrain from using nuclear weapons. The targets of choice will be limited largely to urban areas and economic centers. The implication is that NSNC will involve the indiscriminate destruction of urban areas and the infliction of enormous civilian casualties. Economic facilities, such as oil fields, also will be destroyed.

Fourth, outside powers will hesitate to offer their services in negotiations, but they will be forced to be involved if the use of nuclear weapons is imminent. Once nuclear weapons have been used, there will be no choice. The involvement of outside powers will be certain.

Fifth, if the stakes are high enough, outside powers will enforce an end to NSNC even if they have to use their own nuclear weapons. The costs of the unrestrained use of nuclear weapons anywhere in the world is hardly something that the western industrialized powers can countenance.

Constraints on our thinking

The state of our thinking about NSNC is governed by the paradigm that governed US–Soviet relations in the cold war. The only paradigm that we have for NSNC is derived from the superpower nuclear crises in the 1950s, 1960s, and 1970s. The crisis paradigm borrows heavily from the theories of deterrence and the various 'theologies' about the employment of nuclear weapons that gained prominence in the 1960s. It is profoundly unsettling, however, when we realize that conventional thinking about NSNC is one-dimensional because it ignores the cultural, historical, and political factors that govern the behavior of states in nuclear crises. The deep historical and religious differences among emerging nuclear powers will make it more difficult to de-escalate NSNC.

The more important observation is that terminating a crisis between the emerging nuclear powers in the next several decades will not necessarily be relevant to the events that could transpire in a US–Soviet nuclear crisis. These states may have grievances that are not amenable to the rational actor 'doctrine' that governed US–Soviet conduct in the cold war crises and controlled the process of escalation.

Our understanding of the role of *de-escalatory measures* in nuclear crises borrows heavily from the logic of nuclear deterrence that grew out of the cold war. Embedded deeply within that paradigm are two assumptions: first, that the use of nuclear weapons is a patently irrational act, and second that states will end a nuclear crisis as quickly as possible in order to avoid the use of nuclear weapons. We simply cannot assume that states will act in a rational fashion in a crisis.

If it is true that the superpowers have a rational approach to nuclear weapons and nascent nuclear powers do not, the worrisome prospect is that the consensus among the superpowers on the need to control a nuclear crisis does not extend to the potential antagonists and regional powers. Nor do these states have the range of means, including the ability to control the release of nuclear weapons, that will be necessary to control a crisis. These states do not have, at present, the mechanisms that ensure that nuclear weapons are not released without authorization by lower-level commanders. Without such controls, states will have a difficult time controlling nuclear weapons in a crisis.

Influence of nuclear weapons

How do we judge whether states will become involved in nuclear crises? It is essential that we consider their history of involvement in war, including those they have fought, who they have fought and why, and their conduct in those wars. One could conclude that they will act in the future much as they did in the past, and the possession of nuclear weapons will not deter them from becoming embroiled in crises or change their propensity for confrontation and conflict. The alternative interpretation that has powerful antecedents in American and Soviet history, is that nuclear weapons change the thinking and behavior of states and make their earlier historical propensities irrelevant. It is inevitable that past behavior offers some useful insights into their willingness to use nuclear weapons in a crisis.

To be sure, there is no compelling evidence that a nuclear-armed state will engage in the kinds of actions that were common before they possessed nuclear weapons. It may well be that the possession of nuclear weapons induces a degree of caution – not unlike that demonstrated by the superpowers – that only those with nuclear weapons can understand or feel. The point is that we should be skeptical about the potential causes of NSNC because they are based for the most part on extrapolations of how those *which have not owned nuclear weapons may act in crises once they possess nuclear weapons.*

It is only fair to note that there is no empirical solution to the dilemma of how to predict whether nuclear-armed states from radically different cultures and traditions will be involved in NSNC. We do not know if nuclear weapons will moderate the behavior of states. We can hope, however, that Iran and Iraq, while reckless in their willingness to use chemical weapons, will become cautious when it comes to nuclear weapons.

NOTES

1. The opinions expressed in this chapter are the author's alone and do not reflect those of The RAND Corporation or of any agency of the US government.
2. We run the risk of construing the issue too narrowly if the focus is on nuclear weapons, for there is a range of weapons of mass destruction, including chemical and biological agents, that states can use. The threat by Iraq to use chemical weapons against Israel if attacked could precipitate a nuclear crisis if it led Israel to retaliate with nuclear weapons. I want to stress that non-superpower nuclear crises do not necessarily involve two nuclear powers, but can easily occur if only one of the antagonists possesses nuclear weapons.
3. See Jeffrey Richelson, 'Air Force Tries to Shoot Down Its Own Spy', *Los Angeles Times,* 9 April 1989, p. V-3.
4. We are not concerned explicitly with the proliferation of nuclear weapons of which much has been said and written over the years, but with the structure of crises that involve states, other than the superpowers, that possess nuclear weapons and the means to deliver them.
5. 'Pakistan and India on Nuclear Knife-Edge', *Intelligence Digest,* 4 May 1990.
6. 'Just a Touch of War Fever', *The Economist,* 7 April 1990, p. 47.
7. See Aaron Karp, 'The Frantic Third World Quest for Ballistic Missiles', *Bulletin of the Atomic Scientist,* June 1988, p. 19.
8. See 'Missile Epidemic', *The Economist,* 23 September 1989, p. 16.
9. South Africa agreed in early 1990 to sign the Non-Proliferation Treaty, although its value is questionable given South Africa's reported nuclear weapons capabilities. R. Jeffrey Smith, 'S. African Nuclear-Arms Work Detailed', *Washington Post,* 27 September 1990, p. 16.
10. See Robert C. Toth, 'U. S. Worried by Nuclear Security in Unstable Soviet Empire', *Los Angeles Times,* 15 December 1989, p. S-7.
11. There could be several stages to the alerting of nuclear forces, like the American DEFCON. Each of these levels of alert, were they to exist, could offer additional points for intervention during NSNC. But for these purposes, we shall treat nuclear alerts as a single entity conceptually even if a more detailed review of alerts might provide opportunities for de-escalatory measures.

12. The proliferation of satellites and other sensors may improve the intelligence-gathering capabilities of the new nuclear powers.
13. The surprise attack has been a well-worn assumption in strategic analysis for decades. That does not change the fact that it is difficult to believe that NSNC will emerge without some warning or a clear provocation. This may reflect the bias, inherent in observations on the nature of superpower politics over several decades, that NSNC are more likely to emerge gradually from a variety of circumstances.
14. At the same time, it is easy to imagine continued reticence of US and other world leaders to preemptively attack a nation that has threatened others with weapons of mass destruction. The worldwide political repercussions would be enormous.
15. Bill Keller, 'US and the Soviets As Allies? It's the First Time Since 1945', *New York Times*, 8 August 1990, p. A8.
16. These are broad and illustrative examples. Other chapters in this volume outline specific de-escalatory measures, many of which involve nuclear forces.
17. 'India and Pakistan on Nuclear Knife-Edge', *Intelligence Digest*, 4 May 1990.
18. Michael Wines, 'New Strategies to Stem Proliferation of Weapons', *New York Times*, 30 September 1990, p. A13.

9 Conclusions

Joseph E. Nation

Our objective in this volume was to examine a range of issues involving de-escalation and confidence-building. In particular, we addressed the following questions:

- What roles can or should confidence-building measures play in nuclear crisis de-escalation?
- Have these or other measures been useful in the de-escalation of past crises or in the termination of conventional wars?
- Do Soviet and US views, including those of military leaders, differ about the utility of CBMs?
- How might behavioral factors influence de-escalation?
- Are CBMs likely to become more or less useful as force structures are changed?
- Can we apply the lessons from de-escalating US–Soviet crises to non-superpower crises?

This final chapter offers general conclusions and research findings. However, rather than addressing these questions individually or linearly, conclusions are presented in a format that ties together common themes and findings. This chapter also offers areas for further investigation.

9.1 CBMs ARE USEFUL ACROSS A BROAD SPECTRUM

Confidence-building measures are potentially useful management tools for a broad range of concerns in international relations, although much of our research shows that there are clearly drawbacks to CBMs. Carefully-crafted CBMs can provide positive results in military, political, economic, and cultural spheres by fostering mutual understanding, creating an environment for further cooperation, decreasing fears of an adversary's aggressive intent, and in some instances, constraining an adversary's potentially aggressive actions. Although this volume concentrates on CBMs involving military forces, a strong argument can be advanced that CBMs outside the military realm are even more critical in preserving peace and avoiding war. These CBMs can create an environment in which aggression is a virtually unthinkable means to resolving disputes, and in which accidental war resulting from false warnings or misunderstandings is an even less likely event than it is today. These types of CBMs cannot achieve this alone, but they can help greatly.

CBMs that involve military forces are also clearly useful across a wide spectrum – from peace to crisis to war, but their potential contribution may be more significant in avoiding or ending wars than in fostering better relations in peacetime. CBMs that involve military forces in peacetime reduce the probability of already extremely unlikely events (e.g. an unpremeditated or accidental nuclear or conventional attack) and their contribution seems relatively unimportant. As such, these CBMs do not *create*, but *reflect* the positive aspects of political relations. CBMs in crisis and war, on the other hand, may reduce the probability of moderately to highly-likely events. For example, CBMs can constrain deliberate aggression by introducing operational restrictions and making offensive operations more difficult. Similarly, CBMs can reduce the risks of accidental war by reducing the probability of incidents spiraling out of control and leading to war. More important, CBMs involving military forces in crises may provide useful signals of intent.

CBMs and crisis de-escalation

CBMs, or more accurately, 'packages' of complementary CBMs, can contribute promising mechanisms for successfully de-escalating a serious crisis. CBMs can lift the 'fog of termination' and influence human factors, especially perceptions, and they can also provide mechanisms that both reduce the risks of incidents and limit an aggressor's military options. Adherence to established CBMs, so called 'rules of the road', can also provide useful signals of a desire to see a peaceful end to a crisis. CBMs alone cannot resolve crises, but their contributions can be very important.

The most important actions in crisis de-escalation may be the introduction of or the continued adherence to militarily 'insignificant' (what one author calls 'squishy'), symbolic CBMs. For example, a declaration to end the crisis peacefully, although of no military value, could be an important step. Similarly, regular high-level contacts in which representatives try to hammer out differences could be useful. These 'squishy' CBMs may influence perceptions favorably and, perhaps most important, they may demonstrate the good faith of the parties involved and provide additional time for negotiations to address the central political disputes in the crisis.

Militarily insignificant CBMs may, in fact, be the most important in the eyes of political leaders. In past crises, political leaders have been largely ignorant of the military context of crises, noticing only the most dangerous or threatening military developments. Leaders have been far more concerned with the contextual aspects of crisis management, changes in perceptions, and other less tangible factors. For example, leaders have viewed verbal threats to escalate a crisis as a far more credible and noteworthy indication of intent than most military actions. This emphasis on largely symbolic factors appears to be common in both US and Soviet leadership styles.

The important role of largely symbolic CBMs does not mean that CBMs involving military forces are unimportant. Yet most of the measures that involve military forces discussed in this volume are indeed militarily *insignificant*; that is, they do not affect the capability to conduct threatening offensive military operations. For example, returning one or two SSBNs to port, cancelling scheduled missile test launches, or restricting airborne alerts may demonstrate a willingness to wind down a crisis, but they do not necessarily prevent preparations for or the execution of a surprise attack.[1] Similarly, rules of engagement, including those for air and naval forces, do not necessarily constrain offensive operations.

There is substantial reluctance to consider militarily significant de-escalatory measures in a crisis.[2] For example, returning mobile ICBMs and increasing their otherwise very low vulnerability could invite escalation rather than de-escalation. A common concern throughout this volume is that increased vulnerability such as this decreases the ability to generally achieve one's military objectives, and specifically to 'cover' all targets should war occur. If indeed the ability to cover all hard *and* soft targets is highly desirable, then increases in vulnerability are inappropriate. On the other hand, a very strong case can be advanced that less ambitious objectives, such as covering all soft targets and perhaps some hard targets, permit the consideration of militarily significant de-escalatory measures (e.g. the return of a substantial number of forces to home bases or to routine training and patrols). Whether the ability to deliver warheads with at least 400 equivalent megatons (one 'McNamara', a phrase coined earlier in this volume) is a reasonable objective is an issue that will undoubtedly continue to divide many analysts and decision-makers. The adoption of this less ambitious objective, signalled by the introduction of militarily significant CBMs, seems reasonable, particularly if other events point toward an increasingly likely peaceful resolution.

CBMs, accidents, and incidents in crises

Perspectives on the usefulness of CBMs in crises depend largely on the perceived risks of accidents or incidents leading to conflict. Although it is not supported generally in this volume, some analysts and citizens have expressed concern that a lone accident or incident in a crisis could precipitate a deadly, yet unintended conflict. Incidents or accidents, or perhaps more likely, a series of incidents between US and Soviet forces, could lead to re-escalation and war in a superpower nuclear crisis. And it is in this regard that CBMs may be useful in crisis management.

However, the dangers of accidents and incidents in crises leading to unintended conflict may be overstated, at least according to the historical record. Leaders in past crises have apparently not been overly concerned with this potential problem, despite their general concern with the dangers of incidents. In fact, leaders appear only to have taken notice of the most serious incidents, and no convincing argument has been made that this outlook will change. Leaders would certainly take note of incidents, such as a violation of their airspace, but an incident alone would be unlikely to lead to a rapid re-escalation of the crisis and even less likely on its own to lead to war.

But even if leaders take notice of only the most serious incidents or accidents, there is some concern that the likelihood of accidents or a series of accidents in peacetime or in a crisis is increasing. As one author has argued, nuclear weapons modernization has increased the danger of an unintended or accidental launch of nuclear weapons in peacetime and crisis. Certainly, press reports from recent years have elevated our concerns, but even these reports do not suggest a growing danger. In fact, there are technical reasons that suggest a falling probability of dangerous events.

A large-scale system failure could cause a false alarm and lead to unintended war. But as pointed out earlier in this volume, the apparent attack would have to be large, the trajectories of the attacking missiles would have to be credible, and the launch would have to be detected by more than one sensor. And without a launch-on-warning policy, the dangers of an accidental war erupting are decreased even further.

While the dangers of accidental war resulting from warning-system errors have probably decreased, the dangers from incidents involving forces at sea, in the air, and perhaps on the ground have probably not changed appreciably. Leaders may not pay close attention to most incidents, but even innocuous incidents could at worst derail the de-escalation process and at best contribute to its undoing. In this regard, rules of engagement may be very helpful and one of the most important steps in de-escalation.

There is, of course, a contrary view to the usefulness of ROEs in crises. One of the purported contributions of ROEs is their establishment of specific guidelines for how forces operate and interact. In the absence of ROEs, an incident might be explained easily as a wholly unintended event. With ROEs, incidents could be interpreted as deliberate or perhaps more sinister events. Yet on balance ROEs are probably very useful tools for three reasons. First, they reduce the potential number of interactions at a time of heightened mistrust and thus reduce the likelihood of unintended crisis re-escalation. Second, adherence to ROEs provides a signal of the desire to keep the crisis in bounds and to work for a peaceful solution. Finally, even if some established ROEs have been violated, those remaining, especially those that are militarily significant, can signal a strong intent to resolve the crisis without the use of force.

In addition to rules of engagement, the United States and the Soviet Union should consider additional ways to reduce further the risks of incidents in crises. Perhaps most important, they should establish more sound operating and de-escalatory procedures. Although not explicitly labeled as CBMs, these would do much to build confidence.

In short, accidental nuclear war resulting from failures of warning systems is probably an unlikely event, even in a crisis. But the dangers from incidents involving forces is still present. Some measures, particularly rules of engagement and the introduction of sound operating measures can contribute to reducing these risks and to providing signals of intent. Although their contribution would probably be marginal since leaders appear to notice only the most serious events, even this marginal contribution should be welcomed as a way to reduce the risks of crisis re-escalation and accidental war.

9.2 THE COMPLEMENTARY ROLES OF STRUCTURAL AND OPERATIONAL ARMS CONTROL

CBMs may be useful tools across a wide spectrum and at various stages of conflict, but CBMs cannot accomplish much on their own. In particular, de-escalating a crisis – indeed managing any stage of a crisis effectively – seems difficult at best and impossible at worst if structural arms-control efforts fail to create a stable crisis environment. In a world where an aggressor stood to gain a significant advantage by attacking first, leaders would be understandably unwilling to increase the vulnerability of their forces – even if only marginally – if these actions resulted in a perceived or real disadvantage. CBMs are most effective when a more comprehensive approach to arms control, including the integration of structural and operational arms control as evidenced in the Conventional Forces in Europe talks, is undertaken.

START may not be consistent with de-escalatory CBMs

The ongoing START negotiations appear to lack this integrative approach, although this in no way suggests that the START agreement will result in a less stable crisis environment. To the contrary, liberal counting rules for bombers are intended to create incentives to encourage bomber development, and it is widely believed that US and Soviet forces in the late 1990s will be essentially invulnerable. Pressures to launch on tactical warning should fall dramatically, and this should result in a far more stable environment. (These effects may be mitigated by other factors explained below.) The main point is that START addresses primarily the size of arsenals rather than the interaction of arsenals and operational characteristics.

Large reductions in warhead levels, as envisaged in START II or subsequent agreements, may affect crisis-stability and the prospects for crisis de-escalation adversely. Larger reductions that lead to very low US and Soviet warhead levels may diminish crisis-stability, and in particular, stability in crisis de-escalation. The principal reason for this undesirable outcome appears to be an increased concern that lower warhead levels preclude even the most modest increases in vulnerability that result from some de-escalatory measures. Declines in force survivability that might be deemed insignificant at current warhead levels may, after deep cuts, seem far more destabilizing.

START may also pose problems for crisis de-escalation because of its stringent compliance mechanisms. On-site inspections will play a particularly important role in enforcing the agreement, and these could upset opportunities for crisis de-escalation. The potential for down-loading ICBMs combined with on-site inspection provisions could be a recipe for crisis destabilization. In a START II agreement, these problems could worsen as warhead levels fall further, incentives to circumvent warhead limits increase, and concerns about compliance rise sharply.

The complementary roles of different CBMs

Just as operational and structural arms control should be integrated into a broad agenda, a complementary package of transparency measures and constraints on operations appears to work best in hedging against the problems of both accidental and deliberate conflict. Transparency measures and constraints on operations decrease false positive (i.e. non-aggressive intent is inaccurately interpreted) and false negative signals of intent (i.e. aggressive actions are inaccurately interpreted), respectively. Robust verification measures work across both of these categories.

9.3 LIMITS OF CBMs

Although CBMs make several important contributions to crisis de-escalation, there are clearly limitations and some dangers. CBMs can send the wrong message, they can be misinterpreted, and their usefulness can vary greatly depending on the source of the crisis or if violations of existing CBMs have occurred.

Perhaps the most dangerous conclusion to draw from the potential accomplishments of CBMs – and one I do not intend to convey – is that CBMs alone can resolve crises. As argued throughout this volume, CBMs are one part of a comprehensive arms-control regime designed to foster stability, to orchestrate an orderly de-escalation of forces, and to avoid war. As argued strongly in some earlier chapters, CBMs treat the symptom rather than the problem. The problem – a serious *political* dispute between two nuclear powers – can only be resolved by a *political* solution. Even constraint measures, although they might help create a military stalemate by forcing an aggressive adversary to choose between an attack with less than optimal forces and possible detection of forces readied beyond levels permitted, do not address the central dispute. CBMs may provide breathing-room for negotiations aimed at resolving the problem, but they can do little if the political dispute cannot be resolved.

The usefulness of CBMs may depend on the source of the crisis

Many CBMs are clearly beneficial in effectively preventing accidental wars by keeping open lines of communication and opportunities for consultation throughout a crisis. Indeed, the potential benefits of CBMs that increase transparency may be very high considering recent superpower developments.

However, transparency measures might be counterproductive in the event of a surprise attack since there is a danger that these could be used for deception. Moreover, they could prove to be problematic if a state employs a confusing and difficult-to-interpret balance of measures to demonstrate conciliation and resolve. For example, a state that wishes to demonstrate strong resolve with a number of declaratory principles, but still seeks a peaceful solution, could find that its actions lead to escalation, rather than de-escalation of the crisis.

Constraint measures, on the other hand, may be more useful regardless of the source of the crisis. Stringent limits on military capabilities that are easy to verify and difficult to circumvent can help greatly. For example, even if an adversary has an aggressive intent, constraint measures restrict military options and can thus contain the stalemate until it is resolved politically and reduce the probability of war.

CBMs can send the wrong message

Although many CBMs are intended to reduce the risks of accidental war, others work principally as signalling devices, and they attempt to deliberately blend a reasonable amount of conciliation with a demonstration of resolve. The danger here, of course, is that this complicated blending of signals may be interpreted as a sign of weakness and this risks a re-escalation of the crisis. The difficulty in constructing a useful, balanced packaged of CBMs is finding the appropriate emphasis on demonstrations of conciliation and resolve.

It has historically been difficult to find this balance. In fact, offensive signals of resolve have often been dominant. In the Russo-Finnish war, the Hungary–Suez events of 1956, and the 1973 Middle East War, credible offensive threats were necessary in order to bring the conflicts to a close. There is no reason to suspect that credible demonstrations of resolve would not be necessary in ending a nuclear crisis and avoiding unwanted escalation, although one also suspects that risk-taking in nuclear crises might occur far less often than in conventional wars where the consequences of re-escalation are clearly less.

Finding the appropriate balance between conciliation and resolve is probably extremely difficult if conventional force operations have occurred or if they are threatened. CBMs that involve conventional forces or peripheral operations could easily endanger the balance between demonstrations of conciliation and resolve. For example, constraints on naval forces, such as rules of engagement or restrictions on anti-submarine operations, could endanger or compromise their more narrow objectives, unintentionally signal weakness, and lead to a re-escalation of the crisis. The introduction of CBMs involving conventional forces may be impossible if they compromise or reduce substantially conventional force objectives. In the end, good faith and militarily insignificant measures can probably help and should be considered.

CBMs that increase vulnerability substantially may not be appropriate

Most of the authors argue that conciliation shown by increases in force-vulnerability is inappropriate. Invulnerability may be the best confidence-building measure from a theoretical standpoint since decision-makers would be less pressured to react with force to early reports of aggressive actions. In a crisis, pressures to launch on warning should decrease, but decision-makers might also *expect* an attack, and thus also be more likely to launch on warning. Increases in the perception of the costs of going second, and especially increases in force vulnerability can increase pressure to launch on warning, even in response to a false warning of attack. An acceptable level of vulnerability might permit decision-makers to ride-out a suspected attack rather than to launch on warning in order to achieve their military objectives.

On balance, one hopes that decision-makers would recognize the tremendous destructive potential of their forces even following the ride-out of a nuclear attack, and this might diminish pressures to launch on warning. For example, just as in peacetime, even after a surprise attack against the United States in a crisis, several *thousand* strategic warheads capable of inflicting massive damage would survive and deny an aggressor any meaningful advantage.

CBMs may be less useful after violations have occurred

How useful might CBMs be in crisis de-escalation if troublesome violations of existing measures had occurred? At best, violations might be interpreted as a failure to communicate orders to standing forces and the violations might be largely ignored. Adherence to other CBMs that had not been violated would undoubtedly increase in importance.

At worst, however, violations might derail the de-escalation process, although existing, non-violated CBMs could also play an increasingly important role in de-escalation. The reinstatement of violated CBMs might be called upon to form the first critical steps in the de-escalation process, creating a solid foundation for the consideration of additional measures or discussions to resolve the crisis. Continued adherence to militarily significant measures might prove to be very useful steps in de-escalation.

9.4 AREAS FOR FURTHER RESEARCH

De-escalatory measures in the real world

We have undertaken this research effort in a highly theoretical manner in which some de-escalatory measures seem wholly appropriate and logical in our laboratory setting. But how would these measures work in the real world in a serious nuclear crisis? Clearly, problems of classification and dated historical evidence cast doubt upon these theoretical constructs. But of more concern, operational cultures and the divergence between theoretical and actual operations may diminish the usefulness of these de-escalatory measures.

These de-escalatory measures may be less able to accomplish their objectives in the real world. A review of past crises illustrates the surprisingly small attention paid to the *military* significance of one's own and one's adversary's activities. This does not initially suggest an important role for CBMs involving military forces; however, it may be that leaders view these measures – whether they are or are not militarily significant – as important signals. We may have overstated the value of militarily significant measures, but we may have equally undervalued symbolic, militarily insignificant CBMs.

De-escalatory measures in the real world will also almost certainly not flow smoothly down the escalatory ladder as one might hope. Unexpected or uncontrollable events – including shifts in domestic political debates or unexpected developments in allied nations, such as the onset of other political, economic, or military crises – have the potential to derail the process. One hopes that leaders are well aware of factors that can mitigate these negative aspects, as well as those that can make de-escalation more difficult. It may be very difficult to overcome this potentially large theoretical–real world divergence, but closer examination of nuclear force operations and behavioral factors are important first steps.

Negotiating de-escalatory CBMs

Even if de-escalatory CBMs are appropriate measures for ending a crisis, the road to their agreement may be quite rocky. Preplanned measures may be useful in some cases, while *ad hoc* agreements may be useful in others. Pre-planned measures would probably include transparency CBMs, while *ad hoc* arrangements might deal more with constraint measures.

Highly specific de-escalatory measures involving nuclear forces seem unlikely to occur in advance for two reasons. First, it is difficult to anticipate crisis contingencies and to establish and to continuously update specific de-escalatory guidelines. Second, neither the US nor the Soviets appears likely to provide the sensitive information on military operations necessary to establish specific agreements constraining forces since this would require some exchange of sensitive operational data. But more general de-escalatory guidelines involving forces, including those that rely on definitions in existing arms control agreements should be pursued. For example, agreements on exactly what constitutes an alert might be useful in pursuing more specific measures in a crisis.

The bilateral implementation of measures seems highly unlikely, although some general guidelines, such as an agreement to adhere to certain key transparency or declared measures – even in a serious crisis – might be established in peacetime. However, differences in US and Soviet force structures greatly reduce the probability that bilateral measures, such as reductions in bomber or submarine alert rates would be considered. In addition, differences in geography and in military objectives limit opportunities.

Non-superpower crisis de-escalation

Finally, as the world's nuclear club expands, the import of research on how non-superpower nuclear crises can be terminated will increase dramatically. If, as is often suggested, the risks of non-superpower nuclear crises are far greater than those of the increasingly friendly superpowers, much of our effort should be focused here. The roles of doctrine, historical experiences, and other factors could provide us with valuable insight into how non-superpower crises might begin and end. The prospects of superpower involvement – and the potential contributions of superpowers in helping these crises end peacefully – deserve our immediate attention.

NOTES

1. Restricting airborne alerts could, in fact, be interpreted as a necessary step to perform maintenance and to prepare for offensive operations.
2. This reflects concern that militarily significant de-escalatory measures could be interpreted as a lack of resolve and instead lead to unintended escalation. This drawback and other limits of CBMs are discussed below.

Index